on track ...

The Small Faces and The Faces

every album, every song

Andrew Darlington

SONICBOND

sonicbondpublishing.com

Sonicbond Publishing Limited
www.sonicbondpublishing.co.uk
Email: info@sonicbondpublishing.co.uk

First Published in the United Kingdom 2024
First Published in the United States 2024

British Library Cataloguing in Publication Data:
A Catalogue record for this book is available from the British Library

ISBN 978-1-78952-316-4

Typeset in ITC Garamond Std & ITC Avant Garde Gothic
Printed and bound in England

Graphic design and typesetting: Full Moon Media

Follow us on social media:
Twitter: https://twitter.com/SonicbondP
Instagram: www.instagram.com/sonicbondpublishing_/
Facebook: www.facebook.com/SonicbondPublishing/

Linktree QR code:

Dedications

For Steve Sneyd, Michael Butterworth, Pete Faulkner, George Cairncross, Andy Robson, Karen Smithey and Simon Clark, who have always been there with help, support and encouragement.

Other SonicBond books available by Andrew Darlington

Derek Taylor: For Your Radioactive Children
Days In The Life Of The Beatles Spin-Doctor Music Biography
(2020, Sonicbond Publishing ISBN 978-1-78952-038-5)

On Track: The Hollies, Every Album, Every Song
(2021, Sonicbond Publishing ISBN 978-1-78952-159-7)

On Track: The Human League And The Sheffield Electro Scene Every Album, Every Song
(2022, SonicBond Publishing ISBN 978-1-78952-186-3)

& the Andrew Darlington website 'Eight Miles Higher'
www.andrewdarlington.blogspot.com

on track ...

The Small Faces and The Faces

Contents

Introduction

Mod.

When Pete Townshend said, after seeing the Mods gather at Margate, that it was the closest he'd ever felt to patriotism, we knew exactly what he meant. This was our tribe. Our time. Our generation.

Mods were 'modernists', a teen youth culture focused on music, fashion and scooters. They were Social Influencers before there was such a term.

'Mods used each other as looking glasses', said George Melly in *Revolt Into Style*, 'they were as cool as ice-cubes'.

Mod was reflected in the glossy *Rave* magazine, but it was a grassroots thing that relied on an intuitive knowing of what was and what was not cool. It might have begun in London, but every city had its Mod club where the Lambrettas and Vespas gathered. In Hull, it was 'The Goldola' coffee bar.

I confused the local barber by asking for a Small Faces haircut – parted slightly off-centre and back-combed on top, when all he knew was short, back and sides with maybe a square neck for the more exotic choice.

When I first saw a music clip of Marvin Gaye lip-synching 'How Sweet It Is' I couldn't identify this swinging, finger-popping, smartly dressed, smiling, slick performer as R&B, surely that was grizzled oldsters like John Lee Hooker, Howlin' Wolf, Muddy Waters or Bo Diddley? When the weekly music paper *Record Mirror* began running an R&B Top Twenty, my friend Patrick couldn't understand why it was listing Otis Redding, The Miracles, Wilson Pickett, Sam & Dave... what about Lightnin' Hopkins, Buddy Guy and Elmore James? But this was the new Stax and Motown R&B to which the Mods made their stylish dance moves. This was what was happening.

American records... or Jamaican Ska, was the music of choice. But Soul Bands such as Geno Washington & The Ram-Jam Band, Jimmy James & The Vagabonds or Zoot Money's Big Roll Band hit all the correct hand-clappin' foot-stompin' funky-butt accelerators for hipsters, flipsters and finger-poppin' groovers. Then there were the groups, The Who, Action, Attack, Creation, The Richard Kent Style in Manchester... and The Small Faces. They oozed cool. They looked sharp, young, cool and poised on the extreme edge of now.

Mod was street-level. It was not top-down. It was ground up. It was a spontaneous teen subculture generated by the kids themselves. It had nothing to do with star role models. It took into account designer labels and fashion style guides but had nothing to do with Class. It was all about intuition. Respect was granted for hip awareness.

'It was just a case of all me mates were Mods, and I was a Mod', said Steve Marriott, 'we took pills ... stayed up all night. The Scene club until midnight. Then, the Flamingo for the all-nighter ... it's very easy to say that The Small Faces were the leaders of it, but we weren't. We were just Mods' (to Paolo Hewitt).

'Very exciting times, the sixties; there'll never be another time like it, I'm sure', agreed Ronnie Lane.

The Darlings Of Wapping Wharf: The Small Faces

Small Faces. Big Sound. None of them were above five feet six inches tall. But despite being a group of diminished stature, this will not be a short history.

In the sleeve notes to the double CD collection *Small Faces: The Decca Anthology 1965-1967,* respected music writer Paolo Hewitt points out that 'it all happened in a very short space of time. At the start of 1965, they were complete unknowns. One year later, they were famous.'

Ronald Frederick 'Plonk' Lane was born in Plaistow on 1 April 1946, 'a funny guy too, and even though he could be excitable, he was a lot more relaxed than Steve' (Marriott, according to Ian McLagan). Why 'Plonk'? For the same – but opposite – penis-related reason that Tich of Dave Dee, Dozy, Beaky, Mick & Tich was called Tich. To Pete Townshend, Ronnie 'liked the same music as I did: he liked to drink and smoke a little grass; he was funny, sincere, artistic, creative, gifted and down to earth. In some respects, he was a typical London East Ender.'

After leaving school at 16, Ronnie met drummer Kenney Jones (born 16 September 1948 in Whitechapel) at a local pub. Kenney 'was quieter, but once he got started, and when he got a word in edgewise, he was hilarious' (Ian McLagan). The two promptly formed a beat group called The Outcasts. Initially playing lead guitar, Ronnie quickly switched to bass guitar, and when he was prospecting for a Harmony bass, he visited the Manor Park 'J60 Music Bar', where he happened to meet bright and sparky employee Steve Marriott.

'I'd like to have a look at that bass over there', said Ronnie. 'Oh, that's the best bass in the shop. That's a great bass!' said Steve. An animated banter about the merits of various instruments ensued, during which they discovered a mutual interest in James Brown, Sue Records and Bobby 'Blue' Bland. Lane bought his bass and accepted Steve's invitation to visit his home after-hours, where he was impressed by Steve's extensive collection of Motown and Stax records. 'This opened my ears considerably', recalled Ronnie.

Steve was dark and dynamic, small but 'larger than life. A cartoon of a person' (according to Ian McLagan). At that time, he was a member of an R&B group called The Moments. Formed in late 1963 when he was still only 16, The Moments started out as the Frantiks, or sometimes the Frantik Ones, but later became Steve Marriott & The Moonlights until they finally settled on the Moments. With Steve was Johnny Herve, Tony McIntyre, Colin Green and Dennis Thompson. Marriott would sometimes invite girlfriend Adrienne Posta to share vocals with him on duets. They'd met when they were both 'Italia Conti Academy' pupils.

The Moments even got as far as recording a revived version of Cliff Richard's debut hit 'Move It'... written by Ian Samwell, who would later figure in The Small Faces story. Former Shadows' drummer Tony Meehan was induced to help with production. Despite the single being hawked around several major record companies, it generated no interest, and the track was never released. When the despondent Thompson and Herve quit, Marriott changed the group's name to Steve Marriott & The Moments. The new lineup now had Barry Hewitt on bass, Tony McIntyre on drums, Steve on lead vocals and rhythm guitar, plus former Johnny Kidd & The Pirates guitarist Johnny Weider and Allen Ellett on keyboards and vocals. An EP, *Steve Marriott's Moments*, issued on 6 October 2008 (Acid Jazz AJX210S), gathers 'Money Money', 'Good Morning Blues', 'You Really Got Me', and 'You'll Never Get Away From Me.' Their increasing R&B orientation attracted the attention of manager Tony Calder – who would also later figure in The Small Faces story as co-founder of the Immediate label.

The Moments played gigs as frequently as six nights a week, including spots at 'The Flamingo' and 'The 100 Club', each earning a wage of £30 a week – £10 more than Don Arden would pay Steve as a member of The Small Faces! They generated a loyal Mod following around their East End stomping ground with forays into Essex. At 'Attic Fanatics' at 'The Attic Club' – 1A High Street, Hounslow – punters paid 3/6d to see the 'Raving R&B' of Steve Marriott's Moments at 7:30 pm on Tuesday, 18 August 1964. They began writing their own blend of Soul and fast & furious R&B. Written jointly by Marriott and Ellet, their next recording endeavour was called 'A Touch Of The Blues.' The other half of Immediate Records and machiavellian Rolling Stones manager Andrew Loog Oldham saw them play and was sufficiently impressed with Steve's vocals that he agreed to produce the record, although it lingered unreleased.

Steve briefly changed the group's name to the Wondering Ones around March 1964 but promptly changed it back to The Moments in time to play a historic gig at the Rainham 'Albion' where Ronnie Lane's Outcasts happened to share the bill.

Oddly, Steve's debut on vinyl had come singing 'Consider Yourself' as the Artful Dodger in the New Theatre original cast recording of the *Oliver* musical, with Ian Carmichael as Fagan (World Record Club TP151 in 1962, CD reissue Old Thundridge Records RIB001, 2013). Producer Shel Talmy writes:

> Steve Marriott was one of the most talented artists I've worked with and also one of the most mercurial. His mood changes were legendary, kinda like dealing with an unexploded time bomb and not knowing when it was skedded to go off!'
>
> According to the many things written about Steve, he was mad about music from a very early age and had become fairly proficient on both guitar and harmonica (mouth-harp) by the time he was thirteen.
>
> What he didn't know was that in 1962, Steve's father spotted an ad placed in a London newspaper by Lionel Bart, author of the very successful 'Oliver', based, of course, on the classic Charles Dickens novel *Oliver Twist*. Bart was searching for a replacement for a major 'Oliver' character, the Artful Dodger. Mr Marriott hadn't told his son what he was doing when he applied for an

audition, so Steve was surprised when he was selected to 'demonstrate his wares'! From all reports, Steve was undaunted and as a Buddy Holly fan, chose to sing 'Oh Boy', then showed his versatility by singing the Connie Francis hit 'Who's Sorry Now'!' Needless to say, he passed the audition. (quoted with the kind permission of Shel Talmy).

'Any kid off the street could have got a part in *Oliver*. It wasn't hard', commented Steve dismissively in *NME* on 15 December 1984.

An issue of *Fabulous 208* magazine (dated 11 June 1966) bemoans the lot of child stars, singling out Steve Marriott for special attention. 'Steve was a star at twelve. You can imagine what laws there were to 'protect' him then. It was don't do this, don't do that. There were laws going right back to the days of child labour in the mines! ... it's great that the law protects the interests of the young, but must they go so far? Aren't you allowed to grow up at 16, and be responsible, and prepare to give something to society?'

In later productions, the Artful Dodger role was taken by future Monkee Davy Jones on Broadway and by Jack Wild in the movie.

But first, The Moments recorded an opportunistic American cover of The Kinks' 'You Really Got Me' for that same World Artists label, b/w 'Money Money' (WA 1032). Steve acquits himself well, but no one can really replicate Dave Davies' manic guitar break on the Kinks original, so he plays harmonica instead. For the slinky B-side, a Don Charles and Alan Caddy song, he throws in his trademark 'come on, children' and 'come on now, sing your song' plus another harmonica solo. Both sides eventually turn up as 2003 bonus tracks on the collection *Small Faces* (Charly Records SNAP 149CD). The Moments 'You Really Got Me' was also later salvaged onto the 2010 compilation *Hits Of The Sixties* (Disky MP 906471), while 'Money Money' turned up that same year on *Dig The New Breed* from the Acid Jazz label AJXCD223. In February 2006, 'Money Money' also became part of a Steve Marriott triple-CD retrospective, *Tin Soldier* (Castle Music CMETD935), which gathers Humble Pie and Packet Of Three material, too.

But when the single bombed, Ellet promptly quit the group. Then, in October 1964, in a bizarre move, the Moments told Steve Marriott he was no longer required! They considered Steve lacked the maturity to make it. Steve went on to greater things. The Moments never had their moment in the big time.

Give Her My Regards – Steve Marriott single

'Give Her My Regards' (Kenny Lynch) 1:55 b/w **'Imaginary Love'** (Steve Marriott) 2:15

Released: 1963, Decca F 11619, Belinda Recordings. No chart placing

The 1960s was a trip.

The sixties was a decade that tells a story in ways that other decades do not. On a rising curve from the poverty and post-war austerity of the preceding decade, the world was expanding. It's a storybook narrative that begins with pages in crisp black and white before it moves through a gradual evolution of rising expectations into new explosions of gaudy colour.

The essential point to grasp is that it was a period of a great opening up from the conformist drabness of the years that preceded it. There was an optimism that things were getting better year-on-year... unless it was all going to get blown away by a thermonuclear apocalypse! Disposable income, although still slight by comparison with what was to come, was rising sufficiently to purchase those shiny new consumer luxuries, such as the Dansette portable record player.

And 1963 was the seismic watershed year for British Pop. There had been earlier inspired stabs at authentic rock 'n' roll, with Johnny Kidd & The Pirates 'Shakin' All Over', Vince Taylor & His Playboys 'Brand New Cadillac', Marty Wilde's 'Bad Boy', Cliff Richard & The Drifters 'Move It.' But overnight, the cosy, insular world of Cliff Richard, Adam Faith and Billy Fury was rendered obsolete. Although 'Love Me Do' was issued and charted in the final months of 1962, it was The Beatles 'Please Please Me' that was the detonation point in unleashing a tsunami of new beat groups – Gerry & The Pacemakers, Billy J Kramer With The Dakotas, The Searchers, Freddie & The Dreamers... and as the year extended there were the first chart appearances of The Rolling Stones and The Hollies.

Throughout this period, Kenny Lynch was a popular, personable singer who scored chart hits with 'Mountain Of Love' (1960), 'Puff' (1962), his cover of the Drifters' 'Up On The Roof' (1962), and 'You Can Never Stop Me Loving You' (1963). 'He was really easy-going and a lot of fun to be around', recalled Ian McLagan, 'he also had a Rolls-Royce which he drove to gigs.' Kenny had used that Rolls-Royce to travel from one date to the next as part of a 'Package' tour bill headlined by Helen Shapiro but supported by The Beatles, which first indicated just how massive the Fab Four would become. Kenny's amended version of The Beatles 'Misery' became the first A-side cover of a Lennon-McCartney song, and although it didn't chart, it suggested there was potential there.

As sharp to spot talent as he was to take advantage of the opportunities it offered, child thespian Stephen Marriott had the irrepressible confidence and vocal ability to turn one of Kenny's slightly catchy songs into a contender for those pocket-money pennies.

As a bit-part actor, Steve was typecast as the cheeky, chirpy Cockney urchin with a sharp attitude. He'd appeared in the 'One Bob, One Job' episode of Richard Hearne's mild knockabout BBC-TV comedy *Mr Pastry's Progress* (21 April 1962). He followed it with a role in the softcore police drama *Dixon Of Dock Green,* which starred veteran actor Jack Warner in an episode titled 'The River People' (9 February 1963), written by Ted Willis, which meant that Steve was already a face on the scene.

The Moments' early musical style was heavily influenced by Buddy Holly. The Kenny Lynch song 'Give Her My Regards' is a Buddy Holly pastiche with strummed guitar and Steve incorporating the Holly vocal hiccup, similar in some ways to Tommy Roe's Holly-esque hit single 'Sheila.' 'I was a bad one, lived for my own fun', Steve sings, as he admits to neglecting the girl he should have valued; now he wants her back, hoping that it's not too late. The B-side demonstrates that Steve already had not only songwriter ambitions but the abilities, too. Again, there's The Crickets' distinctive signature Jerry Allison drum-riff as Steve sings about the idealised love he has yet to meet. A press release from the time quotes Steve as saying, 'I think Buddy Holly was the greatest. My voice is very similar to his, but this just happens by accident. I certainly didn't try to copy his style.'

Altogether, it makes an attractively respectable little 45rpm combination; although it failed to register at the time and proved something of an embarrassment to the later Steve Marriott, it was nevertheless drawn into the official Small Faces discography when both sides were included as bonus filler material on the 1996 2CD *Small Faces: The Decca Anthology 1965-1967* (Decca 844 583-2). 'Give Her My Regards' was also gathered onto the intriguing double-vinyl *Hard-Up Heroes* (1974, Decca DPA 3009/10) compiled by *NME* journalists Charles Shaar Murray and Roy Carr, celebrating obscure and wonderful gems by 'those bands who made it, the ones who didn't and those poor unfortunate souls who wasted the most precious years of their youth sleeping rough on clapped-out equipment in the back of broken-down Bedford vans, ruined their digestion with motorway grease and were always six months behind with their HP payments.'

Meanwhile, Steve went back undeterred into his thespian career, with roles in the TV-series adaptation of the Richmal Crompton 'William' books (as 'Bertie Franks'), in which other wannabes Dennis Waterman and Adrienna Posta have roles, as well as the Peter Sellers' Boulting Brothers movie *Heavens Above* as an uncredited 'Jack' amidst a rollcall of British movie stars, Eric Sykes, Irene Handl, William Hartnell and Roy Kinnear. More to the point, the teen-exploitation movie *Live It Up!* (1963, retitled *Sing & Swing* for its USA release) features Steve as wisecracking 'Ricky' – who gags 'me Tarzan, you Jane' and 'don't call us, we'll call you.' He's one of four GPO dispatch riders who formed a Pop Group called The Smart Alecs. They rehearse on the 'rooftop rendezvous', doing a neat little Shadows footstep routine, although Steve only gets to play drums – for Heinz, on the song heard just before the end credits! The movie stars the charismatic David Hemmings, while the Joe Meek soundtrack includes Gene Vincent, Kenny Ball & His Jazzmen, peroxide-blonde Heinz Burt, The Outlaws (with Ritchie Blackmore, Chas Hodges and Mick Underwood) and attractive songstress Patsy Ann Noble who received radio-play with her featured song 'Accidents Will Happen.' Peter Glaze, the comedy actor in TV's popular *Crackerjack* kids' show, is there too. Future Jimi Hendrix Experience drummer Mitch Mitchell can be glimpsed as 'Andrews', and Dave Clark of the Dave Clark Five is there as 'recording manager.'

Among other bit-part appearances, Steve also played 'Arthur' in one 1964 episode ('The Scousers') of the Sid James BBC-TV sit-com *Taxi!*

Meanwhile, Kenny Lynch went on to become a significant songwriter. He would return as a significant part of The Small Faces story and then he was one of the faces on the cover art for Wings' *Band On The Run* album (1973, Apple PAS10007), and he would later exploit his talent for comedy in partnership with Liverpool comedian Jimmy Tarbuck – albeit involving some dubious racist routines.

The Early Decca Years

Whatcha Gonna Do About It? – Single

'Whatcha Gonna Do About It?' (Ian Samwell, Brian Potter) 1:59 b/w
'What's A Matter Baby' (Clyde Otis, Joy Byers) 2:53
Personnel:
Steve Marriott: lead guitar, lead vocals
Ronnie Lane: bass guitar, backing vocals
Kenney Jones: drums
Jimmy Winston: Hammond organ, backing vocals, rhythm guitar
Released: 6 August 1965, Decca F 12208
Highest chart position: UK: 14 (on chart for 12 weeks)

Unlike The Who, whose Mod image was extensively conflated by their manager Peter Meaden in order to exploit the growing cult, The Small Faces were real East End Mods. They grew out of their mutual love of the Mod's favourite music – R&B and Soul. According to Steve, 'we got the following because we were Mods ourselves.'

In early 1965, following his adventures with The Moments, Steve formed the nucleus of a new lineup with himself as lead guitar and vocals, Ronnie Lane on bass, Kenney Jones on drums, and recruiting friend Jimmy Winston on guitar. James Edward Winston Langwith (born 20 April 1945) was fundamental to the band's evolution, not only because his parents owned the Manor Park 'Ruskin Arms' pub (Steve lived at 26 Strone Road, opposite the pub), where they rehearsed and gave occasional performances. Jimmy's role was soon shifted to become their keyboard player.

Why Small Faces? Ace Face was a Mod slang term for a well-respected member of the In-crowd. After all, the debut single by The Who – when they were still called The High Numbers, was the July 1964 'I'm The Face' c/w 'Zoot Suit' (Fontana TF480). And why Small? Because of their diminutive stature! The lineup debuted at the Kensington Youth Centre on 6 May 1965, although they were not billed because they were not yet named. Two days later, they played the same venue, but this time as The Small Faces – the name suggested by Steve's Italia Conti girlfriend, Annabel. Outside the London circuit, they played the Manchester Twisted Wheel (20 May), two dates in Sheffield – a Working Men's Club (21 May) and the more Mod King Mojo Club the following day. For Steve, the hard times were brief, 'I hardly ever had any money to pay the rent, and when the landlord came round, I used to stir my dog up a bit and make him growl fiercely', he told *NME*-journalist Keith Altham.

Then, among a hectic schedule of gigs, they played a series of dates at Leicester Square's The Cavern In The Town Club. According to Paolo's account, Steve recalled how 'Ronnie drew a picture of a Mod in a parka with 'Small Faces' painted on the back, like it was on Kenney's drumkit, which Ronnie had also painted. We put it outside the gig, and it brought all these Mods in.' Pat Meehan was a 'beady-eyed cold fish' according to Ian McLagan, but he was also assistant to ruthless manager Don Arden. He was attracted by the furore and saw the group rehearse at Maurice King's Starlight Room Club. On Meehan's recommendation, Arden himself subsequently went to The Cavern In The Town gig, immersed in a pressure cooker of crammed bodies dancing to intense raucous volume. He stepped up to the four-piece and invited them to his office on 10 June.

It was a big deal. He was a predatory wolf with an expense account and a fake American accent. The foursome took the tube to Carnaby Street, climbed the stairs of 52-55, next door to John Michael's menswear designer shop – home of suits with brilliant silk linings and pink shirts with small button-down collars, and stepped into the outer office of the Arden empire where they were invited inside to sign to his 'Contemporary Music' agency.

Already manager for The Animals and The Nashville Teens, Don Arden had a ferocious reputation. 'He was kind of a Jewish teddy bear, I suppose', recalls Kenney Jones in Arden's *Daily Telegraph* obituary on 24 July 2007, 'you liked him immediately because he was enthusiastic and he talked about what he could do and what he couldn't do and whenever he said 'I'll do this, I'll do that' – he did and it came true.' True to his word Arden managed to secure them a Decca contract. He also set up accounts for them at the major trend-setting Carnaby Street outfitters.

For their debut Decca session, the group had already swiped the riff from Solomon Burke's 'Everybody Needs Somebody To Love' and added a title from a 1964 Doris Troy single – 'Whatcha Gonna Do About It?', but they needed lyrics. Ian Samwell had a fascinating history stretching back to the very dawn of British rock 'n' roll when he wrote 'Move It', the debut hit for surly young Rocker Cliff Richard, following it with 'High Class Baby' and 'Dynamite.' Later, he discovered and did production work for the trio called America, including their massive hit 'Horse With No Name.' While born in Billericay, Brian Potter was a working songwriter who would later team with Dennis Lambert and relocate to Los Angeles, where they wrote and produced for The Four Tops and Glen Campbell. Meanwhile, the lyrics they jointly sketched for The Small Faces are minimalist – 'I want you to know that I love you, Baby, want you to know that I care', but the track required no more.

There was an original take recorded during July in the IBC Studios at 35 Portland Place where The Action, The Kinks and The Who had worked. With a distorted feedback play-in, the 'alternate version' is included on the remastered 2012 Deluxe 2CD Edition of the debut album. But it was redone at Pye Studios, where the finished released master was completed. The track is basically a drumbeat with Steve's vocals across it, with a slight riff, a break, a touch of organ and backing vocals and that's it, yet it has the power of a mini opus. The demotic phrases that Steve throws in – 'sing the song now', which invites the harmony chorus voices, then 'here they come again' for the later chorus, while 'tell the truth' seem spontaneous in a gospel kind of urging way. 'Tell the truth' – like 'own up', was part of the group's inner vocabulary. At the same time, the long, grating, sustained thirteen-second guitar solo was promoted as part of the pop art innovative freakery that The Who were showcasing on their second hit single 'Anyway Anyhow Anywhere', which had dropped out of the top 40 four weeks prior to The Small Faces entering the chart at number 33 (9 September).

The two tracks also form a blueprint for creative energies surging through the decade. Because The Small Faces were broaching an all-happening chart topped by The Rolling Stones '(I Can't Get No) Satisfaction', above The Beatles' 'Help', Bob Dylan's 'Like A Rolling Stone', The Animals, The Kinks and The Byrds' 'Mr Tambourine Man'. Chart competition seldom came as intimidatingly awesome. Yet The Small Faces climbed to number 29, then number 22, 19 and 15 before peaking at number 14 (14 October). The B-side takes Timi Yuro's original and gives it a slinky make-over. Drum shots lead into a nagging bass-throb before the pleading vocals. Lyrically, she broke his heart; now it's her turn to cry when her new lover lets her down. Del Shannon, Bobby Hatfield and Elkie Brooks also do versions.

I've Got Mine – Single

'I've Got Mine' (Marriott, Lane) 2:51 b/w **'It's Too Late'** (Marriott, Lane, Jones, Winston) 2:37

Released: 5 November 1965, Decca F 12276. No chart placings

The label of the Decca 45rpm was deep blue, with silver lettering.

It might be assumed that the momentum achieved by an attention-grabbing debut hit single would provide sufficient traction to at least register the follow-up some chart visibility. But apparently not. Trend competition was intense. Some ascribe at least a degree of the previous success to Arden's payola, which may well be true. Steve confided to Paolo Hewitt of the *NME* on 15 December 1984, 'I'll tell you something though, without Don Arden, there wouldn't have been The Small Faces. We have to say that. I think he managed us very well, money regardless. And screw money; money only gets in the way… what he actually did was put us over very well and opened a lot of doors. Without those people, you wouldn't get anywhere.'

Fabulous, the 1/- colour fan magazine, in an 18 December 1965 issue supposedly edited by the Walker Brothers, ran features on The Small Faces, Zoot Money, Francoise Hardy, and PJ Proby.

Dateline Diamonds was a low-budget teen exploitation film directed by Jeremy Summers and shot in black and white. Kenny Everett appears as himself, as the DJ broadcasting from outside territorial limits aboard the Radio London ship 'MV Galaxy.' Pirate Radio was a hot, contentious issue at the time. Official hostility was balanced by teenage enthusiasm. There's a tenuous plot involving using the floating pirate radio station to smuggle diamonds from the UK to Amsterdam, but it's largely a heist romp drawing in the smartly-suited Small Faces, 'just back from their fabulous American tour' (sic) who perform 'I've Got Mine' at a Radio London promo-night in

Watford's Rank Ballroom. Jimmy Winston plays a big, shiny Rickenbacker. Kenneth Cope stars as the group's manager; he was the conniving Jed Stone in long-running TV Soap *Coronation Street* and is also featured in a couple of *Carry On* films. Patsy Rowlands also had 'Carry On' roles on her CV. Conrad Philips, the former TV 'William Tell', is there, and a young Kiki Dee sings.

As the first result of the Marriott-Lane writing partnership, the single is an incredibly compressed production with the mixing-desk settings shoved way over into overload until the sound smoulders with burning energies. There's controlled aggression in the drums and a burbling liquid little organ motif that insidiously recurs throughout. Steve testifies, 'I've Got Mine' as the backup voices add a supportive 'You get yours.' It builds to the 1:57-minute point where it stops dead and pauses, only to erupt anew, with Steve's frantic exhortations, 'every day, Babe, I just sit and cry… Oh no, no, no, no, I can't stand it no more.'

Ironically, it reached number 24 on the pirate Radio London chart, but as their lists were not compiled from sales, it didn't really matter.

The tune would later be reconfigured into the instrumental opening title track of the classic 1968 album *Ogdens' Nut Gone Flake*. Meanwhile, credited to all four members of the group, the B-side is also turned up to warping levels of distortion over a dense drumbeat, with Steve's nerve-shredding vocals, 'my Daddy told me there'll be girls like you, I guess my Daddy had his hard times too.' Covered by the Scarborough-based neo-psych B.L.O.W. on the 1996 *Long Ago's And Worlds Apart: A Tribute To The Small Faces*, they retain the low burring bass that deforms the production into galvanising extremes.

A band's internal chemistry is a frequently overlooked aspect of their longevity. The Who, despite being made up of four corrosively explosive characters, fit together like Lego. When Mick Taylor quit The Rolling Stones, the press was rife with rumours that his place would be taken by Eric Clapton or Jeff Beck. Yet they chose former Face Ronnie Wood, a great guitarist sure, but more importantly, an amiably safe-pair-of-hands mate content to simply play rock 'n' roll. As producer Shel Talmy tells the tale, one of his favourite sixties Mod bands, The Creation, were torn apart by personnel instability, with members coming and going at a rate that plagued and frustrated their potential. To work together, in claustrophobically close confines to each other over long tours, the members of the group must get on tolerably well.

So, shortly after the failure of 'I've Got Mine', Jimmy Winston left the group and was promptly replaced by Ian McLagan. There's been controversy over whether Jimmy jumped or whether he was pushed. It's said that his termination was due to snubbing Steve during the filming of an episode of *Thank Your Lucky Stars*. But Ronnie Lane states in an interview that he was fired: 'our original organist… wasn't working out. He couldn't play – I mean, none of us could play, but he was keen. Jimmy Winston couldn't play, and on top of it, he had an ego as if he could play the piano, so he had to go!

We chucked him out of The Small Faces.' (Ronnie Lane, *Small Faces Talk To You: The Story Of The Small Faces In Their Own Words*). Kenney Jones later adds that 'he (Jimmy) got above his station and tried to compete with Steve Marriott.'

As it was explained when Ringo Starr replaced Pete Best on the Beatles drum chair, Jimmy was a great keyboard player, but Ian McLagan was a great Small Face.

Sha-La-La-La-Lee – Single

'Sha-La-La-La-Lee' (Kenny Lynch, Mort Schuman) 2:56 b/w **'Grow Your Own'** (Marriott, Lane, Jones, McLagan) 2:17
Personnel:
Steve Marriott: lead guitar, lead and backing vocals
Ronnie Lane: bass guitar, backing vocals
Kenney Jones: drums
Ian McLagan: Hammond organ, piano, backing vocals
plus
Kenny Lynch: backing vocals
Released: 28 January 1966, Decca F 12317
Highest chart position: UK: 3 (on chart 11 weeks), Germany: 15

One night at... it might have been the Bag O' Nails, or possibly the Cromwellian – no, it was the Scotch of St James, where the mid-sixties' bright young things graze. And Long John Baldry, one of the respected 'Fathers of British Blues' – was eloquently and loudly mocking The Small Faces for almost hitting number one with 'Sha-La-La-La-Lee' – as a 'soul sell-out.' 'Look – here's Steve Marriott, the Soul singer – Sha-La-La-La-Lee!' 'It hurt', admitted Steve. Long John was hitless, of course, but therefore pristinely purer, vindicated by being untainted by crass Pop. They knew it, too. For Long John was a tall, dapper, smart-dressed Blues-shouter of impeccable credentials, growling out Blues breaks long before it became the trendy thing to do – his roots as a folk and jazz singer, with guitar and harmonica, but mostly voice, extended way back into the fifties clubs and coffee bars. Although The Small Faces would be vindicated when Baldry began scoring even more schmaltzy hits of his own – 'Let The Heartaches Begin' indeed.

For the Small Faces, it had been an eventful six months. A cult hit single. A failed follow-up. An exit. A new arrival. Ian McLagan (born 12 May 1945 in Hounslow) was a self-confessed 'cheeky little sod' with 'more front than Jayne Mansfield, and no shame whatsoever.' But he had a taste for Buddy Holly. He ducked out of piano lessons arranged by his mother, but once he heard Booker T & The MGs' 'Green Onions', he was forever hooked. There was a *Melody Maker* advertisement by the Regent Street Boosey & Hawkes emporium offering a Hammond L101 spinet organ on a two-week free trial, an offer he promptly took advantage of, after which 'I lost my mind and I'd never find it again.'

Ian started out with The Cherokees while doing an art course at Twickenham Technical College, but discovered Thelonious Monk and the *Muddy Waters At Newport 1960* album, then found The Rolling Stones playing at Giorgio Gomelsky's 'Crawdaddy Club' which became 'a turning point for me.' With his group, renamed The Muleskinners, they supported the Stones when Ian booked them for the college end-of-term dance. Fuelled on Purple Hearts, French Blues and uppers (or leapers), they also played back-up to Howlin' Wolf, Sonny Boy Williamson and Little Walter while Ian was hanging out at all the trendiest clubs. He also got to play backup for Kenny Lynch! He worked with a band called Boz & The Boz People (fronted by Boz Burrell, later of Bad Company) but quit due to their lack of ambition... just in time to be summoned to Don Arden's office on 1 November 1965 and offered the vacant space in The Small Faces.

The only problem was, he was no Mod, more 'the art-student type in a brown corduroy jacket and blue jeans without a pot to piss in.' That could be remedied. Ronnie restyled his hair, and a trip to Toppers and Lord John boutiques soon had him suitably kitted out.

The letter column of *Fabulous* magazine, on 1 January 1966, included one sub-headed 'Small Faces Clothes' that read 'Could you please tell me where The Small Faces buy all those fab clothes they wear?' signed Jill Upton (Leeds). Letters editor Maureen responds 'Well Jill, Steve Marriott tells me that the boys don't have any special shopping centre. If they see something that catches their eye, then they go and buy it!'

Then, the four-piece were ready to bounce back to even higher highs. No producer is credited on the label of the single, although it is widely accepted to be Kenny Lynch. And it represents a shift from hardcore Mod credibility to teen screamage pop stardom. Maybe 'I've Got Mine' was too densely structured, too intense? Maybe it was necessary to loosen up and be a little more playful. Fortunately, the reliable Kenny Lynch was on hand to furnish a catchy hook. After all, Manfred Mann joked about his string of hits being '5-4-Hubble-Diddy', with nonsense choruses that go 'Sha-La-La' and 'Doo-Wah-Diddy-Diddy.' Kenny's song had a simple singalong chorus, too; it's easy to imagine how a lesser band could have reduced the song to inconsequential blandness. But not so The Small Faces.

A crashing, discordant guitar chord, rimshot drums, little organ trims around the edges, and Steve Marriott's raw, totally convincing vocals. They take the rather trite song by the teeth and shake it up into something instantly radio-ear-grabbing. There's a break as the organ plays a little descending riff, then a slicing guitar line, as Steve throws in his 'sing my song' and 'c'mon children' ad-libs. There's a demotic lyric that catches the street dialogue of the time. 'Picked her up on a Friday night...' In the banter between mates, that's the way it was phrased. That's the one-to-one unsentimental way that meeting a girl was related, a smart anecdote. Then 'I asked her 'where do you wanna go?''... 'well, we went someplace, I don't know.' Just the correct amount of vagueness. It might have been to a Mod club, dancing to Motown records, or simply to a coffee bar. The location is less important than the fact of being there, together, in the sharp dazzle of the moment. But Kenny does not neglect the vital denouement of all those Romance-In-Pictures story magazines such as *Mirabelle* or *Roxy*. In just two simple, unelaborated lines, 'wanna know how my story ends?' with a break for the chorus chant, then 'well, we invited just a few close friends.' Marriage is the song's neat, closing, happy ending. No more clubbing, no more Dexies, Purple Hearts and blackbombers. Just the prospect of, as Squeeze would later artfully phrase it, 'nights by the telly' with the 'nappies smelling.'

There was a keen eye on the female record buyers. And they responded in hysterical droves. Overnight, The Small Faces were less than also-rans. They were stars. On the *Melody Maker* chart on 12 March 1966, they even hit number one, with Ian quoted as saying, 'We can't believe it. We're all jumping about hitting each other. It's tremendous.' On the *NME* chart, they were rated at number two, while *Record Retailer/Record Mirror* placed them at number three. This time, there would be no mistakes, no false moves, no miscalculations. For the eternity of a couple of years at least.

The B-side, credited to all four members of the group, is a snappy instrumental groove that nods its trendy head in the direction of Booker T & The MGs or Georgie Fame & The Blue Flames. While the meaning of the title might be up for discussion – what exactly is it we are being advised to grow? – it's the perfect soundtrack for dancing or cranking up to maximum volume at the house party while Mum and Dad are away. Ian recalls that 'we didn't have a B-side ready, but Steve had an idea for an instrumental twelve-bar that became 'Grow Your Own.' He loved the sound of the Hammond so much that he gave me free rein to go nuts in a solo. Surprisingly, hardly anyone caught on to the references to pot, our audiences possibly being too young, although we considered ourselves to be such devils.'

Sorry She's Mine – Single

'Sorry She's Mine' (Kenny Lynch) 2:58 b/w **'It's Not What You Do (But The Way That You Do It)'** (Winston) 3:00

Released: 1966, Decca F 12410

Produced by Glyn Johns. No chart placings

Meanwhile, Jimmy Winston, released from his Small Faces duties, went straight back in the studio with producer Glyn Jones and a Kenny Lynch song his former bandmates were also recording, which might be seen as a smart move, although chart response was negligible. There are many Small Faces characteristics in the Mod madness of hard drum and guitar lines, although Jimmy invests the vocals with a slight Jamaican twinge, a Ska influence that recurs on his self-penned B-side, which also flaunts a mid-point break, deep-bass and respectably killer guitar solo.

Hey Girl – Single

'Hey Girl' (Marriott, Lane) 2:17 b/w **'Almost Grown'** (McLagan, Jones, Lane, Marriott) 3:09
Released: 6 May 1966, Decca F 12393
Producer: Don Arden
Highest chart position: UK: 10 (on chart for nine weeks)

The cover of *New Musical Express* dated 6 May 1966 was dominated by a full-page advert for 'Out Today! A Great Double Event!' announcing 'this year's most exciting LP *Small Faces* and The New Single 'Hey Girl.' Hear these wonderful discs by The Fantastic Small Faces.'

Launched as part of their set at the '*NME* Poll-Winners' concert at Wembley Stadium, it was a brash, confident record, its grooves crammed full of energy and cheek, drum shots and guitar detonations. Del Shannon had scored with his song 'Hey Little Girl' as recently as March 1962. This record is set to a different tone entirely. Laddish? As laddish as scooter boys on the kerbside watching the miniskirt girls saunter by, young, male, testosterone-fuelled and hepped-up, but out for fun, living for the bright moment. But hey boy, hey girl, the kids are alright! Steve takes the lyric; the others do the 'hey, hey, hey' to add raucous call-and-response emphasis. There's a middle-eight that says, 'when I think of what I've missed, it makes me laugh inside, all the girls that I ain't kissed, just to keep my pride.' Not so much regrets, but a moment's thought of missed opportunities. It's a glorious pre-punk power-noise, as cheap and tacky as hell, to be played at full volume. An intoxicating inhale of city breath rifted with neon, cigarettes and Lambretta-exhaust, hard asphalt and a sky high with stars.

'Almost Grown' is a title borrowed from Chuck Berry tacked onto another sharp improvisational blues-'n'-soul dance instrumental, cooking up a storm that strongly features Kenney Jones' drums and McLagan's organ. There's a single thrown-in throwaway vocal line, 'I love you, you love me, don't you mess with 1-2-3'... and a rather camp 'oh! don't talk that way' in the fade, which means whatever you think it means. Studio banter...?

The label credits their notorious manager as producer, although this may simply be a courtesy. By now, The Small Faces knew their own way around the studio. Just before Christmas 1965, they collectively moved into 22 Westmoreland Terrace in Pimlico (no passport required!), close by Victoria Station, a group house rented by Arden for them in which to bond and rehearse, share music and dope. Together, in one big house, just like The Beatles in *Help*! Only Kenney, who'd barely turned seventeen, was a regular visitor rather than a resident, as he still stayed for the most part in his parents' home.

While Ian was still part of Boz & The Boz People the group had been one of the acts supporting The Byrds on their first UK tour. An affable David Crosby had come around the dressing room offering them friendly joints. Later, the Byrds' ground-breaking proto-psychedelic single 'Eight

Miles High' peaked in the UK chart in June 1966. The lyric, 'nowhere is there warmth to be found, among those afraid of losing their ground' references Ronnie Wood's band The Birds, who'd taken legal action against the American five-piece concerning the 'Byrds' name, and then 'rain grey town known for its sound, in places small faces unbound' which was a direct namecheck for The Small Faces! Both records were simultaneously on the same chart that Frank Sinatra's 'Strangers In The Night' dislodged The Rolling Stones 'Paint It, Black from the top spot. On 2 June, 'Hey Girl' was number ten, while 'Eight Miles High' was number 30 – to peak the following week at number 24.

The sixties storybook narrative was opening up into a vista of new pages, soundtracked by a solid wall of screamage girls. Of course, bobbysoxers had screamed at Frank Sinatra. Dungaree dolls had screamed at Elvis. But as the decade passed its midpoint, the screaming girls' phenomenon only intensified to hurricane proportions. With the advent of ever-shorter miniskirts and the promise of contraception, after decades of repression and imposed conformity, it represented a massive cathartic scream of released energies, an inarticulate speech of the heart amplified into collective mania. For musicians – for The Beatles – what was at first a stunningly positive yea-saying response rapidly became a barrier that prevented their stage performances from even being heard above the dense scream-barrage.

Even by mid-1964, the first Beatles-propelled Merseybeat wave was receding, with Billy J Kramer & The Dakotas, The Swinging Blue Jeans, Gerry & The Pacemakers, The Fourmost and The Merseybeats all slipping out of the charts, only to be replaced by an even more intense barrage of newer louder and hairier groups. The music was not about to relent, nor was the attitude that went with it. It only became more outrageous with the advent of The Kinks, The Animals, Manfred Mann, and The Pretty Things. If Gerry Marsden was the kind of boy your Mum would approve of, The Rolling Stones – lest we forget – were a kick in the teeth for everything that was respectable. The beat boom was confirming the best hopes of British teens, and the worst fears of their parents. 1965 marked the explosive arrival of The Who, The Yardbirds, Them (with Van Morrison), and then The Small Faces. While the newspapers fulminated against Mod, for The Small Faces, the fan-mania was still a fun source of satisfaction. Still a part of the game. Still a reward.

Yet there were hazards. *Melody Maker*, on 23 April 1966, carried a news item about 'fans seriously injured Small Faces drummer Kenney Jones and singer-guitarist Steve Marriott on Monday when riots broke out after the group played at Streatham's Silver Blades Ice Rink in London.' Kenney's dislocated shoulder was treated by a Harley Street specialist. Steve was knocked semi-unconscious and spent two bed days recovering. The injuries threatened dates on their tour with Crispian St Peters and a duo called The Truth.

Hits Vol.5 (EP)

Released: 1966, Decca EP DFE 8663

Tracklisting: The Small Faces ('Hey Girl'), plus Los Bravos ('Black Is Black'), The Animals ('Don't Bring Me Down'), The Alan Price Set ('I Put A Spell On You')

Boasting an impressive beat group roster of signings, Decca adds the most recent Small Faces hit to The Animals' second single for the label since re-signing from Columbia, giving the Goffin-King song a burning fuzz-tone guitar treatment, joining their former keyboard player Alan Price, who was forging his own solo chart profile. Los Bravos were a curious one-off, a Spanish group with German singer Mike Kogel, who scored a massive international hit with 'Black Is Black' (Decca F 22419).

Small Faces

Personnel:
Steve Marriott: lead guitar, lead and backing vocals
Ronnie Lane: bass, backing & lead vocals.
Kenney Jones: drums
Ian McLagan: keyboards, backing vocals.
Jimmy Winston: keyboards, backing vocals, rhythm guitar
Plus:
Kenny Lynch: backing vocals on tracks 3, 7 & 12.
Released: 11 May 1966, Decca Records LK 4790
Highest chart position: UK: 3 (on the LP chart for 25 weeks), Finland: 8

When Ian McLagan was confirmed as a member of the four-piece, he was disappointed to discover his pay grade was actually reduced from £30 to £20 a week!

Only the energy levels were confrontational. There's an argument that rock music had never been driven by such a raging anger of energies before or since. For The Who. And The Kinks. The Pretty Things, Creation and The Rolling Stones. It was a generational thing.

The album was recorded, mixed and mastered in just three days. 'Incredibly', admits Ian, 'most of the tracks on that album were done while we three hooligans were tripping out of our tiny minds and with Kenney on leapers. If it sounded like a party, it really was!' The sleeve photo was taken on the Thames Albert Embankment outside Decca House, against some graffiti faces that Steve had artfully embellished with spliffs.

The Small Faces played the Marquee Club on Wardour Street on 26 April 1966, with Liverpool's The Clayton Squares as support. Entrance was 7/6 for members and 8/6 for non-members.

In the spirit of punk nihilism, The Sex Pistols would later remake The Small Face's breakthrough hit with John Lydon sneering 'I want you to know that I HATE you baby…' as an acknowledgement of their predecessors.

Side One

'Shake' (Sam Cooke) 2:55

When Ronnie Lane spoke of the group's early repertoire, including Otis Redding's 'Shake' – of course, he meant Sam Cooke's 'Shake', the song by the smooth soulster who'd been shot in a dubious motel incident and died on 11 December 1964. 'Shake' was one of the various dance-craze shots that had rippled through teendom in the wake of The Twist's seismic global success, although the dance-move instructions are fairly limited, 'let your body loop-de-loop, put your hands on your hip, come on and let your backbone slip, move your body like your hip… and just shake!' I've never quite understood how to let your backbone slip. Nevertheless, The Supremes had done 'Shake' as part of their 'tribute' album, *We Remember Sam Cooke* (April 1965, Motown

MT629, UK Tamla-Motown TML11012), but Otis Redding gave the song a Memphis horns-driven Stax make-over for his *Otis Blue* album (1965, Atlantic ATL5041) – and would do a soul-stirring gotta-gotta-gotta live version at the 'Monterey Pop Festival' 17 June 1967.

The Small Faces take the Otis album version as their template. 'You listen while I'm talkin' to you, I'll tell you what I'm gonna do, there's a new thing going around, I'll tell you what it's putting down.' Kenney thumps out walloping beats like he's playing on oil drums. Ronnie takes the vocals, which is a generous democratic gesture – much as Ringo was allocated one song on each Beatles album – but he lacks Steve's biting leather-lunged projection. Although Ian McLagan contributes an effective organ solo, subtlety does not figure; the track has the raw, spontaneous attack of a live small-club session. This is what it must have been like to witness The Small Faces play in those cramped, sweaty Mod venues during the long, hot summer of 1965. Meanwhile, R&B shouter Rod Stewart, who had been dropped by Decca following one failed single, issued his own version of 'Shake' b/w 'I Just Got Some' in April 1966 (Columbia DB7892) as his third single, with an arrangement credited to Brian Auger. Even more bizarrely, at the late date of 1973, the American Pride label issued a 45rpm Small Faces single 'Shake' b/w 'Runaway' (PR1006), as a special Disc Jockey sampler from their LP *Early Faces* (Pride PRD0001).

'Come On Children' (Jones, Lane, Marriott, Winston) 4:20

A stand-out example of just how good interactions within the original four-piece lineup could be. There's a long, raucous play-in that leads to what appears to be almost improvised lines of vocal, 'I feel alright, y'know I feel alright', and Steve's preaching-style exhortations… throwing in snatched lines from the 1940s song 'You Are My Sunshine', which has been variously recorded by Gene Autry and Bing Crosby, but perhaps more relevant was a 1962 R&B interpretation by Ray Charles.

Why introduce those sampled lines? It's as though the track evolved from an intense jam session, and whatever came to mind was sucked into the stream-of-consciousness song construction. In a confessional out-loud mode, Steve speak-sings 'as I lay sleeping baby, I dreamed I held you in my arms, when I woke up, I found I was mistaken, do you know that I hung my head and I cried.' They alter the dynamic thrust for a slow-down, then a slow, gradual build – 'you ready?' before it re-explodes back into the mega-riff. Closing into a final 'I wanna hear it, own up each and every one of you, don't it make you feel – alright!'

There's a blistering alternate 3:23-minute version issued on a French EP (November 1965, Disques Decca 457091), which increases the impression of extemporisation with 'everybody got problems, Baby… but you and me, child, don't you know it – 'cos woman you need lurve, you're gonna get it' either edited off or not included on the official album version. A live version, captured 9 January 1966 at the Belgium *Twenty Club*, was included on a 2021 album issued on Nice Records, curated by Kenney Jones himself, which flaunts yet more ad-libs.

'You Better Believe It' (Lynch, Ragovoy) 2:19
When it comes to constructing Pop, Kenny Lynch knows his way around song structures tied into a catchy hook, which the delivery and performance elevate into an edginess that takes it way beyond its natural limitations. Jordan 'Jerry' Ragovoy was a jobbing songwriter with a string of classic hits to his credit, taking in Irma Thomas, Lorraine Ellison ('Stay With Me'), Garnet Mimms & The Enchanters, The Rolling Stones ('Time Is On My Side') as well as Elvis Presley (the *Girl Happy* movie theme). Together, the duo concocted an irresistible minor work of relentless euphoria about a girl who 'can stop the rain and make the sun come out.' Inevitably there's a 2:49 alternate version on the album's expanded 2012 CD edition with a strongly featured organ solo from Ian. But when Steve tells you to believe he loves that girl, you believe it.

'It's Too Late' (Jones, Lane, Marriott, Winston) 2:37
Yes, it was the B-side of failed single 'I've Got Mine', one of three previously-issued tracks on the album, and yes, it was one of five tracks remaindered from the Jimmy Winston lineup – with Ian McLagan featured on the other seven – but it slots seamlessly into the vinyl Side One sequencing. Among other statistics, Kenny Lynch adds backing voice to three tracks – 'You Better Believe It', 'Sorry She's Mine' and 'Sha-La-La-La-Lee.' It's never too late.

'One Night Stand' (Lane, Marriott) 1:50
Thom Keyes was an American-born SF writer who contributed stories to the British magazines *New Worlds* ('Election Campaign', January 1965) and *Science Fantasy* ('Xenophilia', June 1965). But his debut novel, *All Night Stand* (1966, WH Allen) bypasses alien worlds for a scurrilous foray into the Pop milieu, 'The definitive novel about rock 'n' roll, the picture of a group that isn't The Rolling Stones, The Beatles, The Animals (or The Small Faces), but has features in common with all of them – a swift rise to success and an outrageously irreverent view of life.' The Mayflower paperback edition cover blurb claims it as 'THE BEAT SCENE... Observed as never before against the long, lonely landscape in which it is set', encapsulating the novel's sleazy flavour of overnight groupie encounters.

This brief but forceful product of the Marriott-Lane writing partnership is quite equally candid, 'times have changed and my name's in lights', Steve brags to his overnight girl, 'I'm the king of my new-found world', so she should not expect a relationship, nothing more than a fleeting sexual fling; after all, she's nothing more than 'a one night stand, yeah.' Sudden fame released beat groups into a testosterone-fuelled playground of compliant nubile girls. There can be few who didn't take advantage of the sensual delights on offer. But few were as honest about it as this track!

'Whatcha Gonna Do About It?' (Samwell, Potter) 1:59

Ready Steady Go! was the place for clued-up, trend-hungry teen-birds and fashion-sharp young Mod wannabes in the provinces. A film of the four Small Faces looning down Carnaby Street is an object lesson in hip, young and trend awareness. Ronnie Lane does that 'Harry Worth' TV visual gag of using the mirroring effect of a corner shop window to seemingly levitate. Fleets of migrating scooters with mirrors and aerials take off as though telepathically coordinated in shoals that weave from the kerb into traffic. On Saturday, 7 August 1965, The Small Faces make their TV debut on ITV's *Thank Your Lucky Stars: Summer Spin*. By Thursday, 16 September, they take 'Whatcha Gonna Do About It?' onto BBC's *Top Of The Pops*… and on the following day, I watch them on *Ready Steady Go!*, mesmerised by that extenuated fuzz-guitar solo, and by the effortless cool they exude.

Ian McLagan makes his TV debut doing 'Whatcha Gonna Do About It?' and 'I've Got Mine' on the less-than-trendy kids' show *Crackerjack* (17:00, 12 November 1965). Delivered in the BBC's rather patronising style, introduced by host Leslie Crowther – later of *The Price Is Right* – and diminutive comedy actor Peter Glaze, the show that night also featured Valerie Walsh and guitarist Bert Weedon. Yet at the time, prior to streaming, cable or domestic video machines, with only two mainstream TV channels (BBC2 had launched 20 April 1964), an appearance on the immensely popular *Crackerjack* would guarantee an immense audience of potential teen and pre-teen record-buyers. Their credibility was redeemed by doing another *Ready Steady Go!* session the same day, doing 'I've Got Mine' live.

Side Two

'Sorry She's Mine' (Lynch) 2:48

Jimmy Winston might have filched this song to launch his own solo career, but this driving version has the edge. There's another guy coming sniffing around his girl ('gir-er-er-irl') with nefarious intent, but Steve warns the interloper off, advising him don't waste your time, fella, try to win her and you'll lose. She may be a free spirit, she goes around dancing all the time. But this is no controlling situation. In a slower mid-section, he admits, 'she may go away from me for a little time, but she runs back home to me just to prove she's mine.' With snappy drums and fugacious organ break, this is a strongly assertive take on another of Kenny Lynch's catchy melodic inventions. And of course … hey-hey-hey, he's not sorry at all.

'Own Up Time' (Jones, Lane, Marriott, McLagan) 1:47

'Own up time' was a kind of coded in-group catchphrase they used to mean 'tell the truth.'

When Ronnie Lane owns up that 'none of us could play, but we were keen', he was underestimating the group's collective synergy. Rock music was never supposed to be about virtuosity, although some musicians and fans would be temporarily deluded away into believing that. As a fully interactive four-piece, The Small Faces instrumental tracks were always a joy. This was recorded 'with Ronnie and Steve standing on chairs, and you can hear the screaming and shouting at the beginning. There was nothing worked out; it was just a jam', recalls Ian.

But it was more than just a jam and never quite the backing track that they never got around to adding vocals to. Based somewhere around the Booker T & The MGs Memphis Sound, each corner of the quartet plays an equally essential part, with Ian's liquid Hammond organ lines jostling around Steve's brittle shrapnel guitar bursts tied into Ronnie's deep-down gut bass and Kenney's solid drum pattern. They fit together as integral as jigsaw pieces. It's a precise non-verbal expression of all the flash, passion and claustrophobia of the time. The fade comes way too soon ...

'You Need Loving' (credited to Lane and Marriott) 3:59
This epic recording has a complex history as well as a litigious future. Listen to this track now and there's an instant recognition buzz to the blistering incandescent sonic attack of the opening cut of Led Zeppelin's mega-selling second album, with Robert Plant's orgasmic howls and its huge electronic swirling mid-section. The very first time I heard it on the radio, I was mesmerised. I bought the album entirely on the strength of that one hearing.

Both tyro Robert Plant and studio musician Jimmy Page hung out at Small Faces gigs. They were followers, taking notes and picking up techniques. 'You Need Loving' was a part of The Small Faces' earliest setlist. There's no way the Led Zep duo were not familiar with the track. Yet the original liner notes of *Led Zeppelin II* (October 1969, Atlantic 588198/ USA SD8236) credit the song to the four Led Zeppelin band members. Following litigation, another writer name was added to the credits, that of Bluesman Willie Dixon. Hence, the plot complexifies.

Own up time, the real trail goes back further still, all the way back to 1962 when Muddy Waters recorded the Willie Dixon song 'You Need Love' as Chess 1839, as a slow, insidious crawl. It is this original vinyl disc that The Small Faces took and reconfigured into 'You Need Loving.'

The Small Faces had adapted a Solomon Burke riff as the spine for 'Whatcha Gonna Do About It?' That was a case of smart appropriation. No copyright had been infringed. While Traditional Folk and Blues songs, where the authorship has long since been lost in the mists of time, are continually being reclaimed and reinterpreted with the addition of the simple, convenient credit 'trad: arranged by' – 'House Of The Rising Sun' and 'Scarborough Fair' both became massive hits, for The Animals and by Simon & Garfunkel by this process of cultural assimilation. That is the way music evolves. But this was not the case with 'You Need Loving', where the authorship was beyond doubt and clearly documented.

The Small Faces do not use the same earth-shaking riff as the Led Zeppelin track, but it's recognisably the same song. It's far bigger than its 3:59-minute playing time and more dense than a thimbleful of neutron star molecules, with full-frontal guitar assault powered by handclap-augmented drums. Steve's soul-wrenching vocals take lines from Willie Dixon but also 'eeny-meeny-miney-moe's into a segue of 'Land Of A Thousand Dances' with its reeling list of the Pony, Mashed Potato, the Watusi and other trendy dance-fads. Issued months before the classic hit by Wilson Pickett with the Muscle Shoals rhythm section and the Memphis horns, The Small Faces use the original Chris Kenner version without the 'na-na-na-na' hook borrowed from Cannibal & The Headhunters before delving back into a climactic 'You need loving' closer. The Wilson Pickett single became the go-to dance record at every Mod club across the land. Hell, I even danced to its irresistible energy rush myself. But for The Small Faces, this track is the album's motherlode, driven by analogue mischief and opportunism while playing tag with the sound barrier itself.

Robert Plant vs Steve Marriott? It's an amusing game, although comparisons are odious. They're both formidable high-volume vocalists. Marriott has maybe a greater degree of control whereas Plant has a more histrionic manic nirvana edge. But when this album was recorded, Robert Plant was still a year away from making his own debut solo singles, the slow bluesy 'Our Song' b/w 'Laughin', Cryin', Laughin'' (March 1967, CBS 202656) and 'Long Time Coming' b/w 'I've Got A Secret' (July 1967, CBS 2858), neither of which made the slightest ripple. The Small Faces got there first. They defined the possibilities that others would use as the jumping-off point for their own adventures. It will stand.

Ian finishes the long and convoluted history with, 'I hope someone got paid along the way because I know we didn't.'

'Don't Stop What You're Doing' (Jones, Lane, Marriott, Winston) 1:55
A prowling echoey guitar figure, Steve seizes the lyric about the high-flying bird that just flew in through the window and told him that her love is strong, as Ronnie and Jimmy Winston coo in the background like The Miracles behind Smokey Robinson. It's way too brief by far, 'I got something to tell ya, are ya listening?' Steve urges – and yes, we're listening, we were grabbed from the first groove, then 'play the Blues!' and they play 'the sweetest song you ever heard.' Perhaps this is just a throwaway track recorded early on in the first sessions, but it proves just how volatile the collective chemistry could be with the four playing on cruise control.

'E Too D' (Lane, Marriott) 3:02
The very earliest Small Faces set list was made up of 'Come On Children' and 'You Need Loving' plus their cover of Marvin Gaye's Motown hit 'Baby Don't

You Do It', which was also a part of The Who's early live set. Then there was 'Ooh Poo Pah Doo', originally recorded during an Allen Toussaint-produced session by Louisiana Blues singer Jessie Hill in 1960 for the Minit label, although it was subsequently done by many others, including The Shirelles, Etta James and Rufus Thomas. Another song, for which Jimmy Winston took the hoarse rowdy vocals, either improvising or forgetting the lyric, was called 'Jump Back', written and recorded as 'Jump Back Honey' in 1952 for the Okeh label by 'Queen Of The Boogie' Hadda Brooks, and covered the same year for Capitol Records by Ella Mae Morse.

The other song the early Small Faces based their set around was the live jam 'E Too D', named – and misspelt – for its two-chord progression. For the recording session, Ian recalls how 'Steve's fiery guitar thrashing at the beginning still sounds great, and it's a wonder he didn't break more strings because both he and Ronnie used solid glass plectrums that were as thick as threepenny bits and didn't bend at all.'

'Sha-La-La-La-Lee' (Lynch, Schuman) 2:56
Later in the second half of the song, where 'I held her close and asked her again if she was gonna be my baby', it's that single word 'again' that differentiates the line from its use earlier in the song. A minimalist approach. Why go to the trouble of writing a new verse when you can simply repurpose what you have already? Or more generously, maybe the singer, Steve Marriott, despite the song's strident bravado, is uncertain about the girl who looks good and moves so fine, the girl he's just picked up, and he needs the reassurance of her repeated answer 'Oh yeah, Oh yeah, Oh yeah, Oh yeah, Oh yeah…'?

Conclusion
The first CD edition in July 1988 by London Records 8205722 included four bonus tracks taken from three singles B-sides and one A-side; 'What's A Matter Baby', 'I've Got Mine', 'Grow Your Own' and 'Almost Grown.' Fifteen of the 16 tracks were in mono, the exception being a stereo mix of 'Sha La La La Lee.' It was first remastered for CD in 1997 by Deram Records, with bonus tracks of alternative versions of 'Shake', 'Come On Children', 'Whatcha Gonna Do About It', 'Own Up Time' and 'E Too D.' *Small Faces: Fortieth Anniversary Edition* (2006, Decca) boasted twenty-three tracks, including singles A-Sides and B-Sides, 'What's A Matter Baby', 'I've Got Mine', 'Grow Your Own', 'Hey Girl' and 'Almost Grown.' A 2012 double-disc *Deluxe Edition* featured outtakes, non-album singles, alternate versions and mixes, with remastering, while the overall reissue was overseen by surviving band members Ian McLagan and Kenney Jones.

The 1966-67 Decca Singles and EPs

All Or Nothing – Single

'All Or Nothing' (Marriott, Lane) 3:04 b/w **'Understanding'** (Marriott, Lane) 2:45

Released: 5 August 1966, Decca F 12470

Highest chart position: UK: 1 (on the chart for 12 weeks)

This is the single that deposed The Beatles 'Yellow Submarine' from number one, allowing *Melody Maker* to headline 'Faces Sink Sub!' While *Disc*, on 10 September 1966, announced 'Small Faces Leap to number one', while adding support features 'Gary Walker: Wining & Dining', 'Sandie Shaw: The Things I've Missed', while Gene Pitney claims that he 'Hates That 'Money' Thing.'

Suppose the challenging proposition was to take the commercial hooks that Kenny Lynch had supplied but combine them with inventive and challenging rock music, 'All Or Nothing' delivered in spades. This is the undisputed peak of their Decca period, with integrity and commercialism poised in acute equilibrium, yielding no quarter to either. The instrumentation is sparse but so tight it achieves density; Kenney's opening drum-roll, Steve's guitar, Plonk's bass and Ian's keyboard are immaculately interdependent and balanced against each other. The song exploits the range of Marriott's pleading vocals, from the restrained first verse that allows the timbre of his voice to be heard, erupting into the full-throttle hurt and passion, 'You'll hear my children say!' he roars into the harmony chorus, urging 'ya gotta gotta gotta keep on trying, yeah!' The perfect Pop 45rpm record is a thing of awe and wonder. Compressing all those vital hit ingredients down into a precise 3:04-minute burst of sound.

There's an atmospheric video of the group lip-synching the hit on the streets of what seems to be Stockholm, supposedly busking; it's chilly, plumes of their breath hang in the air, Kenney wears dark shades, Ian wears a long patent leather coat, passers-by toss coins, during the 'bop-bop-bop' break an elderly lady walks past in a big black hat and spectacles... Steve, in corduroy jacket, mischievously follows her, aping her gait as the others grin. It catches the group's pure play element in a spontaneous moment trapped in time.

Later, they would replicate the track's little guitar lick on 'Afterglow Of Your Love' as a reminder of just how far they'd come. Paul Weller would also allude to the riff.

There had been a Frank Sinatra song called 'All Or Nothing At All', but that was in the prehistory of 1939. This was NOW!

The Small Faces always combine a strong A-side with a value-for-money flipside, and 'Understanding' is classier than most, to the extent that The Sex Pistols would use the song as part of their early set (a live version recorded at the London *Nashville Rooms* on 3 April 1976 was included on the Sex Pistols 2002 Virgin box-set). In that, it's a mature plea for compassion and reasoned debate in a relationship – 'when people ask me what love's all about, there's one thing I can say' – to Ronnie, 'we thought we were laying it down for people, but we didn't know... we were trying, I suppose' (to *DISCoveries*, November 1989), yet it's also an awesome blast of power-pop that lifts off with a 'la-la-la' riff, throws in Steve's trademark 'Come on children, I want to hear you one more time', and even takes a midpoint break for the kind of ref's whistle that techno rave celebrants would revive a couple of decades later. It is a strong enough track to have made A-side status in its own right. In fact, the B-side of 'All Of Nothing' was revived by The Tony Jackson Group – and the ousted original singer with The Searchers does a credible version of 'Understanding' on a 1967 Portuguese EP 'Just Like Me' (Estúdio EEP50013), reissued in the UK as part of the 1991 *Just Like Me* compilation (Strange Things STCD10003).

'You see, I love this life I lead', sings Steve, as The Small Faces play a heavy schedule of gigs: the prestigious 'Sixth National Jazz & Blues Festival' on the Windsor Racecourse Meadow (Friday, 29 July 1966) on a bill with Spencer Davis, The Soul Agents, Geno Washington & The Ram Jam Band for just 10/-. Cream debut on the Sunday bill with The Action and The Alan Bown Set; they play despite deluging rain. Then The Small Faces play the Redruth Flamingo (3 August), the Leicester Granby Hall (5), the Nelson Imperial (6), the Blackpool South Pier (7), the Bath Pavilion (8), the Malvern Winter Gardens (9), then record an insert for TVs *Scene At 6:30* (10 August) and for *Top Of The Pops* the following day. Then more gigs, the Lewisham Odeon (12), the Finsbury Park Astoria (13) and a return to the Blackpool South Pier (14).

Fabulous 208 (13 August 1966) called The Small Faces 'the hippest boys in the business' as they prepared to top the *Ready Steady Go!* bill (Sunday 14 August), with reports that 'both Steve and Kenney have bought their own horses, and that in the future the group hope to purchase a riding stable. Steve and Kenney have stabled their horses out at Epping and as soon as they get a day off, they're out there getting in plenty of practice.' Adding 'funny, but I keep getting visions of four Small Faces on horseback, riding along the M1 on their way to gig!' The photo accompanying the gossip shows them drinking glasses of celebratory champagne.

Rave, in August 1966, has a tailor's dummy cover centre, tagged 'This is a dummy. Either side is a Small Face! Inside, there are more Small Faces...' Ronnie in colour-patched jacket stands to the left, Steve in brown stripes to the right.

NME carried a 'Small Face A Week' series through September 1966. Written by Keith Altham, it began with Steve relating how 'once Plonk and I tried dishwashing in Joe Lyons, but we went off our heads there after twenty-four hours', followed by 'Mystery Man' Ronnie 'Plonk' Lane. There was even a picture-strip telling of The Small Faces story titled 'It All Happened To Steve.'

The Small Faces were now the ace faces that London Mods turned to as The Who became progressively more hairy.

Hits Vol.6 (EP)

Released: 1966, Decca EP DFE 8667

Tracklisting: The Small Faces ('All Or Nothing'), plus Lulu ('Don't Answer Me'), The Alan Price Set ('Hi-Lilli Hi-Lo') and Jonathan King ('Just Like A Woman').

17 October, The Small Faces miss the first two tour dates – the Aldershot and Romford ABCs – due to a dispute over billing with the headlining Hollies. The tour continues with both bands sharing equal billing. Paul Jones and Paul & Barry Ryan are also playing.

Small Faces (New Zealand EP)

Released: 1966, New Zealand Decca

'Sha-La-La-La-Lee', 'Whatcha Gonna Do About It' and 'All Or Nothing'

'This is the first proper record we've done instead of all that Mickey Mouse stuff like 'Sha-La-La-La-Lee'', Steve told Richard Green in *Record Mirror* as 'All Or Nothing' topped the chart. 'We take writing far more seriously now than we used to. I don't think there is anything The Small Faces could do to improve 'All Or Nothing.' With some of the other numbers we could have done a much better job if we could spend more time on them.'

My Mind's Eye – Single

'My Mind's Eye' (Marriott, Lane) 2:06 b/w **'I Can't Dance With You'** (Marriott, Lane) 3:12

Released: 11 November 1966, Decca F 12500

Highest chart position: UK: 4 (on chart for 11 weeks), Netherlands: 13, Sweden: 17, Germany: 24

Dreaming days with minds ablaze. Introspection isn't something necessarily associated with The Small Faces. Yet here they are, dreaming their dreams away. 'People running everywhere, running through my life, I couldn't give a care because they'll never see all that I can see with my mind's eye.' It's said this track was intended for album release, but Don Arden decided the group needed a single in time to meet the profitable Christmas market, and this demo was eminently suitable – particularly as it filches a long passage from the Christmas song 'Gloria In Excelsis Deo', which is described as 'fluidly sustained through 16 notes of a rising and falling melismatic melodic sequence.'

I remember enthusing when the single came on the jukebox in The Tiger pub after a day's college in the Hull old town, and my Mod friend Patrick said, 'yes, I always liked this Christmas song.' I didn't quite understand his enigmatic comment until I related it to the 'Hosanna in excelsis' chorus. And yes, it clicked. The recording is admittedly raw, but has the undeniable spark of rough spontaneity and the cheekily blatant theft works as prime-time Small Faces.

It entered the *NME* chart at number 20 on 19 November 1966, rose to number nine, then to number six, to peak at number four on 10 December beneath Tom Jones' 'Green Green Grass Of Home', Val Doonican's 'What Would I Be' (!) and The Beach Boys epic 'Good Vibrations.' It hung around into the New Year charts. Despite its success, its release was viewed as a betrayal that incurred the group's displeasure and was a factor in their break from both Decca and Arden. 'I Can't Dance With You' is a moodier Soul workout with full fatback percussion from Kenney and a precise organ-break from Ian. Steve warns, 'look out, girl' while demanding, 'which way you wanna go, ha, to the left or the right?' before Ronnie joins him for the harmony chorus. The lyric slyly uses 'dancin'' as a metaphor for 'romancin'', directed at an undecided object of his amorous attentions, cautioning her 'you know you're steppin' out of sight.' It constitutes a good-value flip-side and was later gathered onto *The Small Faces: The Early Years* compilation (1988, See For Miles SEECD247). The Valentines, a band recording in Australia for Perth's Clarion label, did a cover of 'I Can't Dance With You' as the B-side of their debut single version of Arthur Alexander's 'Everyday I Have To Cry' during the summer of 1967. Despite the power-tonsil vocals of Bon Scott, who went on to front AC/DC, their interpretation offers no match for Marriott's fervent delivery.

Small Faces (French EP)

Released: 1967, French Decca

Tracklisting: 'My Minds Eye', 'I Can't Dance With You', 'Shake' and 'One Night Stand'

'Basically, it's rock 'n' roll – course it is', Ronnie Lane told *Melody Maker*. 'I suppose our roots are in the old Stax and Otis Redding records. They are still the Guv'nor sounds. Those were exciting times when Motown and Stax were happening, and The Stones and Who came along.'

The Immediate Years

My Way Of Giving – Single (B-side by Chris Farlowe)

'My Way Of Giving' (Marriott, Lane) 2:33 b/w **'You're So Good For Me'** (Oldham, Rose, Skinner, Bell) 2:17
Released: 27 January 1967, Immediate IM041. Producer: Mick Jagger
Arranger: Art Greenslade. No chart placings
The B-side, written with two members of Twice As Much, was lifted from the album that Oldham had pretentiously titled *The Art Of Chris Farlowe* (IMLP006). The raspy-voiced soul singer, already highly regarded within the cult London R&B scene, was taken up by Andrew Oldham as a star in the crown of the Immediate roster and – gifted a Jagger-Richards song and production – promptly took 'Out Of Time' (IM035) to number one. He followed it with another Rolling Stones song, 'Ride On Baby' (IM038), which achieved a less impressive number 31. Then it was Steve & Ronnie's turn! They provide a strong original composition. There's massive thumping percussion, then Farlowe's big blustering vocals, with Steve and Ronnie's voices clearly audible in the backup chorus. The single secured Chris a *Top Of The Pops* slot backed up by his regular band, The Thunderbirds, which included Albert Lee's guitar and a young Carl Palmer on drums. Despite this, the single only crawled up to a disappointing number 48.

I Can't Make It – Single

'I Can't Make It' (Marriott, Lane) 2:12 b/w **'Just Passing'** (Marriott, Lane) 1:15
Released: 3 March 1967, Decca F 12565
Highest chart position: UK: 26 (on chart for seven weeks)
'After two whirlwind years clowning around London in the mid-sixties, playing up their image as speed-loving Mods with tight tunes and even tighter suits, The Small Faces finally grew up in 1967' said Gordon Thomson to *Observer Music Monthly* in June 2004.

From Soul, style and scooters, by now, the group had met Andrew Loog Oldham, who seemed to be everything that Don Arden was not. Arden was a gangster enforcer; 'we were in fear for our physical well-being', admitted Ronnie. Oldham was young and hip in dark shades, an idealist with a smooth line of chat and a curriculum vitae that included packaging The Rolling Stones into an acceptably marketable proposition. Steve Marriott had already contributed session harmonica to his Andrew Oldham Orchestra projects, an occasional album indulgence with arranger John Paul Jones that ran to *Sixteen Hip Hits* (1964, Ace Of Clubs ACL1180) and *The Rolling Stones Songbook* (1965, Decca SKL4796). Having already been a catalyst in using Jagger-Richards compositions to accelerate the careers of Marianne Faithful, Twice As Much and Chris Farlowe, Oldham was conspiring with 'prematurely balding desk jockey' (Ian's description) publicist-producer Tony Calder to launch Immediate Records, intended to be a pioneering Indie label designed to exploit Oldham's connections with the hiperati of the London R&B club scene.

Ian noticed that 'if I asked a question he couldn't answer, he'd slide around it with a stoned smile and pass me the joint, which seemed to set the pattern for all of our meetings.' But Oldham promised The Small Faces a more sympathetic ear with an artist's sensitivity to production and studio time. It seemed the perfect proposition. So they jumped.

This single unfortunately fell between the cracks by being caught up in the viciously acrimonious litigation necessary to extricate them from Decca Records and from Don Arden's managerial control. According to Arden's obituary in *The Guardian* on 25 July 2007, 'The Small Faces eventually won their freedom, but all attempts at retrieving royalties due from Arden found them locked in court battles, finally receiving payment only in 1977.'

Both of these tracks were recorded for Immediate but leased back to Decca in order to fulfil contractual obligations as a temporary expediency. As such, the group were dissatisfied with the compromise and refused to perform any promotional work, which explains the low chart position of a lowly number 26. Despite this, it remains an intriguing coupling.

The opening line of 'I Can't Make It' – 'I know how you're feeling' – carries just the slightest trace elements of The Temptations' 'I know you wanna leave me' play in to Norman Whitfield-Eddie Holland's 'Ain't Too Proud To Beg' – perhaps too close to be entirely coincidental. After all, The Temptations were floor-fillers at all the trendiest Mod clubs. But the Small Faces song is a powerful soul-deep work-out in its own right, with Kenney's drums joined by Ronnie's sharp bass-throb; Steve's vocals are as powerful as we've come to expect as he pleads 'I can't make it without you, you know it's true, girl, ha!' over Ian's moody organ, before delivering her the ultimatum 'get yourself together and under control, and take me baby, before I decide to go', with Ian and Ronnie joining in the sympathetic call-back harmonies. There's evidence that they did perform 'I Can't Make It' as part of a short set done for the *Morecambe & Wise* TV show in April, and there's a blistering live clip lifted from the German *Beat Club* broadcast from Bremen. But this is a transitional track, with all the spiky attacking energies of their Decca back-catalogue, while the brief 'Just Passing' is carried on the whimsical breeze of chemically enhanced awareness, a 'feeling of spring like the wing of a bird that is flying.' Steve counts in with 'one and-a two and-a three and-a four and-a' before Ronnie sings in swirly waltz-time punctuated by parps and echo voices. The line 'my mind does go old and I'm looked at, inspected, hated, accepted' is heavily distorted, and when he sings 'the wise men they wrangle, their minds look for angles and meaning', Steve adds his ghost emphasis 'meaning' a moment later. The track closes with bursts of delighted laughter and a ripple of feedback (as with The Beatles' 'Penny Lane' and The Monkees' 'Pleasant Valley Sunday'). At a mere 1:15-minute's length, they could easily have added an instrumental break, then repeated the full 1:15 once again to bring up the playing time, but they didn't. In the same way that

The Beach Boys added the throwaway 1:17-minute 'You're Welcome' to the flip of their July 1967 'Heroes And Villains' single. Or the even more concise track 'Whistle In' at 1:04 on their *Smiley Smile* album. It was a part of the experimental whimsy of the time. The Beatles would later insert brief single-idea tracks onto *The White Album* – 'Wild Honey Pie' at 0:52 – and 'Mean Mister Mustard' on *Abbey Road* at 1:06.

The slight slip in the single's chart profile had no visible effect on The Small Faces' trend-status. *Rave* magazine, in April 1967, ran a feature, 'At A Small Face's Place: Ian McLagan' by journalist Maureen O'Grady. The group commenced a twice-nightly package tour that kicked off at the Essex ABC Romford, with 'The world's no.1 Hit Recorder' Roy Orbison with his own American musicians The Candy Men, 'The Exciting!' Small Faces, plus prettily photogenic vocal duo brothers Paul & Barry Ryan, Sonny Childe with the TNTs (he would later have hits as R.B. Greaves), The Robb Storme Group (who later became Orange Bicycle), plus Jeff Beck with a group that consisted of Ronnie Wood, Aynsley Dunbar and lanky singer Rod Stewart.

Beck quit the tour after just two dates, including one at London's Finsbury Park Astoria on 3 March 1967, where some unseen hand pulled the plug backstage and silenced them. Ian McLagan denied any such act of sabotage. Beck told *Disc & Music Echo,* 'It's not worth appearing on a bill starring such names as Roy Orbison and The Small Faces. You're just playing to fans of these acts. It's a waste of time trying to get across.' He went on to promote his hit single 'Hi-Ho Silver Lining', while his slot on the tour was filled by P.P Arnold showcasing her single 'The First Cut Is The Deepest.' The tour programme profile says, 'The sensational Small Faces, now recognised as the hottest group in the country following their emergence as British champions in the *New Musical Express* 1966 Chart championship, are all set to take over where the Beatles left off…'

(Tell Me) Have You Ever Seen Me – Single (B-side by The Apostolic Intervention)

'(Tell Me) Have You Ever Seen Me' (Marriott, Lane) 2:04 b/w
'Madame Garcia' (Dines, Shirley) 2:50
Released: 7 April 1967, Immediate IM 043. No chart placings

The Small Faces were the biggest small band on the scene. But Pop stardom can be notoriously transient. As Ringo said, 'you're only as big as your last hit record.' Fame can give and it can take away. To have a chance of building a longer-term career within the music industry, it's useful to acquire songwriting and studio-production skills that can be employed later on acts other than yourself. Paul McCartney spoke about how, once the Beatles bubble burst, he and John could continue as a kind of British Goffin-King partnership. That never happened, but it is something that he was thinking about.

Marriott-Lane was shaping up into a very accomplished writing partnership.

Taking a step into the psychedelic lounge, Steve took an interest in the Brit-psych group The Apostolic Intervention, fronted by Angus Shirley (lead guitar) and vocalist Peter 'Dino' Dines (organ). Beguiled by the potential of their sound, he persuaded Andrew Loog Oldham to sign them. Steve subsequently offered an original song – '(Tell Me) Have You Ever Seen Me' to them, much to Ronnie's chagrin. Ronnie intended to use the song on the next Small Faces album. Bass guitarist Bob Argent was unable to play for the session, so Steve stepped in, taking joint producer credits as well with Ronnie.

It starts with the signature Small Faces drum-roll, then kicks into the forceful lyric punched out with a catchy chanted 'hey-hey-hey' vocal riff. The Hammond-led instrumental B-side, 'Madame Garcia', with credits on some pressings claiming this is another Marriott-Lane composition, was recorded in the same session, with Steve's voice again audible in the mix. It has all the high-energy burn of sitting on the cusp of that soul-into-acid phase. The moment the sixties really caught fire.

Although it failed to chart, the 45rpm single soon achieved collectable artefact status and was later salvaged onto a number of compilation albums, including *The Immediate Singles Collection Volume 2: Pop Goes Immediate* (1991, Immediate AK46994) alongside The Small Faces 'Lazy Sunday' and Billy Nicholls 'Daytime Girl'; both sides of the single were included on *Immediate Single Anthology Number 1* (1993, Repertoire), while the A-side was on *Psychedelic Perceptions* (1996, Temple Records) and *Psychedelic Colours Of Sixties London* (2006, Pazazz Records).

Further work by the group failed to live up to expectations, and by the end of 1967, they'd split. Brother of Angus, drummer Jerry Shirley, would again collaborate with Marriott by joining him in Humble Pie.

Patterns – Single

'Patterns' (Marriott, Lane) 2:05 b/w **'E Too D'** (Marriott, Lane) 2:54

Unauthorised release, 26 May 1967, Decca F 12619. Highest chart position: UK: 51

After The Who left Brunswick records, the label issued two further singles from the *My Generation* album even though the group had by then re-signed to Reaction. Although entitled to do so under the initial terms of the contract, this proved an irritating distraction from The Who's newer releases on their new label. The same thing happened to The Small Faces once they'd left Decca and inked to Immediate; their old label continued to milk their back catalogue by issuing this single.

As they were promoting 'Here Come The Nice' with appearances on *Top Of The Pops* on 1 June and *Dee Time* on 8 June, *Melody Maker* reported 'The Faces ex-recording company Decca Records release an old LP track 'Patterns' this week, but the group have dissociated themselves with the record.'

Ronnie Lane is the featured vocalist on the previously unissued 'Patterns', flip-sided with the already familiar album track. Paul Simon had already written and recorded a song called 'Patterns.' This is not that song. Although it's maybe a little more lyrically complex than the group's usual subject matter so far, the patterns are less Paul Simon's degree of pathological pattern-recognition apophenia and more reading body language, 'patterns in the woman's hands that weren't there yesterday.'

Just as TV Time Lord 'Doctor Who' had two fully functioning hearts, the body of The Small Faces had four interdependent hearts. The Small Faces were never simply Steve Marriott's band; they operated as a solid, equal-opportunity four-piece, with Ronnie on hand as second or alternate vocalist. His more relaxed, even-tempered delivery was perfectly suited to their less histrionic material. And the tight vocals, with Ronnie ghosted closely by Steve, make this stand out as untypical of The Small Faces sound. This is likely another reason why record-buyers passed by on the other side.

Real Crazy Apartment – Single by Winston's Fumbs

'Real Crazy Apartment' (Winston) 3:00 b/w **'Snow White'** (Winston) 2:30

Released: 1967, RCA Victor RCA 1612

Produced by Terry Oates. No chart placings

With a vaguely Cream-style guitar thrust, stepping into the New Thing, but with surging keyboard and falsetto backing, this is a genuine heavy Brit-Psych oddity. The jangly guitar B-side retains the swelling burbling Hammond sound to tell the tale of a poor little 'fairest of them all' rich girl on the scene; 'she has got so many clothes, a banker's weight of jewels.' It was later collected onto the second volume of the *Chocolate Soup For Diabetics* (1981, Relics ACID1) album series. Jimmy Winston's subsequent acting credits include the 1968 stage musical *Hair* and as 'Sura' in the 1972 BBC-TV Jon Pertwee-era *Doctor Who* serial 'Day Of The Daleks.' He also featured in the Stephen Frears-directed 'Play For Today: Long Distance Information' (BBC-TV, 11 October 1979), about events at a local radio station the day Elvis Presley died. Winston himself died on 26 September 2020 at the age of 75. Other members of Winston's Fumbs included Tony Kaye, who went on to join a group called The Syn with Peter Banks and Chris Squire, who evolved into the prog rock supergroup Yes.

Hits Vol.7 (EP)

Released: 1967, Decca EP DFE 8675

Tracklisting: The Small Faces ('My Mind's Eye') plus a decidedly untrendy trio of tracks by The Bachelors (the wretched 'Walk With Faith In Your Heart'), Val Doonican's 'What Would I Be' – a track that had charted higher the same week as 'My Mind's Eye' – and Ronnie Aldrich ('Somewhere My Love').

Here Come The Nice – Single

'Here Come The Nice' (Marriott, Lane) 2:54 b/w **'Talk To You'** (Marriott, Lane) 2:06

Released: 2 June 1967, Immediate IM 050

Produced by Steve Marriott and Ronnie Lane
Highest chart position: UK: 12 (on chart for ten weeks), Germany: 24, Netherlands: 28

When was the highest high-point of Mod? Was it as early as the shockwaves of moral panic that ensued following the pitched Mod-Rocker battles on Clacton and Margate beaches across Easter and the Whitsun weekend of 1964, when magistrate Dr George Simpson imposed fines of up to £75 on rioters he condemned as 'long-haired, mentally unstable, petty little sawdust Caesars' who hunted, like rats, only in packs? Which only accelerated the explosions of energy and aggro. Every frame of TV footage, every press-photographed arrest provided a 'Hello Mum' moment of fun. 'After Clacton... a new battlefield, Wild Ones 'Beat Up' Margate: Forty arrested in all-day clashes' howled the *Daily Mirror* front page on 18 May 1964. When Dr Simpson's remarks and the riots themselves landed Britain on the front pages of the world's press, it created a frisson ripple of notoriety that put a strut in every Mod's step.

Or when the *Sunday Times Colour Magazine* ran its eight-page 'Changing Faces' full-colour photo spreads of London Mods in their strange, gaudy new clothes on 2 August 1964.

Being a part of the Mod squad was about as good as it got. But being 'hip' was changing. The whole idea of Mod had been about exclusivity and being different, and suddenly Mod was everywhere. Even *The Daily Mirror* of 'Garth' and 'Andy Capp', the tabloid newspaper that the old guys pull out of their overalls to read during the factory tea break, was running a cover story 'Are You A Mod Or A Rocker: You Have To Be One Or The Other.' As George Melly observed, Mods – as modernists, 'in that they were the forerunners of a general trend' – carried with them their own destruction. As the Mod thing spread, it lost its purity' (in *Revolt Into Style*, Allen Lane Penguin, 1970). And there were new vibrations wafting in from the American West Coast which were redefining it all into a nouveau strangeness. Of course, Mod would not go away. It retreated north to the Wigan Casino, where it kept the faith by morphing into Northern Soul and Scooter Clubs until The Jam and a new wave of Mod bands like Secret Affair reignited it all for a newer generation.

Meanwhile, The Small Faces were restless. As journalist June Southworth pointed out, 'for Steve Marriott, being a Small Face has increased the problem he already had to handle. The problem of being small and young-looking and not to be taken too seriously. Steve is nineteen now' (in *Fabulous 208*, 11 June 1966). He wanted the respect of his music peers. So, The Small Faces took their style-sharpness and adapted it. Welcome to the New Cool.

The hedonistic hard partying that was to prove ultimately corrosive on Steve's talents had deep roots. 22 Westmoreland Terrace was always party-central; 'even experienced smokers like Georgie Fame were surprised at how stoned they could be hours after they left our place', recalls Ian. And how one evening, a dealer brought the dapper Mr Brian Epstein and Moody Blues drummer Graeme Edge to call and then hosted by passing around segments of LSD-spiked orange. Steve reacted badly to the 'trip.'

'He was not what I'd call a particularly balanced person, and he was rarely relaxed, and in the same way that acid can lead you to the heights of illumination and wonder, it can also take you down to the depths of your darkest fears' as Ian explained. But it didn't stop Steve from repeating the experience with some frequency. All of a sudden, there was more in their collective Mind's Eye than ever before.

Lysergic Acid Diethylamide was the new magic elixir. First accidentally synthesised by Swiss chemist Albert Hofmann in the Sandoz laboratories, it was taken up by counter-culture artists and musicians, including Allen Ginsberg, Charles Mingus and Charles Olson, until it reached the American West Coast where the pure strains formulated by Owsley Stanley were championed by The Grateful Dead. Humphry Osmond coined the term psychedelic, and it was proselytised as a catalyst for mystical insight by Timothy Leary in such books as his *The Politics Of Ecstasy* (1968, GP Putnam, ISBN 091417133X) and as a playful way of cleansing what Aldous Huxley called the 'Doors To Perception' by Ken Kesey's *The Electric Kool-Aid Acid Test.*

By the time The Beatles gave their imprimatur and were known to be taking acid trips, it had entered the music mainstream, and rock was flowering in gaudy new directions. The formerly dour Moody Blues returned with 'Legend Of A Mind' on their 1968 album *In Search Of The Lost Chord* (Deram), which is a hymn to 'Timothy Leary', while Pete Townshend of The Who no longer saw himself as a Mod, and adopted the guise of 'The Seeker' on the band's 1970 single, proclaiming 'I asked Bobby Dylan, I asked The Beatles, I asked Timothy Leary…'

The BBC was notoriously itchy-fingered when it came to censoring what it considered material of dubious taste. Sexual references or sly inferences to narcotic preferences were scrupulously excised from their radio playlists. But their judgement could be ludicrously flawed. With the release of *Sgt Pepper's Lonely Hearts Club Band,* the BBC promptly banned 'A Day In The Life' because of its alleged drug references, while failing to notice that the very title of 'Lucy In The Sky With Diamonds' spells out LSD. Maybe the pirate radio stations located just outside territorial waters could flaunt more liberal attitudes, but they had the sensitivity of their advertisers to consider. They could also be unpredictably reticent.

Yet remarkably, The Small Faces escaped the prurient attentions of the morality police despite, as Jon Savage notes, 'their debut single for Immediate, 'Here Come The Nice', was an ode to a Dealer', one who is 'always there if I need some speed' (amphetamines). With the Marriott-Lane writing partnership sharpening, nudged by sharing howls of laughter over the Lord Buckley proto-rap comedy routine 'Here Come Da Nazz' on his 1964 *In Concert* album (World Pacific WP-1815).

The lower half of the *NME* front page on 17 June 1967 was devoted to an advert panel announcing the release of 'Here Come The Nice', showing the fourpiece sitting in a car, Ian and Kenney in the front, Plonk looking out the rear wind-down window, Steve slouched in the back beside him with his foot arrogantly braced against the window arch.

The single's stumble-in piano intro is 'treated' in the studio... just as the descending final fade is extended into a long slow dive, using variable speed studio effects, into a final 'crash' created by striking and strumming piano strings in the way that modern-classical composer John Cage worked with 'prepared piano.' To me, the sequence resembles shoving a piano out of the tower block window, hearing it fall until it shatters on the pavement far below. The song itself has a ticking percussion as Steve's voice insinuates the risqué lyric with harmony back-up; it accelerates into the second verse, 'here come the Nice, looking so cool', and builds with teasing innovation, cheeky in its deliberate game-play subterfuge and crammed with energies more natural than artificial. This is a song that serves notice to the Pop world in general that The Small Faces are moving up a gear, and that this is a band to listen to with renewed scrutiny.

'Listen', yells Steve, demanding your attention, at the opening of 'Talk To You.' If the A-side was charting new terrain, this was the reassuringly familiar undiluted tight group sound, with hard guitar and Steve's spine-shivering vocals backed up by Ronnie and Ian's support voices on a song that pleads for her to hear his words before they fall apart, 'I don't want to share your car, no, no, no, or stop you being a star.' Lifted from the album and short at just over two minutes, this track has a short, short fuse.

From The Beginning

Personnel:
Steve Marriott: lead guitar, lead and backing vocals
Ronnie Lane: bass, backing & lead vocals
Kenney Jones: drums
Ian McLagan: keyboards, backing vocals
Jimmy Winston: keyboards, backing vocals, rhythm guitar
Released: 2 June 1967, Decca Records LK 4879
Highest chart position: UK: 17 (on LP chart for five weeks)

'There's nothing small about the talents of this group', says the *NME* review, 'they capture the R&B idiom exactly.' Yet this is less a cohesive album, more the scrapings and cuttings from the studio floor that the group had left in the Decca archives when they'd quit and moved across to Immediate, padded out by a second (or third) time around for the cream of the singles. 'All in all, it was a rotten excuse of an album', Ian admits, 'even though there are some good tracks.' So, a contractual obligation album – or, as the *Record Mirror* reviewer phrased it, 'a good commemorative album for anyone whose singles have worn out' on 17 June 1966, but there's some fascinating never-before material here, plus some blueprints for ideas that would be developed later. Reissued in August 1984 as Decca DOA2, it was remastered as a CD for London Records 8207662 in 1989, and there was an expanded Deluxe Edition issued in 2012 from Decca/ Universal UMC 278 134-1.

Side One

'Runaway' (Max Crook, Del Shannon) 2:47

'Pop Godfather' Don Arden was fiercely possessive about his boys. After all, hadn't he 'invested' £12,000 in launching their first single by chart-fixing it into visibility? Allegedly. He expected an adequate return on that funding. There are stories about how entrepreneur Robert Stigwood had tentatively sounded out The Small Faces with a tempting management offer, and Arden – the vengeful 'Al Capone Of Pop' retaliated by taking his well-muscled enforcers around to Stigwood's office to 'teach him a lesson' – which consisted of hauling him up out of his chair and dangling him off his fourth-floor balcony as a warning. Another to get a taste of Arden's wrath was then-Yardbird Jimmy Page when he and Keith Moon were speculating about forming their own band, and they suggested Steve Marriott as vocalist. On hearing this, Arden retaliated with a brief but effective veto, 'how would you like to play in a band with broken fingers?' Jimmy sensibly opted for inviting Robert Plant to sing instead.

Naïve and trusting, The Small Faces themselves were living for the moment. It was their disgruntled parents who approached Arden to find out where all the proceeds were going; he straight-facedly told them the group were all junkies and that they used their cash to support their habits. A lie, but 'it put our parents off the track and flung them up in arms against us' as Steve told Paolo Hewitt in *NME* on 15 December 1984.

And now The Small Faces were leaving the control of his 'Galaxy Entertainments Ltd' agency. As though determined to get the last word in, Arden – a failed singer himself, warbles the 'operatic prologue in his Josef Locke' tenor to this live cover of Del Shannon's massive 1961 transatlantic debut hit. Steve ducks out of replicating Shannon's high falsetto peaks and Ian's keyboard lacks the tinny nail-biting shrillness of Max Crook's musitron, yet the group turn in a respectable reworking of the song by the man born Charles Weedon Westover in Grand Rapids, Michigan. After suffering a disruption to his run of hits with the advent of the British Invasion, Del himself had made a major return to the charts as recently as 1964 with his urgent lovers-on-the-run hit 'Keep Searchin' (We'll Follow The Sun).'

While Don Arden's daughter became Reality TV star and *X-Factor* judge Sharon Osbourne.

'My Mind's Eye' (Marriott, Lane) 2:02

At a time when Pop Stars were as much a household name as Kleenex, The Small Faces were by now firmly entrenched in the pantheon of what *Fabulous* magazine called 'Your Fave Raves.' Not quite at The Beatles or The Rolling Stones apex, not quite The Kinks or The Who on the second level, but certainly on the third level alongside Manfred Mann, The Hollies, The Searchers and The Yardbirds. For the group themselves, the attitude expressed by the lyrics says, 'everybody I know says I'll change, yeh, laughing behind their hands, I think they're strange.' They had their own agenda. It was not necessarily thought-out or planned; it was an intuitive thing that reacted in response to the currents of the time, but it was already moving in new directions.

'Yesterday, Today And Tomorrow' (Marriott, Lane) 1:52

An early foray into Brit-Psych, Ronnie Lane sings lead on this heavily phased previously unissued track, with high vocal back-up in every sense of the word, 'why do birds fly high, straight up to the sky?' Although it starts out with a typically dense Small Faces guitar figure, it rapidly upends through Kenney's drum thump and Ian's little keyboard run into a deliberately ethereal eeriness. There's an unpredictable instrumental break with spatterings of acoustic guitar and Steve picking out notes on a stringed Chinese instrument he'd found in a Shaftsbury Avenue antique shop before the track closes with a final splash of drums. The title had previously been used by a 1963 Italian Carlo Ponti anthology movie featuring the delectable Sophia Loren in three roles with Marcello Mastroianni – surely the connection is too precise to be coincidental? And from where the opening lyric 'when the children play, you're so far away' may vaguely have been derived, closing with the haiku-like precision of 'playing had no meaning for so long.' The track maps out the group's further voyages into invigorating weirdness.

'That Man' (Marriott, Lane) 2:14
Another previously unissued vocal outing for Ronnie, dabbling its toes into strange waters. What it means and who the lyric addresses is, at first, anyone's guess. That wild-eyed man at his journey's end… is he still my friend? He has a weary look; is he a living book? Then the singer turns to catch his reflection, and the mirror 'can't tell me any lies.' So, it is a moment of introspective self-analysis? Again, there are typical Small Faces crashing guitars leading into the slightly-phased vocals, with unusual guitar phrases thrown over the top, closing into an almost jaunty jig fade-out, complete with an unhinged 'weee-heee' yell. It shows The Small Faces adventuring into more experimental terrain than we've so far glimpsed. The first shapes of things to come. An 'alternate mix' version of the track, at 2:14, was included on the 'Rarities & Outtakes' Disc 4 of the October 2015 5CD exhaustive compilation *The Small Faces: The Decca Years* (Decca/ Universal Music Catalogue 473-429-6).

'My Way Of Giving' (Marriott, Lane) 1:58
This is the demo of the song they'd given to Chris Farlowe. French Rock star Johnny Hallyday had also done his version – as 'Je N'ai Jamais Rien Demandé' on his album *Johnny 67*. A more complete version was to be included on the first official Small Faces Immediate album … and it would eventually become the B-side of the 1975 reissue of 'Itchycoo Park', which returned The Small Faces to the top ten. This is a strong song with a complicated history. We won't even mention the Rod Stewart version … yet!

'Hey Girl' (Marriott, Lane) 2:16
The 'Blind Date' column was a regular *Melody Maker* feature in which Pop Stars were played a series of new records without being given title or artist details, and they reacted accordingly. Ronnie Lane was subjected to the trial in the 3 September 1966 issue and identified 'I'm A Boy' by The Who ('I don't think it's quite so commercial as some of their others'), 'When I Come Home' by The Spencer Davis Group ('the backing is sort of like Don Covay, and it's a gas'), 'Land Of 1,000 Dances' by Wilson Pickett ('Plaistow is the land of hope and dances. We used to play there in a pub until Stevie broke the piano in a frenzy'), James Brown ('I dig him, but I don't rave about him'), Sandie Shaw ('I don't like knocking people, because I don't like people knocking me'), but he doesn't like The Seekers ('get rid of that one, quick') and he throws Eddie Arnold's 'Tip Of My Fingers' out of the window.

'(Tell Me) Have You Ever Seen Me' (Marriott, Lane) 2:17
Steve sings on this previously unissued track. This was the demo version of the song he'd gifted to The Apostolic Intervention. The drum-roll intro recalls

'All Or Nothing', but the sound is thin, lacking the depth we expect from a full studio mix. A more studio-polished version of the song would appear on their first album for their new label home.

Side Two

'Come Back And Take This Hurt Off Me' (Don Covay, Ron Miller) 2:16

A previously unissued rough-hewn cover of Don Covay's soul composition. Never a major R&B player, Covay was always a respected name among the soul fraternity, where a degree of obscurity only helped enhance a reputation. A Little Richard protégé, he wrote and recorded 'Pony Time' with his group The Goodtimers, which later became a US number one for Chubby Checker, after which he went on to write songs recorded by Solomon Burke, Wilson Pickett and Aretha Franklin. His own gospel-fuelled 'See-Saw', co-penned with Steve Cropper at Stax, became a big record on the Mod dancefloor circuit, its 'up-down all-round' suggesting shapes to throw.

The Rolling Stones creamed off Covay's 'Mercy, Mercy' for their *Out Of Our Heads* album (1965). Then, in a war of the Steves, teenage wunderkind Steve Winwood, with The Spencer Davis Group, had already released their version of 'Take This Hurt Off Me' on their *Autumn '66* (August 1966) album, so it's a case of take your choice of preferred version. 'I'm too young to be in misery' could apply to both vocalists! The Small Faces open with a stronger guitar-barrage, although the dialogue passage 'I knocked on my Momma's (mother's) door' she said 'Stevie come on in (Honey)' '(Son) you don't have to say a mumblin' word, I know your woman left you again (she left my little baby again)' applies equally to both, with cries of sympathetic support from band members mimicking the original voice intercessions on the Don Covay record. You'll forgive my slight bias in favour of Steve Marriott's interpretation.

The strange phenomenon of the UK Blues Boom, with young white boys aping old Delta Blues singers, revitalised first the British music scene through the influence of Cyril Davies and Alexis Korner, into John Mayall, The Rolling Stones, The Animals, Manfred Mann and the rest, from where it was exported in a big way back to the States where it introduced a large mainstream audience to their own neglected wealth of indigenous music. Whether you consider the practice of 'covering' songs done by black American artists as theft or cultural appropriation, the singers and songwriters themselves were usually delighted by the unexpected appreciation and gained from the career boosts and royalties that followed. And if you want the Don Covay original version of this song, it's only a click away on YouTube.

'All Or Nothing' (Marriott, Lane) 3:02

In the entry concerning The Small Faces in her excellent *Rock Encyclopedia* (Grosset & Dunlap, 1971), American music journalist Lillian Roxon opined that 'in England, their physical smallness, natty Mod look, perkiness and sheer accessibility made them number one group with all the new young fans who were already finding the Beatles and Stones too old and too remote to identify with… The Small Faces emerged looking for all the world like the very kids they were playing to – innocent, childlike and vulnerable.' When you listen to 'All Or Nothing' yet again, it's almost possible to be convinced by her theory.

Ian recalls how 'Ronnie slapped his beaten-up Harmony bass to make it boom like congas' while 'Kenney was way ahead of his time on the drums and played like an old pro at 16', he 'ran all over the kit staring wildly into space, leaping out of his head. Old Kenney was one for the blues, all right, and I do mean French blues' (slang for uppers).

'Baby Don't You Do It' (Holland, Dozier, Holland) 2:00
A rare Jimmy Winston vocal and rhythm guitar on this early, previously unissued, Motown cover. It opens with high, spiky guitar, leading into a choppy Bo Diddley beat topped by high falsetto backup voices behind the very competent lead vocal. It's a frantic Mod scramble that captures all the unrestrained energy of their early live club dates. As Paolo Hewitt writes, it's 'as if a speed-driven garage band had just recorded at the Motown studios.' This was a song that had started out as a 1964 single for Marvin Gaye, which also became a standout live favourite for The Who, whose more frenetically bombastic and extended treatment was eventually recorded as the B-side of their 1972 'Join Together' single. Elsewhere, The Band take the song into an entirely smoother musical continuum as an encore performance during their *The Last Waltz* concert movie, with a liquid ooze of voices around Levon Helm singing while playing drums, and Robbie Robertson adds stinging guitar against horns arranged by Allen Toussaint. The favourite interpretation is very much up to the mood of the listener at the time.

'Plum Nellie' (Steve Cropper, Al Jackson, Booker T Jones, Lowie Steinberg) 2:30
A previously unissued instrumental from the Memphis Soul Stew, where the organ squirms like worms. The diminutive quartet played this Booker T & The MGs tune, alongside 'Green Onions', as part of the Swindon Town Hall gig, the first full live set they'd done with Ian McLagan as part of the lineup, 'and it flowed as if we'd been playing together for years. Kenney was a loud, solid drummer, Ronnie had a great ear for simplicity in a bass line and was locked into Kenney, and Steve was a dynamic guitarist and the most soulful singer. He had an old man's voice. There was no looking back…'

'Sha-La-La-La-Lee' (Lynch, Shuman) 2:54
'We'd cut the basic tracks 'live' on one track', explained Ian, 'then overdub solos and backing vocals on separate tracks, leaving the fourth track for the lead vocals, although Steve often got his vocal live, that's how strong a

singer he was.' No Pop Art or social comment, just an essence that even ends happily ever after with implied wedding bells. Well, maybe.

'You've Really Got A Hold On Me' (William 'Smokey' Robinson) 3:16
Searching For The Young Soul Rebels. This is a Miracles single that had been brought to the attention of the British record-buying public at large when it was included on the second side of the *With The Beatles* (1963) album. This previously unissued Small Faces version differs with guitar playing the opening chords where The Beatles and The Miracles had used piano, then showcases Steve at his most pleadingly soulful, with determined keyboard swelling behind his 'please, please, please, please... one more time' and Kenney's ticking percussion.

'Whatcha Gonna Do About It' (Potter, Samwell) 1:57
Back to where the story had begun, Steve still sings as though the sound itself has hold of him. When the track was collected onto the *Hard-Up Heroes* (1974, Decca DPA 3009/10) double-vinyl, the liner notes – by compilers Roy Carr and Charles Shaar Murray – say 'Ladeeez and Gentlemen, we now present the very first Small Faces record which comes complete with Marriott's raunchy squeal and some very topical feedback. The Small Faces ... became the ultimate Mod band.' When *NME* later reviewed a further reissue, on 25 December 1976, Phil McNeill saw this as the group's only major success from *within* the Mod scene, 'the record epitomised their stance, bringing Booker T & The MGs with The Who, Winston's even then almost archaic fat organ thudding up against Marriott's whining feedback, Jones drums rifling high in the mix and Plonk just audible if you turn the bass full up (which, of course, you always did). Plus, naturally, Stevie's unrivalled R&B punk voice.' Some people live in a world where the sixties never ended. Listen to this track again now, and you can almost believe they're right.

Related Releases
Itchycoo Park – Single
'Itchycoo Park' (Marriott, Lane) 2:45 b/w **'I'm Only Dreaming'** (Marriott, Lane) 2:23
Released: 4 August 1967, Immediate IM 057
Produced by Steve Marriott and Ronnie Lane
Highest chart position: UK: 3 (on chart for 14 weeks), Aus: 2, Canada: 1, Germany: 17, US: 16, Netherlands: 3, Norway: 4
To psychedelic historian David Wells, in *Record Collector: 100 Greatest Psychedelic Records*, this is 'one gargantuan spliff-laden flower-power piss-take' ('We'll be able to get plastic sitars in our cornflakes soon', Steve Marriott had grumbled as early as May 1966). 'Itchycoo Park' transcends its sardonic origins by virtue of a beautiful melody, pioneering use of phasing and a genuinely atmospheric lyric from Ronnie Lane.'

Phasing, or 'flanging', was the new fad, a production effect achieved by running two tapes together slightly out of sync, creating the whooshing distortion sound of a fountain going off in your head. The Beatles used it most effectively on 'Lucy In The Sky With Diamonds', and it was taken even further by The Hollies on the 'Lullaby To Tim' track on their *Evolution* album (June 1967). Now, here were The Small Faces 'gambolling off towards Itchycoo Park, clearly out of their trees' according to Jon Savage's liner notes for the 4CD *Mojo Presents: Acid Drops, Spacedust & Flying Saucers* (2001, EMI/Universal Music 07243-5-35078-23-4). Despite the earbait phasing effect creating problems when playing it live!

After a brief strummed lead-in, Steve's voice starts out softly beguiling 'over bridge of sighs, to rest my eyes in shades of green' which – David Wells suggests, 'may well be as evocative an opening line as British Pop has ever produced', before Ronnie and Ian chant questions at him 'what did you do there?' 'what did you feel there?' to which Steve power-responds 'I got high' in a call-&-response dialogue. He slinks into slow innuendo mode for 'they all come out to groove about' before Kenney's burst of phased drums. The track winds down to Steve's sharp 'Ha!' until it constitutes almost three minutes of pure audio magic. It's characterised by nose-thumbing cheek and a frivolously serious assertion of the value of freedom over discipline. If Pink Floyd would later attack the brainwashing aspects of classroom education in Roger Waters' 'Another Brick In The Wall', it could be argued that Marriott-Lane precedes them with a lighter touch.

Typically, The Small Faces' take on the theme has a mischievous tongue-in-cheek subversiveness about its invitation – 'you can miss out school (won't that be cool?)' – and spend the day tripping in 'shades of green.' There are references to Oxford, with going 'over the bridge of sighs' to rest my eyes 'under dreaming spires', despite other suggestions that the subject setting for the song was a disused bomb site in Ilford covered in stinging nettles... or, from Ronnie, that it was 'a working-class East End park called Manor Park.' And the irreverent 'why go to learn the words of fools?' – which sounds like a George Bernard Shaw or Oscar Wilde quote, and articulately rejects the dusty learn-by-rote academia of the colleges and schoolrooms in favour of a healthier return to nature to 'be nice and have fun in the sun.'

It's a part of the anti-university tendency, the argument that formal education is a process of repressive indoctrination, and it's both more fun and more educational to 'feel inclined to blow my mind.' To organically extend mental growth and chemically expand the consciousness. The repeated 'it's all too beautiful' could be a sample lifted from a stoned conversation, seen through the LSD lenses of psychedelic spectacles.

Ronnie claimed to have adapted the melody from an old hymn called 'God Be In My Head' and, as a starting point, took a handful of phrases from a magazine feature he'd found in a Bristol hotel room. Yet, as David Wells suggests, it remains 'the perfect soundtrack for anyone who ever felt inclined to blow their mind or, indeed, feed the ducks with a bun.'

If, as Steve once claimed, Ronnie was the more meditative spiritually inclined member of the group, the B-side, 'I'm Only Dreaming', embodies a more romantic form of dreaming. It's essentially a slow ballad, tricked out in ticking percussion effects, shakers and piping organ figures. There's also what sounds like a cough in the play-in groove. If the smile on his face doesn't mean much to her anymore, their love has all been just a waste of time. Still, he looks to find something in her eyes because 'something's all I need to hold onto.' Then there's a ripping response as he argues back, 'what good does dreaming do when you're nowhere?' The pace and emphasis contour his back-and-forth mood changes as he pleads, 'I still care about the way and the little things you say, won't you please come out to play?' There's a slight dream-sequence echo on his voice and a powerful guitar solo with shuffling horn sounds. Ending on the hopeless admission that 'I'm only dreaming, I'm only dreaming.'

The song shows The Small Faces seemingly effortlessly in control of a variety of gears, even within the space of a single track, in a good-value flipside. Paul Weller does his piano-led version of the song as a 2007 bonus track on his *Wild Wood* album, with woozy strings, as well as performing it live at the Steve Marriott Tribute Concert on 25 March 2012 with Noel Gallagher joining Ian McLagan and Kenney Jones onstage. PP Arnold does her own effective interpretation of 'I'm Only Dreaming' as part of the 'Shindig! Magazine Lockdown Online Music Festival' on 25 April 2020.

'Itchycoo Park' was the only Small Faces single to make significant inroads into the American charts, peaking at number 16 on the *Billboard* Hot 100, and hence it was included on the American version of the UK Immediate *Small Faces* album, rejigged and retitled *There Are But Four Small Faces* (US, Immediate Z12-52002). One of the band's signature singles, 'Itchycoo Park' was a hit in other markets and territories, topping the charts in Canada and New Zealand. Then the song would return The Small Faces to the UK top ten when it was re-released in 1975, and again when M People cut their own electro-dance version, which climbed to number 11 in November 1995 with Heather Small's distinctive standout voice touching new skies.

Meanwhile, for *Rave* magazine in August 1967, 'Setting The Fashion' meant The Small Faces plus The Walker Brothers, The Beatles and The Rolling Stones, as well as the Latest Boy/Girl Fashion fads and fancies.

Small Faces

Personnel:
Steve Marriott: lead guitar, lead and backing vocals (piano on 'Things Are Going To Get Better' and 'Show Me The Way')
Ronnie Lane: bass, backing & lead vocals
Kenney Jones: drums
Ian McLagan: keyboards, backing vocals, bass guitar (on 'Show Me The Way') and guitar (on 'Up The Wooden Hills To Bedfordshire')
Produced by Steve Marriott & Ronnie Lane, with studio engineers Glyn Johns, George Chkiantz and Eddie Kramer at Olympic Studios
Released: 23 June 1967, Immediate Records IMSP 008
Highest chart position: UK: 12 (on LP chart for 17 weeks), Aus: 25

While writing the liner notes for a compilation album featuring 'Green Circles', a journalist who might have been Jon Savage set the scene with 'leaving stuffy old Decca for Andrew Oldham's hip but chaotic Immediate label, yer Small Faces started to sing about youth culture as they really saw it.' To avoid confusion with the equally eponymous Decca LP debut, this could usefully be referred to as *The First Immediate Album*. When it was reissued as a CD in April 1991 by Sequel Records (NEXCD163) it was retitled *Green Circles*, and curiously enough the sides were reversed, so that track one is 'Become Like You', and there are three bonus tracks, the lost B-side 'Donkey Rides A Penny A Jar', plus alternate takes of 'Green Circles' itself, and '(Tell Me) Have You Ever Seen Me.' Journalist Colin Shearman reviews the package for *Q* magazine in July 1991, pointing out that 'The Small Faces' move to Immediate in 1967 was a mixed blessing, allowing them more studio time to develop their music but also losing some of the edge and excitement of the speedier, penny-pinching Decca session… this first Immediate album finds them still feeling their way and at times sounding rather lost in their new-found freedom.' This was also enabled by a step up from IBC's four-track technology to Olympic's eight-track machine. The press ad at the time proclaimed, 'whichever way you look at it, there are only four Small Faces. But there is just one *Small Faces* LP. It's on Immediate.' To me, this is a varied and inventive album that retains enough spark and fire to satisfy the fans of the snarly Decca singles, with enough experimentation to register as part of the new consciousness. The Small Faces played an abbreviated set at 'The Seventh National Jazz & Blues Festival' on 11 August 1967 at the Royal Windsor Racecourse. Closing the Friday night bill, they opened with 'Paperback Writer', which fed into 'All Or Nothing', 'with the amplifiers vibrating and threatening to topple and crush them. Then, finally, the lights went out all over Windsor' as the authorities cut off the power at the stroke of midnight, according to *NME*. The festival's publicity spokesperson blamed the group for turning up late; The Small Faces blamed the administration for keeping them 'hanging about' for twenty minutes after they arrived. The booing audience of 6,000 disgruntled fans blamed anyone who came into sight wearing an official badge!

Side One

'(Tell Me) Have You Ever Seen Me?' (Marriott, Lane) 2:16

For the sleeve notes of *The Darlings Of Wapping Wharf Launderette* (Immediate NEECD311, 1999), David Wells writes 'while acts like Cream and The Pink Floyd were incorporating improvised instrumental freak-outs into their recordings, The Small Faces were honing their pure pop sensibilities via energetic two-minute nuggets like the opening of '(Tell Me) Have You Ever Seen Me.' Yes, we'd heard a demo of this song on *From The Beginning*, but this is the completed studio version, and the difference is instantly apparent. This is a denser, much fuller sound, with Steve's voice taking on a more insinuating quality through the 'words seem out of place' sequence into the hard urban visionary poetry of 'many flowers are breaking through the concrete', which recalls something that Liverpool bard Adrian Henri might once have penned; and just a touch of acid-imagery with 'listen everybody, I can hear them breathing.' It's informative to compare and contrast the two versions.

'Something I Want To Tell You' (Marriott, Lane) 2:10

Kenney delivers sharp, snappy drums, and Ian injects rolling organ as Ronnie plays 'Stand By Me' bass lines and takes the lazy and drunken vocal in an attractively slurred way on this semi-spoken song. She's busy making plans, but 'I don't like what you're running after'; he's rejecting her materialism, 'don't you know that they're not my way?' The something he wants to tell her is 'enough', it's over, 'once again I am alone.' There's a lengthy organ play-out. In days to come, Ronnie would indeed eschew the materialism of the Rock Star lifestyle to become troubadour ringmaster of his own travelling carnival. Although that 'Passing Show' still remained in the future, these lyrics could be seen as an advanced tremor of that rejection.

'Feeling Lonely' (Marriott, Lane) 1:35

The dynamics anticipate the 'Afterglow' build, taken slower with Steve at his most pleading as he confesses that loneliness is his 'Achilles heel', although the track is over almost too quickly. It's a miniature that packs a lot into its 1:35 minutes... why the 'green memory'? Then he agonises, 'I feel that I am part of a wheel', which could refer to early symptoms of being trapped in the Popstar lifestyle until it winds down into a less evolved 'Here Come The Nice' close to an abrupt thump.

'Happy Boys Happy' (Marriott, Lane) 1:36

This is an easy-on-the-ear, organ-led instrumental, flaunting a jazzy freedom with precise breaks for piano and pattering bongos. In order to compare and contrast the mono and stereo mixes, the album was later reissued in a remastered deluxe edition made up of the full original mono album, the full original stereo album, plus two generous sides of mono and stereo bonus tracks … including the '(If You Think You're) Groovy' backing track (2012, Immediate/Universal UMC 278-134-5). Recorded during the same sessions, a Bluesy three-minute instrumental titled 'Piccanniny' – with Steve playing harmonica – remained unissued until the 1997 2CD collection *Small Faces: The Masters* (Eagle Records EDMCD 023).

'Things Are Going To Get Better' (Marriott, Lane) 2:39
With a relentless pulsing build, Steve stretches the word 't-h-i-n-g-s' over octaves and adds piano with a pleading lead voice as Ronnie and Ian feed in smoother cooing support vocals. The theme is ostensibly that his life is taking an upward curve now that he's found his girl, but there are clues in 'times change', 'times fly' and 'it's time for a change' to suggest that they're also talking about their own shifting attitude to their music. Recorded 11 January at Olympic Studios, there were numerous takes of what was originally given the working title 'Doolally', and there's a radically different 'Take Fourteen Session Version' with whistling and stronger harmonies on the May 2012 expanded edition of *From The Beginning* on Decca/Universal 278-134-1, which includes a full side of bonus tracks.

'My Way Of Giving' (Marriott, Lane) 1:59
This also had an overlap with the previous outing in rough form on *From The Beginning*, from where it had been used as a demo for Chris Farlowe. Whereas the first take has an appealing rawness, with the cooing 'don't worry Baby' answering background voices, Steve seems to take on something of Farlowe's gravel-voice quality on this more finished Immediate version. It's a torrid reading of the song, where Steve protests that he knows 'the pain of too much happiness.' He protests that he's not a guy who means to hurt, and although at times it seems their love won't work, she must surely see the confusion in his cloudy eyes. With all the drama and dynamics of classic Small Faces, this could just as easily have been a hit single.

'Green Circles' (Marriott, Lane, Michael O'Sullivan) 2:46
Ronnie Lane shares the vocals with Steve. Mick O'Sullivan was a friend of Steve's, who Ian describes as 'little more than a ligger and a freeloader', although his talents extended as far as rolling a decent joint and pouring a fair glass of brandy, as long as he didn't have to foot the bill. At the dawn of the sixties, chart-topping songs had concerns that rarely extended beyond being young, in love and having fun, sunshine, lollipops and kisses. Or the angst and anguish of being a Teenager in Love. When Dusty Springfield sang, 'it happens to be true, I only want to be with you', you never doubt her for a moment.

The advent of Bob Dylan shook lyrics up into more inscrutably surreal areas. No one could make literal sense of the mythopoetic 'Mr Tambourine Man' and then Procol Harum's 'A Whiter Shade Of Pale', but somehow everyone understood they were anthems of the tribe. It wasn't necessary to explain, you just had to feel them on an intuitive level. 'Green Circles' constitutes The Small Faces' first foray into lyrical ambiguity, 'and with the rain a stranger came, his eyes were filled with love and pain.' He's a mystical cypher like Donovan's 'Hurdy Gurdy Man'; it's not necessary to know who the stranger is or to be aware of his backstory. He dreams of circles in the air; he wants the world to be free so that others can share his vision. Until, with the dawn, he went his way.

It's several moves beyond 'picked her up on a Friday night.' It could be a metaphor carrying all manner of profundity. A guru with new messages of freedom, an alchemist with a new ingestible chemical formulation? This track was later collected onto the 4CD *Mojo Presents: Acid Drops, Spacedust & Flying Saucers* (2001, EMI/ Universal Music 07243-5-35078-23-4), where the liner notes call it 'this classic of the LSD-trip canon. As ever, the Faces gave the experience a Cockney tinge: thumb-tack piano and a closing phased-out rave-up. Knees Up Mother Brown Acid, if you will. It was a mode they perfected on the following year's masterpiece, *Ogdens' Nut Gone Flake.*

Among their more collectibly bizarre artefacts was an Italian-language version of 'Green Circles' recorded phonetically for the Italian record market as 'Prati Verdi.'

Side Two

'Become Like You' (Marriott, Lane) 1:58
By now, things were getting seriously good. Steve and Ronnie share vocals on this gentle, acoustic, unrequited love song with a waltz-time lilt. The lyric takes the form of a series of sometimes absurdist questions, 'would my heart be made out of wood' 'if I could be a brick', 'if I could give my best friend a kick' and 'would I know just where I was at, would my brains be where I sat?', with a Dylan-feel to the phrasing – 'if I could throw myself a-way.' The stereo mix features the tambourine more strongly and what sounds like a mellotron solo. It slows to a stop, then circles and Steve laughs – 'hello, they're playing it again', so they take another chorus. When Paul Weller appeared at the London Astoria on 20 April 2001 for the Steve Marriott Memorial concert, he sang a touching version of this song with Noel Gallagher taking the Ronnie Lane role.

'Get Yourself Together' (Marriott, Lane) 2:16
Unless the track was a single that required repeated live promotion, once the group had recorded a piece and listened to it a few times with a critical ear, they never played it again. Recorded 13 December 1966 at IBC Studios,

this warning to a broken-hearted friend was cut at the same session that also resulted in 'Green Circles', with Steve playing a rippling twelve-string acoustic guitar Byrds-style. His vocals are emphasised by repeated exclamations of 'Ugh! Ahhh.' There are differences in the mono and stereo mixes, including the greater prominence of laughter and incoherent vocals during the instrumental sequence of the latter. When a fannish Paul Weller enthused about 'Get Yourself Together' – a track he recorded as part of a bonus EP given with the 1983 Jam album *Snap!* – as being one of his favourite Small Faces numbers, Ian couldn't even remember it and had to hunt out the album to refresh his memory.

'All Our Yesterdays' (Marriott, Lane) 1:53
Although the title of this riotous song can be traced back to Shakespeare's *Macbeth*, it's more likely that they were referencing the then-current Granada TV nostalgia show fronted by Brian Inglis. Steve provides the theatrical introduction, 'and now for your delight, the darling of Wapping Wharf laundrette, Ronald Leafy a-Lane' – incidentally providing the title for the future Small Faces compilation CD, for a Music Hall romp with knees-up party noises going on in the background as Ronnie sings about losing his 'cute Miss Sunshine.' There's an instrumental 'Take seven' of the backing tape included on *The Decca Years 1965-1967* compilation, which shows the fairground hurdy-gurdy organ as a good example.

'Talk To You' (Marriott, Lane) 2:09
Issued as the flip-side of 'Here Come The Nice', this is a walking-on-a-wire kind of nervy high-energy experience with a hard rock riff and an arrogant thrust to Steve's vocals as he throws in his trademark Soul asides, 'you remember me, Baby?' 'you know what I gotta do, got to keep on trying.' An alternate version that runs for fifteen seconds longer was issued as part of the *Here Come The Nice* box set in 2014.

'Show Me The Way' (Marriott, Lane) 2:08
There have been suggestions that Ronnie was the group's George Harrison, with a slight mystical bent. Ian blames an American girl fan who stayed over at Westmoreland Terrace with 'Plonk, being the stallion of the group.' She introduced him to Buddhism and hung a scroll of Chinese symbols on his wall. But his more introspective moments did not find favour with the others. Ronnie's predilection for a softer, pastoral and more psychedelic sound was heavily evident on songs such as this, where he recognised the 'old man in me... as old as the sun' and 'all the truth I have known has been scattered and blown.' Ronnie sings, Steve plays a bit of 'Here Come The Nice' harpsichord piano and Ian plays bass guitar. The song has nothing whatsoever to do with Peter Frampton's later hit of the same title.

'Up The Wooden Hills To Bedfordshire' (McLagan) 2:05
For Ian McLagan's first solo composition for The Small Faces, he recalls the childhood usage for 'up the stairs to bed', and takes it as a cue for 'when you're slipping into sleep.' Ian also sings and plays bass on this track, which has a pastoral psych swing to it, strummed guitar and a kind of noodling inspiral organ. For the American version issued on *There Are But Four Small Faces,* the 'to Bedfordshire' part was deleted from the title for fear of confusing Stateside sensibilities.

'Eddie's Dreaming' (Marriott, Lane, McLagan) 2:54
A tropical sunshine Caribbean-flavoured romp, brass-tinged, with Ronnie dabbling his toes into the warm sand – 'I see the sunshine, the sunshine sees me' (an echo of the old 1954 Stargazers' hit 'I see the moon, the moon sees me' which in turn adapts it from a nursery rhyme), there are Speedy Acquaye's pattering congas and a playful flute passage, but Eddie's only dreaming, Steve and Ian chant 'always dreaming' in supportive emphasis behind Ronnie's voice. As it goes into the repeated horn-riff fade (from Georgie Fame's horn section), submerged voices can be heard commenting, 'I said Eddie's dreaming, he's dreaming again.' The Eddie in question is trumpeter Eddie 'TanTan' Thornton, whose voice can be heard in the fader banter. An American EP TK-193 includes a slightly edited version running to just 2:37.

The 1967-68 Singles and US-only album

Tin Soldier – Single

'Tin Soldier' (Marriott, Lane) 3:16 b/w **'I Feel Much Better'** (Marriott, Lane, McLagan) 3:55
Released: 2 December 1967, Immediate IM 062
Produced by Steve Marriott and Ronnie Lane
Highest chart position: UK: 9 (on chart for 12 weeks), Aus: 3, Can: 38, Germany: 7, US: 73, Netherlands 4, Sweden: 16

Things were becoming more flamboyant. It was all about how you looked, the objective being to break all bonds with the generation that had been shaped by the grey austerity years. As Kenney Jones recalls 'Don Arden gave us a shopping account in every clothes shop in Carnaby Street, which was great as we were always into fashion. We wore the most outlandish paisley shirts we could find, fur coats, flared slacks and pointed boots. Nothing was too wild for Steve.' As regards Kenney's own sartorial style, 'the amount of time he spent doing his hair would come to annoy me' according to Rod Stewart, 'he liked it turned under nicely at the bottom, and curlers were involved.'

The clothes, as George Melly points out, weren't meant to last but to dazzle. Cathy McGowan – styled as 'Queen of the Mods' by the press, set herself up as 'teenage consultant' in which role she was solemnly reported in the *Daily Mirror* as pronouncing 'the kids want clothes to look terrific – and they don't wear them for very long, so it doesn't matter if they fall to bits' (reported in *The Neophiliacs* by Christopher Booker).

And 'Tin Soldier' catches every pulse and throb of the moment. For me, this track – enhanced by the gorgeous P.P. Arnold, is about as good as it gets. This is the greatest 3:16 minutes that The Small Faces ever recorded and one of the greatest tracks of the 1960s. At the same time, the video is a joy that I've regularly revisited with delight.

It opens with Steve's barely-heard count-in, then an ascending keyboard figure, enforced by organ and crashing guitar of growing roaring prowling intensity – Steve yells 'c'mon' and the power-vocals hit, stabbed by guitar-break emphasis. Steve's voice is not only at its most energised but strengthened and lifted to new heights by P.P. Arnold's seamless blending. There's a vague storyline hooked into Hans Christian Andersen's 1838 fairytale 'The Steadfast Tin Soldier', with Steve envisaging himself as 'a little tin soldier that wants to jump into your fire.' But it develops into phrases of their most cleverly wrought poetry, 'all I need is your whispered hello, smiles melting the snow, nothing heard, your eyes are deeper than time, say a love that won't rhyme without words.'

But there's more going on shifting deeper into the layered mix, including the little ticking echo-fade behind the upfront harmonies; Steve plays Fender Telecaster while Ian contributes three keyboards (the studio's Steinway grand, his old flat-top Wurlitzer electric piano, and a new Hammond M100).

This is a 45rpm single structured in interlocking ways that work to maximum fine-tuned effect, working up into the wailing climax build, 'no, I just want some reaction, someone to give me satisfaction, all I want to do is stick with you, 'cause I love you' closing with Kenney's thundering drum-storm. There are few singles that transcend the genre to assume classic status. The Who's 'I Can See For Miles.' The Beatles' 'Strawberry Fields Forever.' Jefferson Airplane's 'White Rabbit.' The Rolling Stones' 'Street Fighting Man.' 'Tin Soldier' is every bit an integrated triumph of rock 'n' roll creativity as any of them. It is simply awesome.

As Pete Townshend was quoted after 'I Can See For Miles' only charted as high as number ten in the UK, 'I spat on the British record buyer', it seems staggering in retrospect that 'Tin Soldier' peaked only one place higher. But it was a peak time, the perfect storm for rock singles.

'Tin Soldier' entered the *Record Retailer/Record Mirror* at number 29, 13 December 1967 – the week The Beatles' 'Hello Goodbye' was number one, with Traffic ('Here We Go Round The Mulberry Bush') and Simon Dupree ('Kites') in the top twenty. It climbed to 18 ... fell one place to number 19, lapping over into 1968 at 19 for a second week, then up to 16 by 10 January, up to 14, to peak at number nine, 24 January 1968. By that time, Georgie Fame was topping the chart with the movie-inspired 'Ballad Of Bonnie & Clyde' while The Beatles double-EP 'Magical Mystery Tour' was in the top ten. The same week, Peter Frampton's Herd peaked at number 15 with 'Paradise Lost.' On the rival *NME* chart, 'Tin Soldier' got no higher than number ten. After that, it was declining figures... 10, 17, 24, then a final appearance at number 33 the week Manfred Mann topped the chart with 'The Mighty Quinn' on 21 February 1968.

The B-side opens with twisty bass figures before oozing into a smooth Motown groove with accelerated spoof doowaddy-waddy and langa-doolanga backing voices referencing old fifties doo-wop harmonies, Kenney takes a precise drum break, then at the mid-point, it upgears into heavy-rock riffing, fades... and returns for a reprise. The playfully stoned lyrics – 'times were so high they were low' puncture any trace of pomposity with 'I'm only writing the rhyme, don't find me taking my time... please pass me my glass of wine'! There's a different mix with an extended fade on the 2014 *Here Come The Nice* 4CD compilation (Charly Records CHARLY 170BX).

When the single failed to chart in America, Canadian group The Guess Who – featuring Randy Bachman – who had already scored heavily with their revamp of the Johnny Kidd & The Pirates hit 'Shakin' All Over', covered 'Tin Soldier' for the US market. The instrumentation closely replicates The Small Faces original, and although vocalist Burton Cummings follows Steve's words and ad-libs, there's no way that his voice can come close to capturing its sheer power.

Steve would revisit 'Tin Soldier' for the June 1981 Humble Pie album *Go For The Throat*, a powerful, but in some ways wistful performance, as though it was already a concession to better days. Issued as a single, The Humble Pie version climbed as high as a US number 58 position.

In Another Land – Single by Bill Wyman

'In Another Land' (Wyman) 2:48 b/w **'The Lantern'** (Jagger, Richard) 4:24
Personnel:
Bill Wyman: vocals, bass, piano, Hammond organ
Mick Jagger: backing vocals
Keith Richards: acoustic guitar, backing vocals
Brian Jones: Mellotron, effects
Charlie Watts: drums
Plus:
Nicky Hopkins: harpsichord.
Ronnie Lane & Steve Marriott: backing vocals
Released: 2 December 1967, USA only, London Records 45-LON-907
Highest chart position: US: 62 (Cashbox chart)

The Beatles' *Sergeant Pepper's Lonely Hearts Club Band* was an album that raised the bar across the entire pop spectrum, demanding responses. The Peter Blake cover art includes a doll wearing a shirt that reads 'Welcome The Rolling Stones', inviting reciprocation. The Stones' subsequent psychedelic masterpiece *Their Satanic Majesties Request* (December 1967) is frequently viewed as a career misstep that they would never repeat, yet – as well as smuggling the hidden faces of the Fab Four into its 3D artwork – it includes some jaw-dropping material, not least of which is the inventive American hit single 'She's A Rainbow' (November 1967). A second American single was this track, which was issued by Bill Wyman and was one of the few Rolling Stones tracks the bass player wrote and sang for the band.

The album was recorded across the summer months of 1967 which was a troubled period for all concerned, complicated by the celebrated drug bust and court appearances, so it was unpredictable which band members would even turn up for scheduled studio time. '2000 Light Years From Home' was supposedly written by Mick Jagger in a Brixton prison cell. Engineer Glyn Johns recalls that 'In Another Land' was recorded on an occasion when only Bill Wyman arrived in the Olympic Studio, unaware that the other Stones had already cancelled, so recording went ahead with session musician Nicky Hopkins playing harpsichord and both Steve Marriott and Ronnie Lane clearly audible in the mix. Other members of The Rolling Stones were subsequently overdubbed onto the tape, with Brian Jones on mellotron. Trippy and stoned, heavily phased and rifted with trendy dream imagery ... it closes 'then I awoke, was this some kind of joke? I opened my eyes, much to my surprise', to fade out with the sound of Bill Wyman snoring! If it was both psychedelic and a jokey satire on psychedelia, it was also a cosmic joke, with all the absurdist profundity that the term implies. It still sounds amazing to these ears.

To Kenney Jones 'there was a real camaraderie between the bands. It wasn't about competition. It was peace and love. There was no division between work and play either. We were in and out of each other's studios, having a play on this or that. It was a beautiful, friendly time.'

28 January 1968: During a chaotic tour of Australia, a plane carrying The Who and The Small Faces landed in Melbourne en route from Adelaide to Sydney. The flight was delayed for three hours due to claims of drunkenness and unruly behaviour by the bands. The flight eventually continued on to Sydney – with two security guards on board to make sure the boys behaved themselves.

The news of their misdemeanours preceded them to the New Zealand leg of the tour, where Pete Townshend recalls, 'Steve Marriott had a (21st) birthday party and decided to do a Keith Moon and throw a TV set off his balcony. It landed on the pavement just as a police car drove by. The police came directly to our room, and we opened the door, thinking we were done for. To our astonishment, they were very cheery, didn't even mention the TV set, wished Steve a happy birthday and left us a case of beer so we 'wouldn't think the Kiwis were as inhospitable as them miserable Aussies! In newly married Ian's account, it was a record player that Steve threw through the French windows onto the balcony!

Ben 'Plum' Pridden, one of the members of The Who road crew, was made to sing 'rooty-dooty-di' while he was humping gear. Ian McLagan thought it was catchy enough to steal...

Lazy Sunday – Single

'Lazy Sunday' (Marriott, Lane) 2:55 b/w **'Rollin' Over'** (Marriott, Lane) 2:09

Released: 5 April 1968, Immediate IM 064

Produced by Steve Marriott and Ronnie Lane

Highest chart position: UK: 2 (on chart for 11 weeks), Aus 5, Can: 42, Ger: 2, USA: 114, Netherlands: 1, Norway: 7

Reportedly, The Small Faces themselves were unhappy with this A-side being issued as a single, believing its playful irreverence fails to conform to their projected heavier, more serious aspirations. But for this writer, it's a track that captures the mood of the time to manic quintessential perfection. And it remains one of the group's most recognised, played and anthologised tracks. It's a catchy and easily singable song, one of the most inventive interactions between – first Steve and Ronnie's writing, plus Ian and Kenney's constructive interplay, that is also a production of some considerable complexity, for which they plundered the BBC sound effects archive to create a wonderful collage of mischievous changes.

It opens with Steve complaining that he doesn't get on with his neighbours because 'they make it very clear, they've got no room for ravers'... cue the sound of riotous partying. The angry next-door residents 'stop me from groovin', they bang on me wall, they're doin' me crust in.' Note the vernacular because backstage at a *Top Of The Pops* session, Graham Nash of The Hollies had teased that Steve did not sing in his natural Cockney accent. So, the dropped-in dialogue 'Gor Blimey, hello Mrs Jones, how's your Bert's lumbago?' with Plonk responding 'mustn't grumble' is done in the kind of *Monty Python's Flying Circus* charlady drag-voice. It supposedly quotes the talkative domestic, Marge, employed to help out at 22 Westmoreland Terrace. There are also amusing musical quotes from F.J. Ricketts' 'Colonel Bogey March' and the riff from The Rolling Stones' '(I Can't Get No) Satisfaction' played on comb-&-paper in pastiche tribute.

The track was later collected onto the compilation *Happy To Be Part Of The Industry Of Human Happiness* (November 1969, Immediate IMLYIN2) alongside tracks by Amen Corner, The Nice and Humble Pie ('Alabama '69' and 'Cold Lady').

Subtitled 'Part II of Happiness Stan' 'Rollin Over' makes for a powerful flipside, the mono mix has a more focused intensity that brings out the trilling piano in the extended fade.

Rave, in December 1967, priced at just 2/6d, has Steve Marriott as cover star with a 'Pop round-up on Faces' feature, as well as The Monkees, Move, The Who, Scott Walker, and 'Our Christmas Present To You: Psychedelic Poster Inside!'

There Are But Four Small Faces (USA only)

Personnel:
Steve Marriott: lead guitar, lead and backing vocals
Ronnie Lane: bass, backing & lead vocals
Kenney Jones: drums
Ian McLagan: keyboards, backing vocals
Plus:
P.P. Arnold backing vocals (on 'Itchycoo Park', 'I Feel Much Better' and 'Tin Soldier')
Released: 17 March 1968, Columbia Records/ Immediate Z12-52002
Highest chart position: 178
Tracklisting: Side One: 'Itchycoo Park', 'Talk To You', 'Up The Wooden Hills', 'My Way Of Giving', 'I'm Only Dreaming', 'I Feel Much Better'
Side Two: 'Tin Soldier', 'Get Yourself Together', 'Show Me The Way', 'Here Come The Nice', 'Green Circles', '(Tell Me) Have You Ever Seen Me?'

There was a 1964 single called 'There Are But Five Rolling Stones' by The Andrew Oldham Orchestra (Decca F11817) credited to Oldham with Mike Leander (b/w Phil Spector's 'To Know Him Is To Love Him' by Cleo). Oldham simply reconfigured the title for this American introduction to The Small Faces, which reshuffled existing tracks into an attractive package. To Ian 'Andrew put together an album... and released it without our consent or permission. We were pissed off when Decca released *From The Beginning*, but now Immediate was doing it too.'

Would You Believe – Billy Nicholls

Personnel:
Billy Nicholls: vocals, acoustic guitar
Joe Moretti: electric guitar
Steve Marriott: electric guitar, background vocals
Big Jim Sullivan: acoustic guitar
John Paul Jones: bass
Ronnie Lane: bass, background vocals
Jerry Shirley & Kenney Jones: drums
Nicky Hopkins, Ian McLagan & Caleb Quaye: keyboards
Released as limited edition: April 1968, Immediate IMCP 009. Later reissued on Billy's own South West Records label (1998, SWCD001), after which it appeared as a slip-case edition through Castle Music (2006, CMQDD1358)
No chart position

A 16-year-old Billy first approached George Harrison for help in placing his songs, but then sought out Andrew Loog Oldham, who was busy launching Immediate with its upbeat slogan 'Happy To Be Part Of The Industry Of Human Happiness.' The resulting album started out as a Loog Oldham vanity project, a commissioned response to The Beach Boys' *Pet Sounds*. The sessions drew in the regular Immediate crew, and despite its initial limited release, the album soon became a highly collectable cult pop-psychedelic album in its own right. *Would You Believe* was described as employing 'a string of virtuoso production techniques, multi-layered harmonies and plenty of Wilson-esque chamber pop instrumentation' with what psychedelic historian David Wells calls Billy's 'gently spiralling vocals skipping over three-minute pocket symphonies in praise of acid (note the acronymic title of 'London Social Degree') and street traders selling 'Turkish cigarettes' ('Portobello Road').

The only one of its 12 tracks not written by Billy himself, the title track 'Would You Believe?' (by Jeremy Paul) is arranged by The Small Faces with recording engineer Alan O'Duffy, and the group members can clearly be heard elsewhere, too. Steve's voice and 'typically fiery lead guitar' are a powerful presence on 'Girl From New York', a track first collected onto the 4CD *Mojo Presents: Acid Drops, Spacedust & Flying Saucers* (2001, EMI/ Universal Music 07243-5-35078-23-4) – a 'Psychedelic Confectionery From The UK Underground 1965-1969', where Jon Savage calls this track 'atypical' because of Marriott's guitar 'and future Humble Pie drummer Jerry Shirley giving the track an aggressive edge.'

The track was also included on the free cover-mount CD for *Mojo* magazine in April 2021. From 6 October 1967, Billy was part of an Immediate 'jet-hop' tour of European promotional dates with The Small Faces, P.P. Arnold and Warm Sounds. He later toured with The Who and had songwriting successes with Phil Collins and Leo Sayer (with his composition 'Can't Stop Loving You (Though I Try)').

(If You Think You're) Groovy – Single

'(If You Think You're) Groovy' (written and produced by Steve Marriott and Ronnie Lane) 3:15 b/w **'Though It Hurts Me Badly'** (written by P.P. Arnold, produced by Mick Jagger) 4:20
Released: 24 Jan 1968, Immediate IM 061
Highest chart position: UK: 41 (4 weeks on chart)

Pat 'P.P.' Arnold arrived in Swinging London as part of Ike & Tina Turner's Ikettes, but when their tour moved on, she stayed here, where her engaging talent for friendship, as well as her awesome vocal prowess, determined her as an integral part of the happening scene. Signed to Immediate, she scored an immediate chart hit with Cat Stevens' song 'The First Cut Is The Deepest' and became co-vocalist with Steve on The Small Faces finest single 'Tin Soldier.' As part of the extended family – 'The First Lady Of Immediate', it was only natural that there should be this further collaboration.

It opens with acoustic guitar and woodwind, then gunshot drums break it into a big production number with horns and gospel voices, but Pat's voice is never less than in total control; it pauses and reverts to acoustic guitar and rattling tambourine before building again, and the elements complement each other immaculately, rising to the big chorus climax, 'if you think you're groovy' she taunts, 'you don't even move me.'

There's a clip from the French TV show *Bouton Rouge*, on 2 March 1968, with The Small Faces themselves miming the back-up with added phased whooshes. She wears the maroon mini dress with white ruffles down the front that she wears in the 'Tin Soldier' video, and it's a breathtaking performance.

And yes, the word 'groove' was still fashionably acceptable back then.

Both sides of the single appear on her 1968 debut album, *The First Lady Of Immediate* (Immediate IMSP 011), alongside 'Though It Hurts Me Badly' and 'Treat Me Like A Lady' produced by Mick Jagger, as well as her hit single 'First Cut Is The Deepest' orchestrated by Mike Hurst.

'Yeah, all that seems like it was another world now', she told me. 'We would go out on those Immediate tours, so all the artists were very much in tune and in touch with each other *and* with all the people who were about at the time. We all used to tour together. We used to work up and down the M1. We used to go to Europe; I remember touring Europe doing all the colour TV shows – when colour TV was first happening. There were all those Music Shows and Festivals and things. It was a special time. But unfortunately, that all changed when Immediate suddenly went bankrupt, and everybody just disappeared with the money and we all got left behind. I guess it was a drag all that, 'cos there was, like, really good things happening there.'

Ogdens' Nut Gone Flake

Personnel:
Steve Marriott: lead guitar, lead and backing vocals
Ronnie Lane: bass, backing & lead vocals
Kenney Jones: drums
Ian McLagan: keyboards, backing vocals
Plus:
Stanley Unwin: narration
P.P. Arnold and Billy Nicholls: uncredited backing vocals
Lyn Dobson: flute
Released: 24 May 1968, Immediate Records IMLP 012
Highest chart position: UK: 1 (on LP chart for 19 weeks), US: 159, Germany: 6

It entered the chart on 15 June and climbed to number one by 29 June, where it stayed for six weeks.

Small Faces
which were in the studios
hallowed be thy name
they music come
thy songs be sung
on this album as they came from your heads
we give you this day our daily bread
give us thy album in a round cover
as we give thee 37/9p
lead us into the record stores
and deliver us Ogdens' Nut Gone Flake
for nice is the music, the sleeve and the story
for ever and ever...

Promoted by Loog Oldham advertising copy with a playful blasphemous edge, branded 'Brightest Selection' and 'Manufactured By The Small Faces', strictly speaking, this is only the third Small Faces studio album and the last with the full original lineup. Yet the distance travelled between those three albums is jaw-dropping. They came a long way in a short period of time. This is the farthest and the highest they would ever get, with tunes soaked in the dye vat at the rainbow's end.

David Wells, in his *Record Collector: 100 Greatest Psychedelic Records*, says, 'if *Sgt Pepper* is widely acknowledged as the high watermark of the British psychedelic age, then *Ogdens'*, which gleefully smashes all the trappings of the era into one glorious amorphous stew, has some claim to being its archetypal period piece' yet 'fortunately The Small Faces remembered the old adage about content over form – look beyond its fashionable trappings, and *Ogdens'* is, first and foremost, a collection of magnificent songs.'

Above: There were but four Small Faces: Ian McLagan, Steve Marriott, Ronnie Lane and Kenney Jones. (*Chris Walter/Wireimage*)
Below: And then there were The Faces: Rod Stewart, Ronnie Lane, Ronnie Wood, Ian McLagan and Kenney Jones. (*Alamy*)

Left: Four fresh-faced and young Small Faces for the cover of their 1966 debut album. (*Decca*)

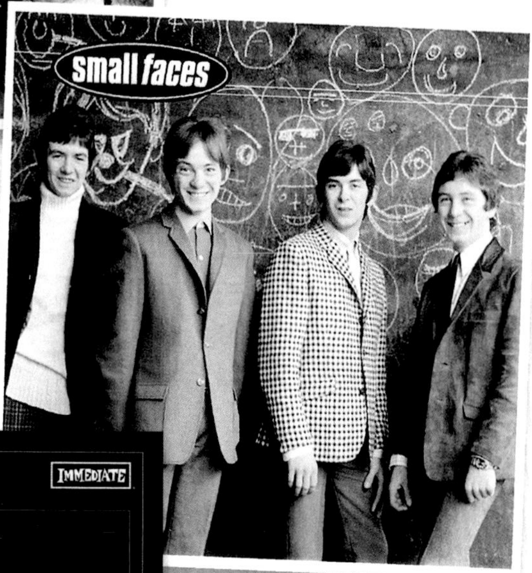

Right: *From The Beginning* was a compilation album released by their old record label after they'd signed to Immediate. (*Decca*)

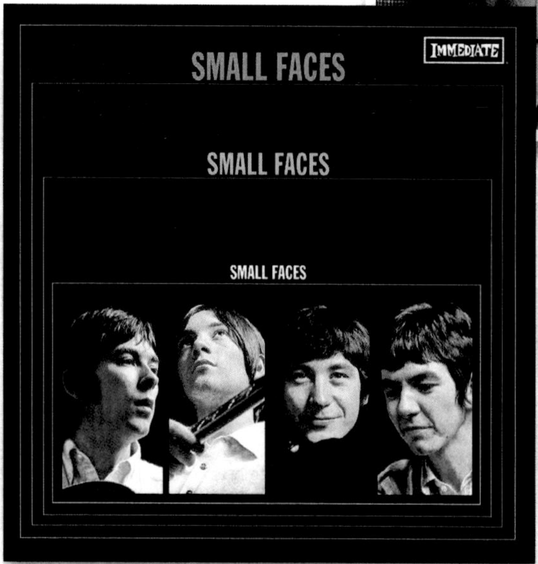

Left: Confusingly, their first album for Immediate bears the same title as their debut album for Decca. (*Immediate*)

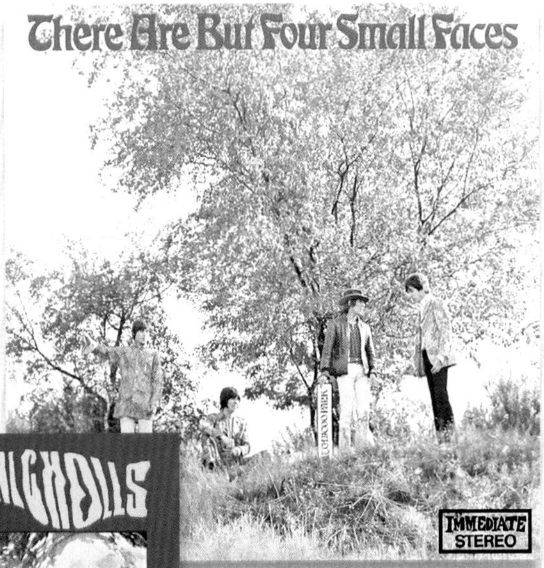

Right: With a new title and a little reshuffling of the track content, *There Are But Four Small Faces* became the band's first American long-player. (*Immediate*)

Left: Billy Nicholls' *Would You Believe* is a neglected classic from 1968, with more than a little input from The Small Faces. (*Immediate*)

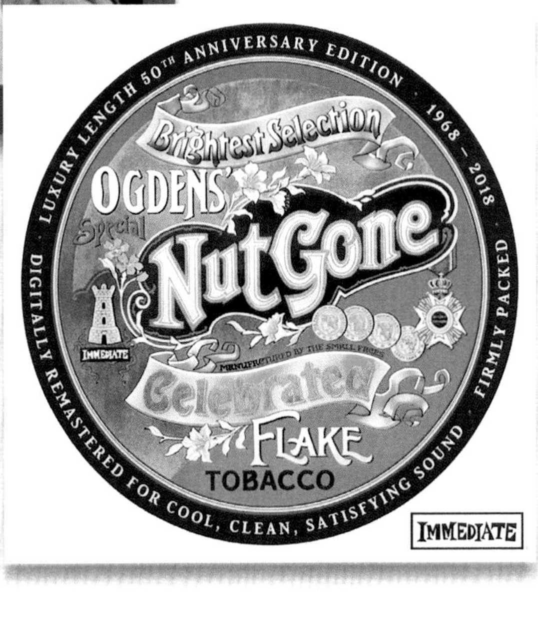

Right: In a year of classic albums, this was The Small Faces' crowning achievement and their only UK number-one LP. (*Immediate*)

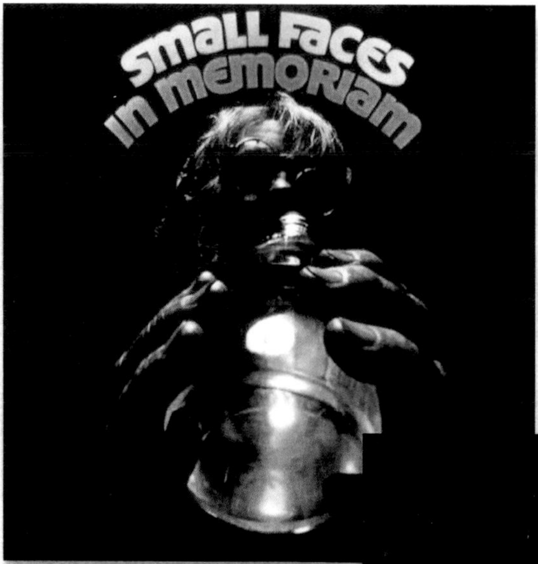

Left: A strange and elusive album, *In Memoriam* was originally only released in Germany. (*Immediate*)

Right: Johnny Hallyday was once billed as the 'French Elvis Presley', yet his 1969 LP *Rivière... Ouve Ton Lit* has some intriguing Small Faces contributions. (*Philips*)

Left: *The Autumn Stone* was a double-vinyl collection of hits, live songs, demos and previously unissued tracks – a treasure trove of wonders. (*Immediate*)

Right: Some say it needed two people to replace Steve Marriott, and for *First Step*, Rod Stewart and Ronnie Wood stepped in to help out. (*Warner Bros*)

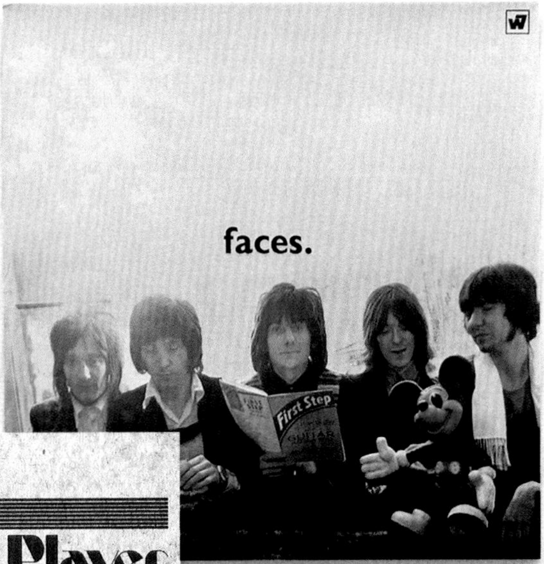

Left: *Long Player*, from February 1971, included Paul McCartney's 'Maybe I'm Amazed'. It's said that Paul didn't realise how good his song was until he heard The Faces' version. (*Warner*)

Right: 'Stay With Me' is the stand-out rocker on *A Nod's As Good As A Wink...To A Blind Horse*. (*Warner*)

Left: Steve Marriott was one of the greatest vocalists of the rock 'n' roll era, caught here singing 'Itchycoo Park', a hit in 1967 and again in 1976!

Right: The Small Faces were an electrifying live band, even when miming on a TV Pop show!

Left: Ronnie Lane – a man of contradictions, yet his writing partnership with Steve Marriott resulted in some classic 1960s hits.

Right: 'Song Of The Baker', as performed on BBC's *Colour Me Pop*, is seen as Ronnie Lane's ode to Sufism.

Left: The SF logo on Kenney's drum kit was a guarantee of quality mod-into-psychedelic rock music.

Right: Kenney Jones was so respected as a rock 'n' roll drummer that he was Pete Townshend's first choice as a replacement for Keith Moon in The Who.

Left: The fourth and final studio album from The Faces included the hit single 'Cindy Incidentally'. (*Warner*)

Right: With Pete Townshend taking advantage of a brief hiatus in The Who schedule – and Ronnie Lane free of his obligations to The Faces – the duo took time out to collaborate on this unique album. (*Polydor*)

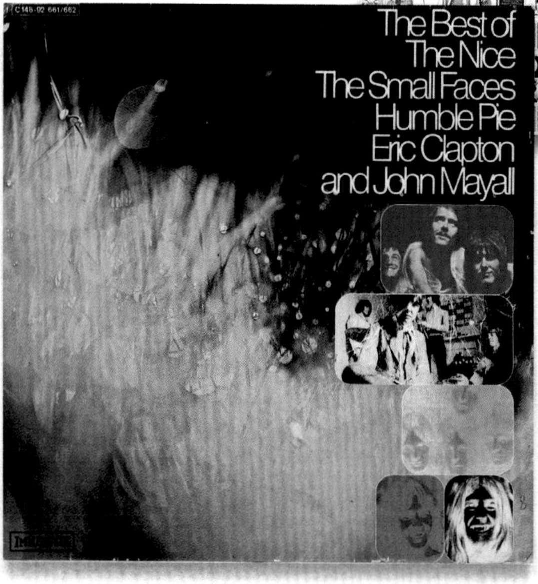

Left: The Immediate label successfully promoted its bands with a series of 'sampler' albums showcasing its artists. (*Immediate*)

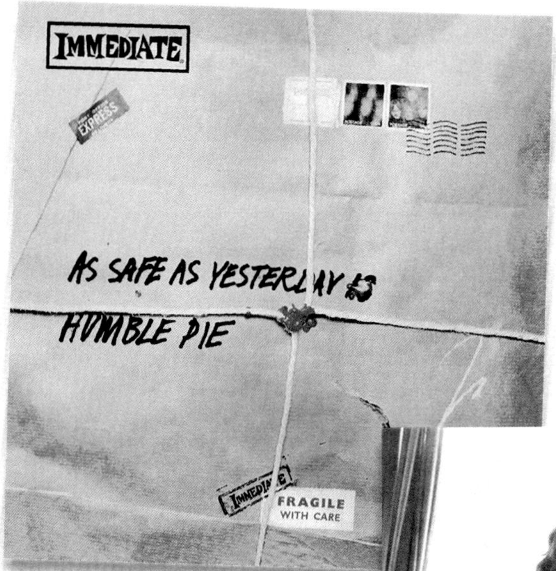

Left: Out of the ashes of The Small Faces and The Herd, allied with Greg Ridley and Jerry Shirley, Humble Pie made a promising debut. (*Immediate*)

Right: The second studio album by Humble Pie, *Town And Country* was issued within months of its predecessor. (*Immediate*)

Left: Adorned with lavish Aubrey Beardsley cover art, how could the third Humble Pie album possibly fail? (*A&M*)

Left: *Rock On*, released in March 1971, was the last Humble Pie studio album to feature Peter Frampton. (*A&M*)

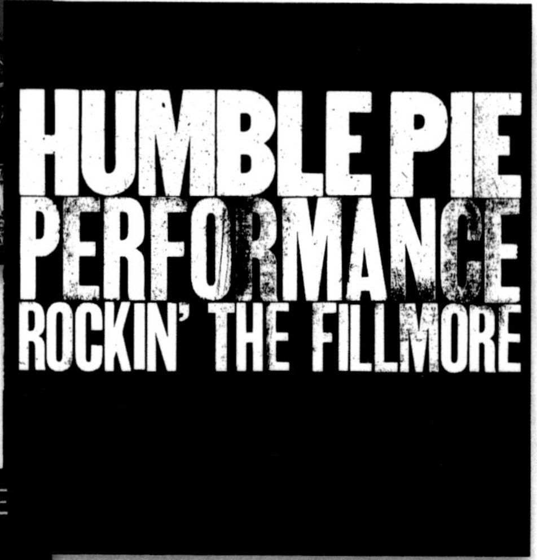

Right: *Rockin' The Fillmore* – an expansive double-vinyl set. After it was mixed, but prior to its November 1971 release, Peter Frampton quit. (*A&M*)

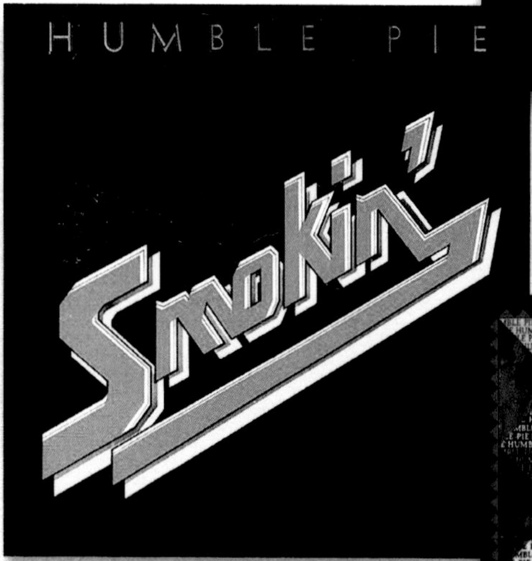

Left: Despite Peter Frampton's departure, *Smokin'* became Humble Pie's commercial breakthrough, peaking at number six in America. (*A&M*)

Right: A double-vinyl release from April 1973, *Eat It* was the first Humble Pie album to feature backing vocals from members of The Blackberries. (*A&M*)

Left: Following its American chart failure, the UK release of *Thunderbox* was cancelled. (*A&M*)

Right: Close to the end of the Humble Pie career arc, *Street Rats* proved to be something of a label compromise. (*A&M*)

Left: In 1980, Steve Marriott convened a new Humble Pie, ironically titled *On To Victory*. (*Jet*)

Right: Despite including a new version of 'Tin Soldier', *Go For The Throat* failed to halt the band's decline. (*Polydor*)

Left: Rod Stewart was a raw rock 'n' roll and R&B vocalist, although his later excursions into disco and the Great American Songbook proved more dubious.

Right: Ronnie Wood came to The Faces from a group called The Birds and he went on to join The Rolling Stones.

Left: Kenney Jones was twice inducted into the Rock And Roll Hall Of Fame: as a Face and as a Small Face!

Right: Rod and Ronnie, when The Faces were DJ John Peel's favourite band.

Left: Ronnie Lane had solo success with his own band, Slim Chance, and the 1974 hit single 'How Come'.

Right: Ian McLagan accurately subtitled his autobiography 'A Riotous Romp Through Rock & Roll History'.

Left: The Small Faces reformed in 1977 – without Ronnie Lane – for *Playmates*. (*Atlantic*)

Right: Neither Rick Wills on bass nor a guesting Jimmy McCulloch on guitar could save *78 In The Shade* from commercial failure. (*Atlantic*)

Left: The 1976 *Marriott* solo album looked back to The Small Faces' 'Wham Bam Thank You Ma'am'. (*A&M*)

Right: With new versions of 'All Or Nothing' and 'Whatcha Gonna Do About It', Steve Marriott gigs with his Packet Of Three. (*Aura*)

Left: This affectionate 1981 reunion for Steve Marriott and the seriously ill Ronnie Lane remained unissued until the year 2000. (*NMC*)

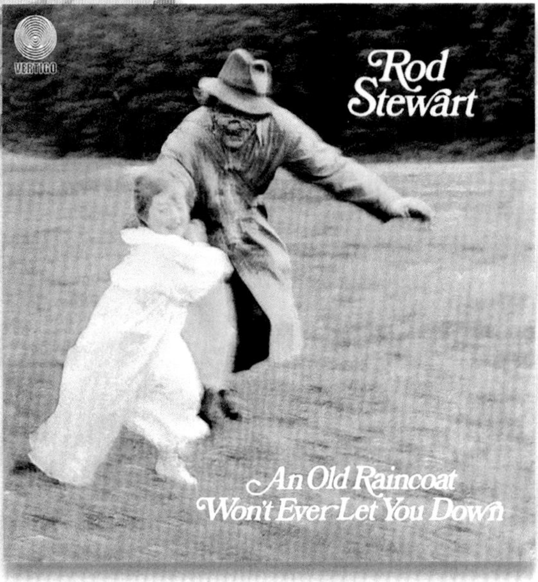

Right: Rod Stewart's first solo album included his Faces bandmates Ronnie Wood and Ian McLagan. (*Mercury/Vertigo*)

Left: Compare and contrast The Small Faces' original 'My Way Of Giving' with Rod's version on *Gasoline Alley,* and draw your own conclusions! (*Mercury/ Vertigo*)

Right: When Rod Stewart scored a global number one with 'Maggie May' from this album, his solo star began to outshine his role in The Faces. (*Mercury*)

Left: 'Think of me and try not to laugh', Rod sings on 'You Wear It Well'. And yes, I do try. (*Mercury*)

Right: *Smiler* was Rod Stewart's final album with a Faces connection ... after this came *Atlantic Crossing* and celebrity on a new level. (*Mercury*)

Kenney Jones recalls how 'it was a very free time. Even our record label, Immediate, reflected the ethos of the day. They let us do what we wanted and gave us as much studio time as we requested. There were constant parties to the point where Steve and Ronnie couldn't work at home anymore as people were always dropping by. So they hired a boat and went down the Thames writing lyrics for *Ogdens*' (much of Side Two was written this way). It was a *Three Men In A Boat* idea, gently putt-putting from Henley towards Maidenhead. The recordings were done at the Pye Studios, with some time at Trident (for 'Rene'), but mostly at Olympic, with Ian playing a small Wurlitzer electric piano on top of his Hammond organ, with Steve playing a Gretsch White Falcon and Ronnie a Harmony bass, both boosted by 100-watt Marshall amps. 'Everyone was always dancing', recalls Kenney, 'watching the band dance was like poetry.'

As part of the concept album theme, the second vinyl side tells a linked fairytale. It was – and remains, in every sense of the word, a success. With the generosity of the Immediate team, this was given the unique product design of a circular sleeve that imitates 'Ogdens' Nut Brown Flake', which was a long-time favourite brand of loose tobacco favoured by those who preferred to roll their own cigarettes.

If marijuana was to be legalised, then Ogden's would likely market it. 'It would be real good dope and your nut would go!' reasoned Ronnie.

Its uniqueness was part of a record label arms race ignited – as usual, by the Fab Four. The Peter Blake cover art for *Sgt Pepper* totalled £3,000 – which works out time-adjusted at around £51,000 today, with a packaging that included a press sheet of various cut-outs: a clip-on moustache, sergeant's stripes, badges and a stand-up card. The Rolling Stones reacted with a moving 3D cover for *Their Satanic Majesties* and a hexagonal sleeve for their 1969 *Through The Past, Darkly (Big Hits Volume 2)*. Both a hexagonal sleeve and The Small Faces circular design stood out when used in a Record Store window display but caused problems when filing the albums on your shelf or in your front-room record cabinet. And – as Mick Farren pointed out, 'the imaginative print job falls apart almost as soon as you handle it'! Jethro Tull had a pop-up inner gatefold for their *Stand Up* (1969) and The Rolling Stones' *Sticky Fingers* (1971) album incorporated an Andy Warhol working zipper that tended to scratch holes in whatever album it was slotted in next to.

Ogdens' Nut Gone Flake was in the vanguard, yet although the sleeve might prove attention-grabbing, it was the music in the grooves that mattered. And the album was both critically and commercially well-received, with both *Disc* and *Melody Maker* nominating it their Album Of The Month. With this album, the foursome had finally shucked off the last vestiges of its Decca-era teenybopper image and come up with a product worthy of the increasingly important album market. Yet, according to critic Johnny Rogan, 'behind the outward success, The Small Faces were still in a financial mess. Oldham had allowed them to indulge their creative whims in the studio for over a year and the recording costs (of *Ogdens' Nut Gone Flake*) proved astronomical' (in his book *Starmakers And Svengalis: The History Of British Pop Management*, 1988, Trans-Atlantic Pubn, ISBN-13 978-0356151380). Nevertheless, Mick Farren, in *NME* on 21 September 1974, concludes that 'it's a milestone in the development of a British idiomatic Rock style that amalgamates our own history of popular, and predominantly working class, songs with black R&B.' On the album chart, it replaced Otis Redding's album *Dock Of The Bay* (Stax) at number one, to be replaced in turn by Tom Jones with his *Delilah* (Decca) by 10 August. Among multiple reissues was the 1983 cassette format from Immediate IMC2001, the 1986 LP from Castle Classics CLALP116, and the Castle Communications CLACT016 expanded CD with bonus track 'Tin Soldier' (Live).

Side One

'Ogdens' Nut Gone Flake' (Marriott, Lane, McLagan, Jones) 2:26
No good idea should ever be abandoned. The Small Faces' second single, 'I've Got Mine', might have failed as a chart contender, but it was a good track. So, this album opens with an instrumental re-working of the song reconfigured to act as a title theme. It now comes effectively decked out in curving flourishes of piano fed through a wah-wah pedal, Kenney's phased drums, and nothing less than a string section orchestrated by violinist David McCallum Snr, who was not only father to the cult TV *The Man From U.N.C.L.E.* star but was the leader of the Royal Philharmonic Orchestra in his own right. He was also one of the violinists featured on The Beatles epic 'A Day In The Life.'

'Afterglow' (Marriott, Lane) 3:31
An interviewer asked Steve who was the woman who'd inspired such a tender soul-influenced declaration of romantic love. Steve didn't remember; he twinkled, 'just some dodgy boiler!' Which was street slang for what in modern parlance might be termed 'slapper.' The track opens with a raggedly drunken singalong sequence – subsequently edited for single release – until it breaks into the song's intoxicating rush. Tight, hard, passionate, the dynamics immaculately sculpted so that the organ cuts in with full force, lifted by the middle eight, and picked out by the little 'All Or Nothing' guitar figure. The Small Faces seldom came better than this.

'Long Agos And Worlds Apart' (McLagan) 2:35
A psychedelic ballad. The voice is distanced as the organ writes enticing squiggles around a lyric that seems to hint at a kind of predestined relationship circularity, 'times could pass me by, I'd sit quite still and pass the time.' If you were played this track as part of the *Melody Maker* Blind Date feature, you might not even guess it was The Small Faces, but you'd still be intrigued. 'Ian McLagan's 'Long Agos And Worlds Apart' suggests a criminally

underemployed songwriting talent' suggests *Record Collector: 100 Greatest Psychedelic Records*, 'while the ensemble playing confirms that The Small Faces were unquestionably a band of equals.' It fades almost too soon, then fades back again for an instrumental reprise.

'Rene' (Marriott, Lane) 4:29

Rod Stewart recalls how this leering Cockney knees-up was a regular raucous sing-along in the group's touring coach. And the relentlessly catchy tune is a perfect fit for that purpose. Rene is a sex worker past her prime, with her story treated in a 'Carry On'-style sniggery Laddish comedy way that could be considered offensive to 21st-century sensitivities. Steve suggests, 'just make your way down to The Crown & Anchor, ask for Rene' while Ronnie uses his mincing comedy voice for 'ohh, hello ducks!', as Steve assures you that 'you'll be well in.' For Rene, 'the docker's delight', the innuendo-laden 'ship's in every night', she's waiting for a stevedore from Tyneside or 'groping with a stoker from the coast of Kuala Lumpur', while a lineup in the warehouse is no trouble at all if you can spare the money. There's some prurient speculation about her dubious parentage of kids of every shape and colour hid in double-locked coal sheds – Steve concludes non-judgmentally, 'I wonder, well, there you go!' The track closes with a lengthy jamming coda. The Wee Faces themselves rarely played tracks from *Ogdens' Nut Gone Flake* during gigs, but it's easy to imagine how this song would have transformed each venue into a Music Hall communal sing-along.

'Song Of A Baker' (Marriott, Lane) 3:15

To David Wells, 'perhaps more than any other Small Faces project, the album acts as a showcase for the entire group rather than just the redoubtable talents of Steve Marriott.' 'Song Of A Baker' is a Ronnie Lane proto-hard rock track, a surprisingly hard-edged ode to Sufism. The lyric is pared back to elements of folk simplicity, wheat, water and salt. Ronnie sings the first verse, to be reinforced by Steve's harmonies for the powerful second verse: 'I can no longer wonder, 'cause I'm driven by this hunger.' He takes the 'Eddie's Dreaming' line 'I see the sunshine, the sunshine sees me' and retwists it into 'while I'm thinking of love, love is thinking for me', then gives it a further dimension with 'the baker will come, and the baker I'll be.' There's a strong bass line and a point of stereo trickery where the left channel drifts out, only to phase back in, reinforced by a flourish of Kenney's drums.

'Lazy Sunday' (Marriott, Lane) 3:05

The line 'I'll sing you a song with no words and no tune, to sing in the khazi while you suss out the moon' – khazi, for those who don't know, is slang for the outside lavatory cubicle located across the backyard, and sussing out the moon is an indicator to the album's second 'concept' side, a trailer or an advance notice of what is to come when the listener flips over the vinyl.

Side Two

'Happiness Stan' (Marriott, Lane) 2:35

The Who had been experimenting with linked mini-operas since their December 1966 'A Quick One, While He's Away', which consists of fragments built into a 9:10-minute musical suite. The original Nirvana duo of Patrick Campbell-Lyons and Alex Spyropoulos issued what is claimed to be the first 'concept album' in the form of the Science Fiction pantomime *The Story Of Simon Simopath* (December 1967, Island IMCD301), although The Beatles had arguably closed the conceptual loop with the reprise of the title track on the second side of *Sgt Pepper's Lonely Hearts Club Band*.

The Small Faces sensibly confine their fairytale concept to just the second side of *Ogdens' Nut Gone Flake*. Although the term 'concept album' was abused during the 1970s into pompous, pretentious, hugely overblown prog-rock excess, the idea concocted by Steve and Ronnie on their songwriting Thames boat-trip was the more modest tongue-in-cheek novelty story of a boy called 'Happiness Stan' and his hunt for the missing half of the moon.

'Professor' Stanley Unwin was not the first choice for a narrator to supply the spoken between-tracks links and fill in detail. Spike Milligan wrote inspired surreal nonsense poetry. But he was unavailable. And amiably droll South-African-born Unwin (7 June 1911-12 January 2002), who had invented his own gobbledygook language made up of malapropisms, gibberish and grammatical distortions, was an ideal alternative. He'd had a walk-on bit-part in *Carry On Regardless* (1961) and eccentric guest spots on *Ollie & Fred's Five O'clock Club* (1965), *David Nixon's Comedy Bandbox* (1966), and the Tommy Cooper TV series *Life With Cooper* (1966), baffling and amusing audiences with his monologue lectures in 'Unwinese.'

The track opens with Unwin ushering us in, 'are you all sitting comftybold two square on your botty? Then I'll begin….' There's lavish harp used in the way that movies denote a dream sequence, introducing Stan, who lives in a Middle Earth kind of 'land of green' in a small Victorian charabanc, 'this the four-wheel folloped ft-ft-ft out the backgrove.' Stan can sit and watch the moon from deep inside a rainbow. But as the moon rises, he sees that 'black had stolen half the moon away', with the dread warning, 'think of black and black will think of you.'

It's pure English psychedelic whimsy at its most appealing, with eccentric Edward Lear phrasing blended to an intricately conjured cauldron of studio sounds, opening up an enchanted toy box of esoteric devices. Steve and Ronnie tiptoe spritely harmonies, there are both anchoring clear and sharp drums with contrasting fantasy phase-ripples and curlicues of fairground organ.

Tongue-in-cheek and playful, surreal and strangely strange, it's not only unlike anything The Small Faces had done before but unlike anything anyone had done before!

'Rollin' Over' (Marriott, Lane) 2:50
'Now, of course, like all real-life experience stories, this also begins once a polly tito....' American psychedelic rock tended to be more blues-based, expressed through long improvisations. Its English counterpart retained an aroma of Victorian pastoral, or the fairy stories that held Syd Barrett 'high on clouds of sunlight floating by', drawn from sensory memories of 'time spent in that room, the doll's house, darkness, old perfume.' Woven in with a dark hint of Aubrey Beardsley perversity.

Although the full 'Happiness Stan' suite was never performed live, The Small Faces played most of it as part of a BBC-TV *Colour Me Pop* series on 21 June 1968, including this track, which was also the B-side of the 'Lazy Sunday' single.

There's a live version included on their *In Memoriam* album. If the opening riff seems to borrow from Jimi Hendrix 'Foxy Lady', that's probably entirely intentional, keeping this journey on the hard side of rock and not losing itself in artsy-fartsy prettification.

'The Hungry Intruder' (Marriott, Lane, McLagan) 2:15
For Stan, "Oh, blow your cool, man!' he dood this deep thoughcus... so gathering all behind in the hintermost he ploddy-ploddy forward into the deep fundemold of the complicading forry to sort this one out matey.' In other words, Stan sets out to investigate the mystery of the missing moon, 'scintillating dangly in the heavenly bode.' He stops to eat on the way when he encounters a hungry fly in the landscape of his tray. There are swirling 'I Am The Walrus' strings around acoustic strumming, with a close-harmony verse giving way to Steve voicing Stan's confused thoughts in a clear Pantomime exclamation, then a word-tumble as he offers the hungry fly a share of his shepherd's pie.

Less of a song in its own right than a bridging sequence in the story arc, it nevertheless retains an undeniable melodic attraction, with dancing flute and rasping cello.

'The Journey' (Marriott, Lane, McLagan, Jones) 4:12
When the fly offers to 'reciprocale' his deep generosity, Stan 'having possessy power of the magicold' rolls up his 'sleevey wavely hand' and recites the spell 'if all the flies were one fly, what a great enormous flyfelolifer that would bold' and the fly grows huge enough for Stan to straddle its back and ride, as it sings a 'deep joy of a songload' in his 'eardroves.'

Kenney's drums trip out the flight as raspy voices sing about 'the sun is surely just a thought away' with gurgly organ and electronic swishes in an extended instrumental passage intended to represent the esoteric flight 'like an escaped velocy of the rocket floatin into orbit' to seek out the oracle not only capable of answering Stan's question but of revealing 'the philosophy of life to itself.' He happens to be the cave-dwelling hermit Mad John.

'Mad John' (Marriott, Lane) 2:48

The acoustic folksy song about the 'old man who lived in the greenwood', complete with its 'ay-diddly-ay-di' refrain, was considered strong enough to be spun off as an American single in its own right. Sure, it remains an integral part of the story, but it also stands as a kind of variant on the theme of Donovan's 'Hurdy Gurdy Man', the mystical, mythical guru figure close to nature and natural wisdom. John had it sussed!

'And so Stan, walk-ed towards the cave, and in his mind, 'mark me word, Mad John.' Deep thoucus on this, all a tremblode, looking into the dark, and peering into the backgrove of black in there, and then appeared, Mad John. In fine fine foldy silken robes, all whitely hair, scintillating beard and dangly, well the beard must have been fruity-four years old, to grow it and grow it, all night lode, what! And he was glowing, with a friendly light, oh dear, joy, and a voice full of the Cockney Cockney Cockney, all joy of life and living, emanate from the cockload of his heartstrings…'

To suggest that the quest is more Enid Blyton than it is JRR Tolkien would probably amuse the instigators. Just as *Oz* magazine took and subverted images of Rupert Bear in knowing collage, it views fragments of childhood through acid's distorting lens.

'HappyDaysToyTown' (Marriott, Lane, McLagan, Jones) 4:17

'Cool to see you man, hah' says Mad John in greeting, 'what's been your hang-up man, huh, I waiting seven whole days for ya. Not still worried about this scintillating moon and dangly, huh, huh?' as ventriloquised in Unwin's unique way. Happiness Stan responds, 'ye, ye, yes, that's why I sortning you out here, tripply tripply out on the back of this fly who told me, huh….' So Mad John 'leaked arms' with Stan and leads him back to the mouth of the cave, looking up into the 'heavenly bode' where he comes to realise the natural cycle of 'as the sunrise in the early mordy, so the recall of the moon in the eve.'

On one level, 'HappyDaysToyTown' is a superbly catchy novelty 'all together!' sing-along Music-hall romp, 'life is just a bowl of All-Bran, you wake up every morning and it's there' which is both silly and oddly profound, with Ronnie and Steve trading verses – 'an enormous mindblast' as the good Professor interjects, bringing the narrative to a party close. 'Boy Blue left his horn stuffing under the settee and brought his mellotrone, and freaked 'em all out.'

The sequence was filmed for the BBC-TV *Colour Me Pop* strand, and it's a joy; with spontaneous laughter, Steve asks, 'can I have a go?' Ron says 'yes' to make sure Steve repeats 'yeah?' Ron says 'sing now' – Steve grins 'nooooyyyyyce', and then all four band members stand around the mike for the communal singing final, twisting for the 'clap twice, lean back, twist for a while' line.

So, a weird and wonderful album of absurd invention, which surely could only have happened at this never-to-be-repeated time and place in rock history.

Immediate Deluxe Edition (2012, Immediate 276-523-5)
Disc One: Full original album in mono
Disc Three: Full original album in stereo
Disc Two: Previously Unreleased
'Ogdens' Nut Gone Flake' (early session version) 2:29
'Afterglow' (alternate USA mix) 3:01
'Long Agos And Worlds Apart' (alternate USA mix) 2:33
'Rene, The Docker's Delight' (early session mix) 4:28
'Song Of The Baker' (alternate USA mix) 2:58
'Lazy Sunday' (alternate USA mix) 3:04
'Happiness Stan' (backing track) 2:58
'Bun In The Oven' (early session mix) 2:12
'The Fly' (take four, instrumental version) 2:00
'Mad John' (take seven, session version) 2:18
'HappyDaysToyTown' (alternate USA mix) 4:17
'Kamikhazi' (take seven, backing track) 2:15
'Every Little Bit Hurts' (early session mix) 3:56
'Ogdens' Nut Gone Flake' (alternate take, phased mix) 2:25

Related Releases
Mad John – Single
'Mad John' (Marriott, Lane) 2:06 c/w **'The Journey'** (Marriott, Lane, McLagan, Jones) 2:50
Released: early 1969, Immediate ZS7-5012 (US), and elsewhere, not issued in the UK
Produced by Steve Marriott and Ronnie Lane
Highest chart position: Aus: 84
A slightly different mix from the version of 'Mad John' included on *Ogdens' Nut Gone Flake*, with an extra repetition of the 'ay-diddly-ay' jig-sequence tacked into the fade. With the B-side lifted intact.

The Universal – Single
'The Universal' (Marriott, Lane) 2:30 b/w **'Donkey Rides, A Penny A Glass'** (Marriott, Lane, McLagan) 2:45
Released: 28 June 1968, Immediate IM 069
Arranged by Small Faces. Produced by Steve Marriott and Ronnie Lane
Highest chart position: UK: 16, Aus: 37, Ger: 35, Netherlands: 12
A remarkable single in many ways. Part-recorded low-fi busking-wise on a portable domestic tape recorder in the garden of Steve's beautiful old cottage in Essex – 'the house was built by Jerome K Jerome who wrote *Three Men In A Boat*' said Ronnie – with the random ambient found-sound breath of wind on the microphone, plus birdsong, and his dogs Shamus & Rufus barking in the background. It also samples bites of conversation, 'Good Morning Steve, well, you won't believe me today', then a hippy-trippy name-dropper

who came around saying 'I just bumped into Mick (Jagger?), he told me you know where to score?' Steve denies it, 'no, not me friend, I mind my own and my own minds me.' Later, studio musicians were dubbed on, not only the blistering electric guitar that stands out in sharp contrast but brass, including Don Fay (clarinet) and Derek Wadsworth (trombone). Only Ian is missing after a brief spat with Steve.

Yet the record's perceived failure proved a severe blow to Steve who later admitted 'the reviews said either it was a stroke of genius or a terrible mistake. And because it wasn't a hit in a big way, it was considered a terrible mistake. And it killed me – I didn't write again for a long, long time. I just went apart in my head.'

While the ironic 'haven't paid my rent yet… sorry, but I haven't got the money anymore' seems to be a snide shot at Immediate, who told the group they were still in debt. Despite being household names, The Small Faces were living on a pittance!

The B-side is based around a swaggering up-front riff, with crazy non-sequitur lyrics – 'unexpected attacks on your nose, can be treated by touching your toes', and a dense instrumental break augmented by saxophone; it's very much in the *Ogdens' Nut Gone Flake* vein. The lines 'I liked my uncle Joe, what a lovely man' seem to be an affectionate family reference, while 'I like wasting my days in a caravan' is either a preternatural glance forward to Ronnie Lane's nomadic phase or a backwards memory of childhood summer holidays in which donkey rides on the beach could well have figured.

Such freedoms were part of the new consciousness in which anything seemed possible – based on permissiveness, affluence and independence. The *Observer* newspaper, dated 28 January 1968, reported the publication of a booklet by Dr Gordon Stewart Prince, consultant in child psychiatry to King's College, London, who opines that 'no more harm is being done by permissiveness, affluence and independence than was done formerly by intolerant, repressive discipline. It is healthier, he asserts, for teenagers to challenge their parents' authority and to want to make their own judgments than to be protected from ever making a mistake.'

Mistakes and false steps were part of that process of growth.

Afterglow (Of Your Love) – Single

'Afterglow (Of Your Love)' (Marriott, Lane) 3:19 b/w **'Wham Bam Thank You Ma'am'** (Marriott, Lane) 3:12

Released: March 1969, Immediate IM 077

Produced by Steve Marriott and Ronnie Lane

Highest chart position: UK: 36 (on the chart a single week), Aus: 95, Netherlands: 19

The single's release was heralded by big splash ads in the music press. The *NME* dated 8 March had a collage-ad made up of various press-cuttings telling the full 'Anthology of Speculation' story – 'Is Steve Marriott quitting The Small

Faces', 'Frampton To Leave Herd', 'No Stevie Merger say Immediate' and 'Steve Marriott is alive and well and living in Essex.'

Issued shortly after the group's terminal break-up had been announced, the single edit of 'Afterglow' was a different mix from the version on the album. The rowdy singalong play-in sequence was deleted, the tempo was modulated, and there was an effective resurgence tacked on after the fade. It was a first-class single in every way, but its presence was overshadowed by the demise of its creators.

The B-side was a previously unreleased full-on rock track that would later feature on *The Autumn Stone* album. A tape of an earlier version of 'Wham Bam Thank You Ma'am', titled 'Me, You And Us Too' with a long instrumental coda, was discovered while compiling a definitive expanded edition of *The Autumn Stone*. It subtitled a 1999 compilation *Me You And Us Too: The Best Of The Immediate Years* (Repertoire Records REP 4818-WG) and was given a limited-edition single release as IM083 in 2016.

On 9 April 1968, The Small Faces recorded their only BBC radio session for John Peel's *Top Gear*, which was broadcast on 14 May and repeated on 19 May; they played 'If I Were A Carpenter', 'Lazy Sunday', 'Every Little Bit Hurts' and also included a slick Booker T-style organ-led instrumental version of The Temptations' 'Get Ready', which was never commercially issued. John Peel contributed his 'ABC Of Beauty' feature to *Disc & Music Echo* on 2 November 1968 as part of the music paper's five-page Underground special, listing The Small Faces enigmatically as 'don't really understand apparent support for violence which I don't believe anyway. Can make good records, though.' I don't believe for a moment that The Small Faces ever supported or advocated violence other than in the sense of a sonic assault!

In October, The Small Faces commenced a UK tour with The Who and Joe Cocker. It was during a performance on 19 October that Peter Frampton sat in with the group onstage, sparking a rapport with Steve Marriott, who wanted more than anything to elevate his rock credibility, annoyingly conscious of the teenybopper tag still associated with The Small Faces, despite their more recent progressions.

But why Peter Frampton? Herd had enjoyed a mordent top ten single with 'From The Underworld' during the autumn of the Summer of Love. It was a re-casting of the classical mythology story of Orpheus and Eurydice (or Orpheus & The Undergrope as Stan (the man) Unwin phrased it), which might not have been everyone's chosen subject for a debut hit. But the group had failed with an earlier single of Jagger-Richard's 'So Much In Love' (1966, Parlophone R5413) – done more effectively by Andrew Loog Oldham's protégés The Mighty Avengers, so Herd subsequently fell under the influence of the Howard-Blaikely writer-producer team responsible for novelty hits by The Honeycombs and Dave Dee, Dozy, Beaky, Mick & Tich, but failed to fly with their song 'I Can Fly' (Fontana TF819).

Yet 'From The Underworld' (Fontana TF856) worked to the extent that it broke The Herd as a chart act – up to number six, with Frampton already proclaimed The Face Of '68 by the fan press. Their even more maudlin follow-up, 'Paradise Lost' (Fontana TF887), fared predictably less well, no higher than number 15, until the embarrassingly bubble-pop bouncy 'I Don't Want Our Loving To Die' (Fontana TF925) returned them to the top five while effectively killing off whatever moody cred they still retained. Even the B-side 'Our Fairy Tale' co-written by Peter with Herd bassist Andy Bown (a future keyboardist for Status Quo) and the organ-led 'Sweet William' – the flip of 'From The Underworld' – were only pleasantly modest.

But for Peter, as Frampton later Tweeted, 'from 'Whatcha Gonna Do About It' onwards, I knew I had to play guitar with him (Marriott) someday.'

Steve's initial plan, for Peter to join The Small Faces as second guitar in order to 'heavy-up' the sound, met with fierce opposition from Ronnie Lane in particular, Ronnie was backed up by Ian McLagan. The impasse left a lasting grudge. Ian paraphrased Winston Churchill with, 'Steve annoyed all of us some of the time and some of us all of the time….' Meanwhile, The Herd were to continue without Frampton. They issued a May 1969 single, 'The Game' b/w 'Beauty Queen' (Fontana TF 1011), which vanished without a trace.

In Memoriam (Germany only album)

Personnel:
Steve Marriott: lead guitar, lead and backing vocals
Ronnie Lane: bass, backing & lead vocals
Kenney Jones: drums
Ian McLagan: keyboards, backing vocals
Plus:
Eddie Thornton and Harry Beckett: trumpet
Derek Wadsworth: trombone
Lyn Dobson: flute
German release: 1 May 1969, Immediate Records IMSP 022
No chart placings

This album is made up of the 'new' previously unissued material that would constitute the bulk of *The Autumn Stone* album, with the hits and familiar material stripped out. The group themselves tried to put a stop to it because 'it sounded as if we were dead'!

Side One

'Small Faces Live' 0:12
The first side of the album was recorded live at the Newcastle City Hall on 18 November 1968, the second of two 'houses'; this 'track' is the stage announcement made by host Jimmy Avakak.

'Rollin' Over' (Marriott, Lane) 2:19
The concert opens with a deluge of teen screams, which continue throughout. Some of the screaming girls and wired boys seem to be overdubbed in an attempt to increase the excitement, to the extent that the initial sound on this B-side of 'Lazy Sunday' is thin with Steve's voice mixed into the background, although it does catch the genuine atmosphere of a live touring band at this period.

'If I Were A Carpenter' (Tim Hardin) 2:36
The sound balance is correcting to an extent by the time they get into their second number, although the first line of the second verse is virtually inaudible, and Steve throws in an 'if I were a miller, Baby' ad-lib. The later 'cleaned-up' version on *The Autumn Stone* gives a better impression of their performance of this classic song.

'Every Little Bit Hurts' (Ed Cobb) 6:22
As Ian plays the introductory organ phrases and there's some inaudible talk-over from Steve before they perform a lengthy, impassioned interpretation of the Brenda Holloway song. There is a brass section, including Lyn Dobson, to add faint colouration. It closes with Steve yelling 'yeah-her-her-hera-now –

Oh YEAH! – feel so good I wanna scream' then 'I want you to sing this with me, you know what it is!' Again, there's some lost between-song dialogue.

'All Or Nothing' (Marriott, Lane) 4:11
Building towards the show's climax, they do the hit virtually straight, as on the record, except the 'bap-bap-bap-baddap' vocal scat is replaced by organ stabs, although it slows then re-builds powerfully… after which Steve's banter is drowned in a renewed tsunami of screams.

'Tin Soldier' (Marriott, Lane) 3:26
Again, the hit is played without embellishments, with Steve's voice rising to an incredible closing peak. This live sequence of songs gives some impression of the authentic experience of sitting in row ten from the stage at the 2,000-capacity Newcastle City Hall on Monday night. Joe Cocker opened the show, followed by The Crazy World Of Arthur Brown and The Mindbenders before The Small Faces preceded the headlining act, The Who.

Side Two
'Colliboshe r' (Marriott, Lane) 3:09
Side Two is made up of previously unreleased tracks recorded between 21 October 1967 and 11 September 1968 at the Olympic and Trident Studios. This instrumental would later appear on *The Autumn Stone*. The individual members of The Small Faces never claimed to be technically brilliant musicians, but the way they interact on these instrumental pieces demonstrates a near-telepathic level of compensatory empathy. Whatever the title 'Colliboshe r' means, it flows smoothly.

'Call It Something Nice' (Marriott, Lane) 2:03
Spikes of electric guitar, shuffles of acoustic guitar. Ronnie and Steve take alternate vocals on different stereo channels, then share vocals. There's a bright, sparkly guitar break and harmonica. Lyrically, it's a refutation of responsibility, 'don't grow to depend on me, don't lean on me 'cause I might let you down', in a similar way to Bob Dylan opting out of a relationship with 'It Ain't Me, Babe.' In total, it's a musically and lyrically inventive track.

'Red Balloon' (Tim Hardin) 4:12
The fragile, beautiful loser Tim Hardin wrote the lyrics 'we met as friends, and you were so easy to get to know.' For The Small Faces, this is the 4:12 version most familiar from *The Autumn Stone* album, which fades out at the end. There's an alternate 4.16-minute mix on The Small Faces *Immediate Years* 4CD box set released by Charly Records (1995), which features Steve's voice mixed higher. To further complicate matters, there's a studio outtake extended to 4.28 minutes, a slightly slower acetate that seems to be taken before studio mixology has had time to smooth the 'rough mix' edges, on

the CD *All Or Nothing* (also known as the *J60* album). Tim Hardin wrote the lyrics 'I haven't any time for children, although I've got a lot.' Make of that what you will.

'Wide-Eyed Girl On The Wall' (Marriott, Lane) 2:48
There's acoustic guitar and handclaps for this moody, previously unissued instrumental, with a hint of horns. None of these tracks were throwaway jams or backing demos awaiting vocal dubs; they were well-worked-out compositions in their own right. This track would make perfect background music for a Swinging Sixties movie montage.

'The Autumn Stone' (Marriott) 3:57
How was it possible to top the artistic and commercial success of *Ogdens' Nut Gone Flake*? How were they to move beyond it and take the next step? As *NME*'s Mick Farren suggested, 'in some ways it was a culmination of all that the band had been working for and, in others, set a final seal on the realisation that their day had passed.' There's a suggestion that, as a reaction to the self-indulgent studio trickery of *Ogdens' Nut Gone Flake*, the next Small Faces album would constitute a simpler back-to-basics approach, as evidenced by this melodic near-solo acoustic song from Steve. As it turned out, we were never going to get that next album, just these luminous fragments.

Rivière... Ouve Ton Lit – Johnny Hallyday

Released: 1969 (France), Philips 844-971-BY
There was a tour through September 1968 with Canned Heat and Tim Rose. Then, through November, as 'special guest stars' on a bill with The Who, Joe Cocker, The Crazy World Of Arthur Brown and The Mindbenders. And if playing the phased passages of 'Itchycoo Park' live was problematic, 'Lazy Sunday' was 'a total joke!'

The final incarnation of The Small Faces as a working unit comes in the bizarre form of an uncredited appearance as the 'Orchestre de Johnny Hallyday' on this album by France's rock 'n' roll star who was once seen as the Gallic response to Elvis Presley, or maybe Cliff Richard.

Glyn Johns was involved as a studio engineer, which might explain why the track listed as 'Amen: Bang Bang' is a reworking of The Small Face's song 'That Man', while two other tracks – 'Réclamation: News Report' and 'Regarde Pour Moi: What You Will' carry a Marriott-Lane writer credit and would reappear on the first Humble Pie album.

In December 1968 The Small Faces played week-long sessions in Paris, with Steve inviting Peter Frampton along for the ride, and all five can be heard playing, in different combinations, and with the French star's regular musicians, across the album. It seems to have been another attempt by Steve to infiltrate Peter into an expanded Small Faces lineup by stealth.

But both Ronnie Lane and Ian McLagan were increasingly opposed to the idea. To Ian, 'when Pete sat in with us one night, it didn't feel like The Small Faces anymore, as nice a chap as he is and a lovely player to boot.' These recordings are – as a result, the last time they all played in the studio together. Back in England, Steve stormed off stage at a New Year's Eve Alexandra Palace concert with Alexis Korner and told the others that he was quitting.

Some might say, what a waste. When The Small Faces imploded, Steve graduated into Humble Pie while the remaining three – Ronnie (bass), Ian (keyboards) and Kenney (drums) fused with two cast-offs from The Jeff Beck Group, Rod Stewart and Ronnie Wood, to re-emerge as the Faces. To replace Steve Marriott required recruiting not one but two replacement members, for Steve had been vocalist as well as lead guitarist. Ronnie Wood was a good guitarist but not a strong singer. Rod Stewart was not a strong guitarist but worked out fine on vocals. Although for direct comparison, check out their two versions of 'My Way Of Giving' (Rod's cover is on his 1970 *Gasoline Alley* album) – Marriott's original vocals are streets ahead of Hot Rod's.

It was the end of The Small Faces. Or at least it was the end of this phase. For they would return… but in the meantime, there was Humble Pie, and there was The Faces. A phase that forms an integral part of the collective story, but deserves less detailed coverage than what had come before.

The Autumn Stone

Personnel:
Steve Marriott: lead guitar, lead vocals, harmonica
Ronnie Lane: bass, backing & lead vocals
Kenney Jones: drums
Ian McLagan: keyboards, bass guitar, backing vocals
Jimmy Winston: keyboards, backing vocals
Released: 14 November 1969, Immediate Records IMAL 01/02
No chart placings

'The birth, spring, summer and autumn of The Small Faces in two albums for the price of one' says the big half-page press ad, 'another Immediate collectors' item in sound.'

After fulfilling outstanding live performance commitments, including a January European tour, they played Birmingham, Coventry, Swansea, Bolton and Crewe before a final show in Devizes. Then, the Small Faces saga was over. The dissolution was formally announced in March 1969. This album was a postscript. Rod Stewart remembers how he and Ron Wood used to listen to *The Autumn Stone* album 'all the time.' Then how, for Ronnie Lane, 'Marriott's departure and the end of The Small Faces had hit him hardest of all and he could be pretty sour and chippy.' Many years later, journalist Max Bell would write, in *Vox* in August 1995, about how the 'Small Faces' brief and ultimately vainglorious career in the sixties virtually serves as a Geiger counter for any prospective working-class heroes about to tiptoe through the entertainment industry minefield.' And yes, they were multiply screwed over. Although this album is essentially a gathering together of old hits padded out with previously unissued live demos and the scrapings from the studio floor, it forms a remarkably cohesive and enjoyable double-vinyl. It was first issued on CD by Castle Communications CLACD114 in 1986, alongside double-LP (CLALP114) and cassette editions (CLAMC114).

Side One

'Here Come The Nice' (Marriott, Lane) 2:57
According to writer David Wells, this single, as included on the American album *There Are But Four Small Faces*, was an attempt 'to see what we could get away with' in flaunting the BBC drug-censorship rules.

'The Autumn Stone' (Steve Marriott) 4:00
A folky, slow, reflective acoustic song from their final recording session together, 11 September 1968, this previously unissued track is different to just about anything else the group ever did. 'We were strangers, and then you came to stay, the sweetest spring dawn morning sings to me.' Some claim it's Chris Wood of Traffic playing flute, but more likely, it was Lyn Dobson.

There's harmonica, and a fast build takes the track to a close. One of the best songs that Steve ever wrote or performed. A demo version called 'Jenny's Song' for Jenny Rylance ends with Steve exclaiming, 'what a fucking gas!' He was not wrong!

'Colliboshes' (Marriott, Lane) 3:12
There's a theory that some of these previously unreleased instrumentals were evolved out of studio jam sessions and that the tapes were later edited into shape and given random titles. That could be true, but if so, it demonstrates a remarkable level of casual proficiency invested in throwaway material.

'All Or Nothing' (Marriott, Lane) 3:03
The number-one single. While it was on the chart, *Record Mirror*, on 20 August 1966, featured a moody colour cover photo of the group with Steve wearing stylish Roger McGuinn 'granny' glasses. Making the cover was a big deal that denoted status. The photo led to a story on the inner pages headed 'Faces shine on new tour.'

'Red Balloon' (Tim Hardin) 4:12
The acoustic guitar sets an air of stripped-down simplicity, but Marriott's chip of gravel in his voice, joined by Ronnie's close harmonies, provides a spine of strength; later, the electric guitar, tinkling keyboard and drums provide depth until the final vocal reprise is taken at a more extreme pitch, followed by a lengthy instrumental fade. Tim Hardin's songs are typically ambiguous; what does the red balloon represent?

The song appeared in the *Mojo* top 100 Greatest Drug Songs compiled by 'djorkaeff' (which lists 'Here Come The Nice' at number five!), who claim that "Red Balloon' is a confessional song about Tim's mixed feelings toward heroin and its effects upon him. Heroin is often sold in balloons, so the 'bought myself a red balloon' line refers to buying and taking heroin. The 'blue surprise' is the adverse effects of heroin. One such effect is the loss of libido or sexual desire – 'took the lovelight from my eyes.' Steve sings the wistful lines 'will we meet one another again, Oh my, I hope so' as if it's a straight romantic encounter. The Small Faces rewrite some of the lyrics, either consciously or – more likely – they were transcribing it from the *Tim Hardin 2* album and misheard the words. This is one of the tracks intended for the follow-up to *Ogdens' Nut Gone Flake*, to be called *1862*. As it is, it was also included on the *In Memoriam* album.

'Lazy Sunday' (Marriott, Lane) 3:06
Taken from *Ogdens' Nut Gone Flake*, the group only found out it was being released as a single while they were touring in Germany! It wasn't a song they'd wanted as a single, considering it just a bit of fun. They were earnest about losing that 'teenybopper' image.

Side Two

'Call It Something Nice' (Marriott, Lane) 2:05

A previously unissued track that got lost in the group break-up and never quite received its due recognition. Ronnie and Steve swap vocals, then share as-tight-as-a-nut harmonies. The title doesn't occur in the song, which is a goodbye message, and there's a story that it was titled as The Small Faces stumbled out of the studio after an all-night session, and the engineer said, 'what shall I call this one?' One of the boys replied, 'Ahh, call it something nice!!'

'I Can't Make It' (Marriott, Lane) 3:06

The 1967 single.

'Afterglow (Of Your Love)' (Marriott, Lane) 3:24

The single mix of the track taken from *Ogdens' Nut Gone Flake*.

'Sha-La-La-Lee' (Kenny Lynch, Mart Shuman) 2:56

The hit single lifted from the 1966 *Small Faces* album. Belgian new wave artist Plastic Bertrand would later revive the song, take it to number 38 on the UK chart and perform it on *Top Of The Pops* on 27 July 1978.

'The Universal' (Marriott, Lane) 2:42

The 1968 single.

Side Three

'Rollin' Over' (Steve Marriott, Ronnie Lane) 2:31

The first of three live tracks as featured on the *In Memoriam* album.

'If I Were A Carpenter' (Tim Hardin) 2:32

This is a live and raucous version of the classic Tim Hardin song. The fragile and doomed Tim Hardin had issued two albums for the Verve label, *Tim Hardin 1* (1966) and *Tim Hardin 2* (1967), which were instantly plundered as a song source by artists across the spectrum. Bobby Darin, former 1950s rocker who had fallen on hard times since the British invasion, launched a critically lauded comeback with his cover of 'If I Were A Carpenter.' The Four Tops would later score with the same song. Rod Stewart, with Ronnie Lane, Kenney Jones and Ian McLagan playing back-up, had a breakthrough hit with Tim's 'Reason To Believe.' Yet just maybe The Small Faces were the most radical interpreters of Tim's songs, following this live recording with another Hardin song, 'Red Balloon.'

'Every Little Bit Hurts' (Edward Cobb) 6:20

This had long been a Small Faces live favourite, recorded for BBC radio sessions and for the *In Memoriam* album. The song had originally been recorded by Brenda Holloway for Motown in 1964. The songwriter – Ed Cobb, a former member of The Four Preps vocal group, went on to write 'Tainted Love', initially for Gloria Jones, but which was a massive electro-hit for Soft Cell, as well as writing hard-core garage songs for The Standells and The Chocolate Watchband. But the way that Brenda Holloway emoted his 'Every Little Bit Hurts' made it a blueprint for lots of aspiring white Soulsters and a litmus test of their abilities. The Spencer Davis Group had a minor hit with the song, at number 41, during March 1965, with a teenage Stevie Winwood aching with inspired sincerity. Rough, raw, and raucous, Steve Marriott vindicates himself every time The Small Faces perform the song.

'My Mind's Eye' (Marriott, Lane) 2:04
The single as included on the *From The Beginning* album. Aware that Decca was striving to promote a more polished version of the group on record than that witnessed during their stomping, raucous live gigs, they were amused when Decca released this pleasingly rough mix of the single instead of a more polished take, apparently in error.

'Tin Soldier' (Steve Marriott, Ronnie Lane) 3:21
The 1967 single that Paul Weller quoted in *Uncut* magazine in September 2004: 'no matter how many times I've heard that song, it still gets me every time. It's so powerful the way it builds up. It still blows me away … I loved the image, the 'fuck off!' attitude, the whole feel to them. They just looked so cool, all four of them, and that rarely happens in a band these days.'

'Just Passing' (Steve Marriott, Ronnie Lane) 1:13
The brief B-side of 'I Can't Make It', on which Ronnie takes the vocals.

Side Four
'Itchycoo Park' (Marriott, Lane) 2:50
David Wells writes, 'while contemporaries like Eric Burdon were exhorting straight society to turn on by flying TransLove Airways to hippy capital San Francisco, The Small Faces suggested that personal revelation could just as easily come while feeding the ducks in an East London park' – with a promo clip shot in Chiswick Park. Wells calls the single, as featured on the *There Are But Four Small Faces* album, 'a transparent send-up of the flower-power scene' that 'transcended its sardonic origins.'

'Hey Girl' (Marriott, Lane) 2:18
The early single as included on the *From The Beginning* album. When Decca produced a compilation maxi-single to jump the Mod revival in 1979, their *The London Boys* (FR13864) included 'Hey Girl' alongside The Birds' 'Leaving Here' and David Bowie's 'The London Boys.'

'Wide-Eyed Girl On The Wall' (Marriott, Lane) 2:47
A previously unissued instrumental. Maybe a playback tape left over after a session, acoustic guitar, Ronnie's bass, and brassy stabs of horns. There is an even more raw extended mix running to 3:32, which has escaped onto a couple of foreign compilations, a 1984 American Compleat Records double-LP – *Small Faces: Big Music* (Compleat Records 672004-1) – and an Italian Rod Stewart CD called *Ridin' High* (1982, International Joker Production SM3985).

'Whatcha Gonna Do About It' (Potter, Samwell) 1:57
The single that started it all as featured on the 1966 album *Small Faces*. Glasgow power-pop band The Jolt issued their own lively version of this song in April 1978 as Polydor 2059-008. While The Pretenders offered it as their own contribution to *Under The Covers: Other People Sing Other People's Songs* (1988, WEA WX146, WEA 242-268-1).

'Wham Bam, Thank You Ma'am' (Marriott, Lane) 3:18
The riff-heavy B-side of the single 'Afterglow (Of Your Love)' pointed its way towards Steve's Humble Pie ambitions, but with incisive little boogie keyboard figures and a playfully catchy 'shang-alang shang-a doo-lang' lyric, with some choppy changes towards the close. After a disagreement with Ian, Steve got session musician Nicky Hopkins to play the piano part. Two versions, one featuring Nicky and the other with Ian, were eventually released. The lyric starts out with what seems to be a groupie theme, 'she was good to those who took off all their clothes and played guitar' but leads into more complex territory with an attack on 'our lives are run by ego freaks, a walking book of rules, he seeks to keep you in your pigeonholes and bash you if your soul steps out of line.' Steve would carry this song over into his future projects.

You Can Make Me Dance, Sing Or Anything: The Faces, With And Without Rod Stewart

First Step

Personnel:
Rod Stewart: 'the voice and banjo', lead and backing vocals, harmonica
Ronnie Lane: bass, rhythm and acoustic guitars, backing & lead vocals
Ronnie Wood: 'the guitars and harp and bass'
Kenney 'Kenny' Jones: 'the drums'
Ian McLagan: Hammond organ, Wurlitzer electric and acoustic piano, backing vocals
Released: 21 March 1970, Warner Bros WS3000 in Gatefold sleeve (UK), Warner Bros BS1851 (US) as by The Small Faces
Produced by The Small Faces, 'in helping the production, we would like to acknowledge Martin Birch, the engineer, and John and Lou', at the London DeLane Lea Studios
Highest chart position: UK: 45, US: 119 (Billboard), and Can: 74

'I never dreamed anyone in Britain would want to listen to me and Woody and three of the old Small Faces', Rod confided to Richard Williams in *Melody Maker*.

On his breakthrough hit single 'Maggie May' the spiky-haired singer mused about his possible futures, 'I suppose I could collect my books and get on back to school, or steal my daddy's cue and make a living out of playin' pool/Or find myself a rock 'n' roll band that needs a helpin' hand.' That he chose the final option is a matter of history. 'We were together for five years and I wouldn't have missed it for the world', recalls Rod in Rod: The Autobiography, 'on a good night, the Faces were something special. On a bad night, we were bloody awful. But with The Faces, being bloody awful could sometimes be even more special than being good' (*Rod: The Autobiography*, Arrow Books, 2013).

Avowed Scotsman Roderick David Stewart (born in London on 10 January 1945) had been kicking around for a while. After attending the same secondary school as Kink Ray Davies, he tried his hand at various professions, including fence-erecting, grave-digging and a try-out for Brentford FC. According to the legend recounted on the liner notes of Long John Baldry's *Right To Sing The Blues* album (1996, Canadian Stony Plain Records SPCD1232), Long John stumbled across the aspiring blues-growler on the midnight platform of Twickenham railway station 'playing harmonica under a pile of football scarves' and busking Muddy Waters. This unlikely encounter provoked Rod to switch from his night job with Jimmy Powell's Five Dimensions to becoming the second vocalist with Baldry's Hoochie Coochie Men.

The Blues Family Tree confusingly complexifies as, soon after that year, as the group broke up, Rod took time out to cut a solo single ('Good Morning

Little Schoolgirl' b/w 'I'm Gonna Move To The Outskirts Of Town' for Decca F11996, October 1964) with a young John Paul Jones playing session-bass. The Yardbirds issued their own version of the same lasciviously risqué Sonny Boy Williamson blues standard at the same time, which divided sales to the extent that neither made the impact it might otherwise have done. Rod was briefly part of The Soul Agents with Roger Pope who would later play drums with Elton John's band. Then Rod rejoined Baldry who took him forward into the new Steampacket project. By then, it was mid-1965, and Steampacket lasted a year as a kind of touring R&B revue with Brian Auger (keyboards), Rick Brown (bass), Mickey Waller (drums), and Long John and Rod as first and second vocalist. With guitarist Vic Briggs and Julie Driscoll waiting in the wings.

There was also Shotgun Express, with ex-Them organist Peter Barden and Liverpool soul-shouter Beryl Marsden, plus drummer Mick Fleetwood and guitarist Peter Green!

Rod joined the moodily unpredictable former Yardbirds guitar star in The Jeff Beck Group, along with Ron Wood, formerly of The Birds, who had enjoyed a single week on the chart at number 45, 27 May 1965, with the frenetic 'Leaving Here' (Decca F 12140). But ironically, the one hit record that emerged from the Jeff Beck alliance – the enduring 'Hi Ho Silver Lining' (number 14, 11 May 1967), had Beck himself singing lead vocals… as with its less successful follow-up 'Tally Man' (number 30, 9 August 1967) with Rod himself relegated to adding backing vocals. They toured America, Jeff and his vocalist sharing a cautious mutual respect; 'there were phases where the two of us struggled to enjoy each other's company', comments Rod with acid humour.

The remains of The Faces were rehearsing in a basement studio owned by The Rolling Stones at 47 Bermondsey Street through the good graces of 'Stu' Ian Stewart. 'Ron Wood was at a loose end after the demise of The Jeff Beck Group' – and he'd had enough of playing bass and wanted to resume playing lead; he 'started going down there with his guitar to join in, and I went along… there was obviously a singer-shaped hole', recalled Rod. He joined on vocals for a work-out around songs from the *Muddy Waters At Newport 1960* album – 'the one with the cover-shot of Muddy standing on the stairs in a fantastically cool white tie', including 'Hoochie Coochie Man', and it was pretty clear they sounded good together. Some of their earliest rehearsal tapes were salvaged onto the 2004 *Five Guys Walk Into A Bar* Faces 4CD box set. During October 1969, they officially became a band, continuing briefly as The Small Faces, 'although the 'Small' had to go because Ronnie and I (Rod) took the average height up to the point where it no longer applied.'

Most people thought that Marriott's departure had dealt The Small Faces a terminal blow, yet the new post-Marriott manager Billy Gaff extricated The Faces from old contractual obligations and negotiated a deal with Warner Bros, and *First Step*, according to Rod, 'sounded exactly like that: a debut album pretty quickly recorded. The fact that there are two instrumentals among those ten tracks gives some indication of the extent to which it was a work in progress rather than a polished jewel.' To Ian, it was thrown together 'with no direction, just a lot of side roads.'

The first real Faces gig was in December 1969 at an American Air Force base in Cambridge. And for a while they were a wonderfully fun live band, boozily shambolic with a gloriously untogether ebullience that made them one of the most exciting John Peel-approved stage attractions of the time. The real fly in their chaotic ointment was Stewart's divided loyalty, with the success of his parallel solo career undermining his commitment to the Faces.

Martin 'the camera' Cook's cover photo for the debut album shows the full new lineup, with Ronnie Wood studying the guitar tutorial *First Step: How To Play Guitar Plectrum Style* by Geoffrey Sisley. All American editions of the album were credited to The Small Faces, and the credit reads 'Produced by The Small Faces', which is either an uncorrected error, a sly in-joke, or a continuity link.

Side One

'Wicked Messenger' (Bob Dylan) 4:08

A song from Dylan's 1967 *John Wesley Harding* lurch into proto country-Rock, The Face's interpretation opens with spooky organ introducing the sparse haunted apocalyptic-threat lyric. Where Dylan is austere, The Faces are effectively rocked up, smoothing out Dylan's eccentric phrasing with thick bass and streamlined organ, yet they retain the brooding atmosphere of the doom-laden poetry, closing with a Kenney Jones drum barrage.

'Devotion' (Lane) 4:56

With lead vocals by both Rod and Ronnie. Rod says that Ronnie 'had a nice voice, but he was no Steve Marriott. And Mac would sing a bit too, but he wasn't even as good as Ronnie.' This is one of four tracks The Faces did for a Radio 1 'The Peel Sessions' on 19 November 1970.

'Shake, Shudder, Shiver' (Wood, Lane) 3:15

'Back with a bang are The Faces' writes reviewer Chris Welch in *Melody Maker*, 'they have retained much of their original appeal, with a much heavier overall sound... some tracks have a strong country feel. Occasionally, they sound a little ragged, but there is drive and strong emotion to compensate.' Rod and Ronnie duet on this raw rocker which is, according to Rod, 'a swaggering blues number with a lyric by Ronnie Lane about how cold his flat was.'

'Stone' (Lane) 5:38

The *NME* review headlined 'Grown Up Faces', singles out this track's 'simpler... country sounds', on which Ronnie takes lead vocal and Rod plays banjo. It continues, 'the group is striving for a heavier sound and getting it. Whether former fans of The Small Faces will like it remains to be seen.'

'Around The Plynth' (Stewart, Wood) 5:52
This was 'a re-fashioned version of the number that Woody and I (Rod) had written for Jeff Beck' – as included on the *Beck-Ola* album as 'Plynth (Water Down The Drain).' It was edited as an American single b/w 'Wicked Messenger.' The track... and the album side, closes with Rod yelling, 'that's yer lot!', which was edited from the US edition.

Side Two

'Flying' (Stewart, Wood, Lane) 4:18
Issued just prior to the album launch, this was the first spin-off single, b/w 'Three Button Hand Me Down.' 'Flying' was a 'slow and brooding rock song, built on descending chords' according to Rod, and was one of the first numbers the formative lineup rehearsed to. According to the lyrics, he's served five years in the County Jail for 'being hungry, tired and poor', but now he's on his way home, carried effortlessly on organ and a spill of shimmering guitar. Kenney's snap-drumming precisely maps the route. The baffled *NME* reviewer said, 'Ian's organ music is the forte of 'Flying', a way-out sort of number.' Maybe this anticipates the mood of his later 'Sailing' hit.

'Pineapple And The Monkey' (Wood) 4:25
'The band take off on a funky instrumental', says Chris Welch, 'and Kenney Jones' drumming is a powerhouse throughout.' For American music critic and author Joel Selvin, his debut contribution to *Rolling Stone* magazine was his review of The Small Faces' *First Step*, where he says they 'play with more control than soul... playing tight changes and neat licks all the way through the record.'

'Nobody Knows' (Wood, Lane) 4:07
Rod shares slow soul vocals with Ron on separate stereo channels, punctuated by Kenney's powerhouse drumming. It stops sharp at the 1:43 mark and then resumes.

'Looking Out The Window' (McLagan, Jones) 4:59
A walking bass intro to a funky instrumental that looks back to Small Faces work-outs such as 'Own Up Time.' Much later, Dave Simpson was to recall in *Melody Maker* on 18 September 1973 how The Faces 'were the quintessential lad's band of their day, as much a part of seventies subculture as George Best's sideboards and the Ford Cortina. Call it inverted snobbery if you like, but their incorrigible, unvarnished swagger and ramshackle bonhomie was the essence of their appeal.'

'Three Button Hand Me Down' (McLagan, Stewart) 5:44
It starts with a bass solo. According to Rod, this was 'a song put together by Mac and me. Everyone was chipping in and we were all coming up with stuff

in different combinations, which was very pleasing.' The conundrum is that where The Small Faces were tight and controlled, The Faces specialised in this loose, improvisational freedom. Maybe it's down to incorporating Ron Wood into the lineup. Or merely the evolutionary up-switch from a focus on 45rpm singles to the greater spacey indulgence of albums?

Bonus Tracks On The 2015 CD Edition:
'Behind The Sun' (Jones, Lane, McLagan, Stewart, Wood) 5:28
An outtake from a 12 May 1970 Western Studios session in California, built on strong blues chord riffing reminiscent of the work song 'Rosie' and buoyed up on Ian's rippling organ. Rod plays to his 'gipsy soul' on a track as good as anything from the album itself. Inventive, to the last fade moments.

'Mona: The Blues' (Lane, Wood), 5:04
Snarling low-down blues instrumental outtake from the same session, with stinging slide guitar. At face value, it has nothing to do with the Bo Diddley song of the same name.

'Shake, Shudder, Shiver' (Lane-Wood) 2:44
Rod and Ronnie share vocals on this BBC session version from John Peel's *Top Gear* show (recorded on 9 March, broadcast on 28 March 1970). One of the first songs The Faces ever played.

'Flying' (Lane, Stewart, Wood), studio Take three, 4:40
'Nobody Knows' (Lane-Wood) studio Take two, 4:24
Without Ron Wood's harmonies, Joel Selvin says that Rod 'sings his butt off. His raspy, sore throat voice lends itself well to The Faces' music. But Stewart's value lies in his unpredictability. His phrasing and delivery are filled with the unexpected.' This is a case in point. 'Now do it', someone yells as Ian plays into the fade.

Related Releases
Flying – Single
'Flying' (Stewart, Wood, Lane) 4:15 b/w **'Three Button Hand-Me Down'** (McLagan, Stewart) 5:37
(Warner Bros WB 8005)
February 1970 UK-only single.

Around The Plynth – Single
'Around The Plynth' (Stewart, Wood) 4:02 b/w **'Wicked Messenger'** (Bob Dylan) 4:05
(Warner Bros 7393)
1970 US-only single.

Had Me A Real Good Time – Single

'Had Me A Real Good Time' (R Stewart, R Wood as 'Bonnie Wood' and R F Lane) 3:55

b/w **'Rear Wheel Skid'** (McLagan, Jones, Stewart, Lane) 3:55

(Warner Bros WB 8018)

Original 1970 mix of the A-side for a November 1970 non-album single.

Maybe I'm Amazed – Single

'Maybe I'm Amazed' (McCartney) 3:15 b/w **'Oh Lord, I'm Browned Off'** (McLagan, Jones, Wood, Lane) 3:48

(Warner Bros 7483)

April 1971 non-album single with the A-side engineered by Bill Lazarus and the flip by Don Sciarrotta.

Long Player

Personnel:
Rod Stewart: lead vocals (the US credits state 'by courtesy of Mercury Records')
Ronnie Lane: bass, acoustic guitars, backing & lead vocals
Ronnie Wood: lead, slide and acoustic guitars, pedal steel guitar
Kenney Jones: drums and percussion
Ian McLagan: piano, organ and keyboards
Bobby Keys: tenor saxophone
Harry Beckett: trumpet on 'Had Me A Real Good Time'
Produced by the Faces at Morgan Sound Studios, except where stated
Released: February 1971, Warner Bros Records K 3011 (UK), and Warner Bros Records WS 1892 (USA)
Highest chart position: UK: 31, USA: 29, Australia: 18, Canada: 34

Where there had once been The Small Faces, now there were two bands – The Faces and Humble Pie, both competing for the hearts and minds of the great Yankee dollar and anyone who ventured the opinion that the main beneficiary of all that sweaty effort would be Rod Stewart, a relative late-comer to the story, was onto a dodgy proposition indeed. Stewart himself defined 'our sloppiness and our looseness – and, more importantly, our attitude towards it – turned out to be the thing that made us vulnerable and appealing, and, in the end, entertaining.'

He suggested that, following Steve Marriott's abrupt departure from the lineup, the other members of the group had a suspicion of lead singers who exploited their musicianship to achieve media visibility, then dumped them to further their own career, something that Rod's subsequent ventures would seem to vindicate. But in the meantime, Rod was effectively straddling two careers as a solo artist and a frontman for The Faces, and for a while at least, everything seemed to be working out just fine.

The release of *First Step* in America coincided with a 38-date North American tour starting in Toronto in March 1970, supporting Canned Heat, followed by Boston and Detroit. The tour bonded the five-piece as a band and resulted in ecstatic reactions from audiences. Hence, the second album should have been more together. Yet 'recording sessions with The Faces always started out in the pub', recalled Rod, and 'quite often we were in the pub longer than we were in the studio.'

This album was issued in a clever facsimile of the old-fashioned card record sleeve.

Side One

'Bad 'N' Ruin' (McLagan, Stewart) 5:23

The first two tracks were recorded on the Rolling Stones Mobile Recording Unit with engineer Martin Birch. A *Record Mirror* review claims, 'Rod Stewart contributes huff-puff phrased vocals over a rhythm setting full of push and pull. The song trucks along with a fair amount of R&B feel and the vocal cuts in and out at will – at perfect liaison.'

'Tell Everyone' (Lane) 4:18
With touches that look forward to Rod's solo hit 'I Don't Want To Talk About It', the instrumentation is razored back to the essentials, with a sensitively carved organ break.

'Sweet Lady Mary' (Lane, Stewart, Wood) 5:45
Rod's lyrics have the sad, reflective quality evident in the best of his solo work, matched to Ron's hauntingly different melody, taking long, graceful sweeps that allow the words to flow.

'Richmond' (Lane) 3:05
Ronnie takes lead vocals, his curious, cheeky voice perched well on Ron Wood's slide work, with a hanging ending that catches the listener off-guard.

'Maybe I'm Amazed' (Paul McCartney) 5:32
Prior to the album, a 3:15 studio version of the song had been issued as a USA single b/w the instrumental 'Oh Lord, I'm Browned Off' (3:48, Wood, McLagan, Lane, Jones) as WB7483. The album version was recorded live at Fillmore East New York on 11 October 1970, on the Electric Lady Mobile Recording Unit, with Rod and Ronnie taking co-lead vocals. It's said that Paul McCartney didn't realise how good his 'Maybe I'm Amazed' was until he heard this Faces version.

Side Two
'Had Me A Real Good Time' (Lane, Stewart, Wood) 5:50
If you ever find yourself wondering why The Rolling Stones chose Ronnie Wood to complete their lineup, it's only necessary to listen to this strutting guitar-driven Rocker to understand. It stops at the midpoint, then begins again with honking horns gliding in around Rod's voice in a seemingly effortless telepathic collision of like minds. It was issued as a single (WB-7442 UK, & WB8018 US) with B-side 'Rear Wheel Skid' (McLagan, Lane, Wood, Jones) 4:50.

'On The Beach' (Lane, Wood) 4:14
The album sleeve is designed to recall the old 78rpm card sleeves, and Ronnies Lane and Wood share lead vocals here with a raspy years-back blues production feel to match, in three sequences punctuated by hanging pauses.

'I Feel So Good' (Big Bill Broonzy) 8:47
Recorded live at Fillmore East New York 11-10-1970, with lots of audience singback participation. 'All right, it's your turn to give something back to us,

now, where are ya!' urges Rod before the band careen into contagious jolting rhythms, chomping guitars and boogie keyboard. This is evidence of why The Faces worked so well as a party band.

'Jerusalem' (Hubert Parry, William Blake) 1:54
Inaccurately credited 'traditional', this comes courtesy of Ron Wood's slide guitar arrangement.

Bonus Tracks Featured On The 2015 CD Reissue:
'Whole Lotta Woman' (Marvin Rainwater) 3:15 outtake.
'Turn the tape machine on', yells someone amid much studio horseplay. Leading into a rollicking outtake of a Number One rockabilly hit from 1958 by the man who claimed Native American Cherokee ancestry, done with more fun than authenticity.

'Tell Everyone' (Lane) 4:00
Take one, sung by Ronnie.

'Sham-Mozzal' (Jones, Lane, McLagan, Wood) 3:12
An early instrumental outtake variant of 'Had Me A Real Good Time' with more upfront piano wrapped around the Rolling Stones-esque licks.

'Too Much Woman (For A Henpecked Man)' (Ike Turner) 5:26
Wrongly credited to Ronnie Wood on the album sleeve, it was also recorded live at Fillmore East, opening with applause and Rod explaining 'Oh right, just warming up' over a jagged guitar intro leading into a raunchy soul-rocker 'born and raised in a slum-filled city' with extended guitar soloing, slowing into just Kenney's drumbeat, before erupting back to full-throttle again.

'Love In Vain' (Robert Johnson) 6:21
Recorded live at Fillmore East, this is the blues classic also done by The Rolling Stones on *Let It Bleed* (1969).

A Nod's As Good As A Wink ... To A Blind Horse

Personnel:
Rod Stewart: lead vocals, harmonica
Ronnie Lane: bass, acoustic guitars, backing & lead vocals
Ronnie Wood: lead, slide and acoustic guitars, pedal steel guitar
Kenney Jones: drums and percussion
Ian McLagan: piano, organ
Produced by the Faces with Glyn Johns at Olympic Studios between March-September
Released: 17 November 1971, Warner Bros Records K 56006 (UK), and Warner Bros Records BS2574 (USA)
Highest chart position: UK: 2, US: 6, Can: 5, Aus: 4

Pioneer Rocker Buddy Holly was also signed to two companies simultaneously, to Decca Records as a solo artist and to the Coral label as lead singer of The Crickets. This was a situation that permitted him to record twice as much material during his brief career as he otherwise could have managed. Rod Stewart was in the same position. There was essentially the same core of musicians for both Rod Stewart and The Faces albums, although he was more free to use additional players on those albums issued under his own name. It was a collaborative process during which song selection must have been a process of the best material going forward for inclusion into whatever project they happened to be working on at the time. So 'Maggie May' could just as easily have appeared on a Faces record. Certainly there was a visible joy as they performed it together on *Top Of The Pops* as it topped the charts, with Rod kicking a football around the stage and DJ John Peel sitting uneasily pretending to play mandolin. For The Faces, it was a peak moment, a refutation to all those snide journalists who'd prematurely written them off as burned-out sixties relics.

Elevated by Rod's trans-Atlantic success with 'Maggie May', this third Faces album conquered in ways that The Small Faces never had – peaking at number two in the UK while reaching a more modest number six on the American album chart. This is also the album that reunited The Faces with producer Glyn Johns, who had helped midwife the *Ogdens' Nut Gone Flake* sessions.

Its spin-off single 'Stay With Me' hit number six in the UK and took them to a US *Billboard* number 17, while it entered the *Cashbox* top ten, the chart that *Melody Maker* carried, achieving an American high that neither The Small Faces nor Humble Pie would ever do. Yet it was inevitably shoving frontman Rod to the fore ahead of The Faces. Although ironically, its success provoked an American cash-in *Early Faces* (1972, Pride PRD0001), made up of old Decca-era tracks – including 'Sha-La-La-La-Lee', 'Come Back And Take This Hurt Off Me', 'Runaway' and 'I've Got Mine', that registered at a US number 176.

Side One

'Miss Judy's Farm' (Stewart, Wood) 3:38

Rod gives a wolf howl. 'Miss Judy, she was moody.' Strutting accelerating guitar. For the *Melody Maker* reviewer, this is 'the best Faces album to date. At last the lads have got it all down on wax. It's worked. Glyn Johns has captured everything sacred to this tumbling unit, and out comes a dishy good-looker designed to be put at the front of record racks, played twice a night and once before breakfast.'

'You're So Rude' (Lane, McLagan) 3:41

Ronnie Lane sings in lascivious seduction mode, 'why, it looks as though there's nobody in... don't you worry, just come right in.' Ian feeds in great organ and piano; then there's some slick Ronnie Wood guitar work and harmonica in the second half outro of this song after the door slam. We assume that Auntie Rene is not the same lady as Rene on *Ogdens' Nut Gone Flake*?

'Love Lives Here' (Lane, Stewart, Wood) 3:04

The lovely guitar lead-in recalls 'Angel', with Ian's organ throwing nostalgic sepia throughout as Rod mourns the imminent 'big ball and chain' that will tear down his childhood home.

'Last Orders Please' (Lane) 2:33

It's fair to say that drinking figures are large in The Faces mythology. Ronnie uses the landlord's closing-time phrase to write and sing about hearing 'Tracks Of Your Tears' playing in the Bar where the former lovers happen to meet.

It's a country-flavoured, easy-on-the-ear romp in the recognisable Ronnie Lane style.

'Stay With Me' (Stewart, Wood) 4:37

Their raucous breakthrough single 'Stay With Me' took heavy flak from feminists over its bragging groupie-baiting, but the irresistibly attacking speed-guitar play-in and rollicking tongue-in-cheek bad taste catches what rock 'n' roll hard-partying was all about. And hadn't The Small Faces already visited the terrain with 'One Night Stand' on their debut album?

Side Two

'Debris' (Lane) 4:36

A 'two, three, four' count-in then acoustic strumming, Ronnie sings a tribute to his bus driver father, Stanley Lane, amid the hardscrabble East End blitz-debris, with Rodney joining on harmony vocals. 'There's more trouble at the depot with the General Workers Union, and you said, 'they'll never change a thing.'' Tasteful guitar work from Ron Wood.

'Memphis' (Chuck Berry) 5:29
A cheerful reworking of Chuck's much-recorded anthem, with slide guitar and Ian's keyboards prominently featured in involved instrumental passages. Phoning six-year-old Marie was initially seen as a harmlessly charming joke, although our more cynical age might see more devious motives.

'Too Bad' (Stewart, Wood) 3:12
Studio chat. Piano. Rod sings about being thrown out of a high-class club because his regional accent gave him away, with Ronnie, Ian and Ron Wood helping out on backing vocals.

'That's All You Need' (Stewart, Wood) 5:06
A tale about Rod's rivalry with his violinist brother that's bound to break your heart, propelled by hard accelerating slide guitar, plus Harry Fowler on steel drums. When Rod hits his stride with The Faces on full-on form, the combination can be a perfect rock 'n' roll equation. And where the reference to 'reading my underground press' may mystify twenty-first-century listeners, it made perfect sense in 1971 at a time when *IT: International Times* and *Frendz* were defining what was and what was not cool.

Bonus Tracks On The 2015 CD Edition
'Miss Judy's Farm' 3:30
BBC radio John Peel *Top Gear* session, recorded 28 September, broadcast 6 October 1971

'Stay With Me' 5:17
From the same *Top Gear* session.

Related Releases
Stay With Me – Single
'Stay With Me' 4:37 b/w **'Debris'** 4:36
Released December 1971, Warner Bros K16136
Single that reached US number 17, UK number six.

Ooh La La

Personnel:
Rod Stewart: lead vocals, banjo and guitar
Ronnie Lane: bass, rhythm and acoustic guitars, lead vocals
Ronnie Wood: lead, slide and acoustic guitars, electric bouzouki
Kenney Jones: drums and percussion
Ian McLagan: piano, organ, harmonium, backing and co-lead vocals
Plus:
Neemoi 'Speedy' Aquaye: congas, shakers and percussion
Produced by Glyn 'See you in a year' Johns at Olympic Studios between September 1972-January 1973
Released: 13 April 1973, Warner Bros Records K56011 (UK), and Warner Bros Records BS2665 (USA)
Highest chart position: UK: 1, USA: 21, Can: 23, Aus: 9

Issued in a complex gimmick sleeve with an animated front and gatefold rear, it included a large 30"x20" poster insert with lyrics, while the 'Other Side' of the record label features a photo of Can-Can dancers while 'This Side' has the track listings for both sides.

In his own defence, Rod Stewart says that at the point he quit, there was no longer a Faces to belong to, which is as maybe. But his solo career was taking off to the extent that the others felt themselves sidelined to backing band status. There was resentment and friction. It also seems that Rod had distractions that resulted in him being absent for three of the album's ten tracks, with Ronnie Lane assuming a more creative input. When Ronnie himself quit, that was the band's engine gone, as Rod and Ron Wood agreed.

There would be a live album credited as Rod Stewart/Faces, recorded at the Anaheim Convention Centre in California, 17 October 1973, with Tetsu Yamauchi replacing Ronnie Lane – *Coast To Coast: Overture And Beginners* (UK Mercury 9100-001, USA Mercury SRM-1-697) – 'Produced out of a hat by The Faces', which balances only three Faces songs against six from Rod's solo albums, plus the Jimi Hendrix song 'Angel.' 'We thank you for your time… and your money' gags our Roderick at the album's close. Yet The Faces staggered on until November 1975 before calling it a day.

The Faces were eventually retrospected by an exhaustive five-CD box set (*1970-1975: You Can Make Me Dance, Sing Or Anything*, Rhino, October 2015). All their studio albums were there: *First Step*, *Long Player*, *A Nod Is As Good As A Wink… To A Blind Horse* and *Ooh La La* in replica sleeves with bonus outtakes plus live and BBC session tracks and a full 'Stray Singles & B-Sides' disc. And there's some startlingly good stuff there. Although arguably the band never fully transferred their onstage euphoria to vinyl, each album has beautifully manic moments that defined their slightly tipsy meld of dignity and camaraderie for a generation of future rockers. The Faces were being spoken of in the same breath as The Rolling Stones as embodying the spirit of rock 'n' roll. As Dave Simpson sums it up in *Melody Maker* on 18 September 1993, while 'Faces wannabes like The Black Crowes, Quireboys et al. sound lamentably dated, The Faces' four albums seem timeless... guaranteed to leave you wide-eyed and legless every time.'

It was during sessions for *Ooh La La* that Ronnie Lane and Ron Wood recorded the soundtrack for a low-budget Canadian movie, music which was finally issued as a duo album in September 1976 as *Mahoney's Last Stand* (Atlantic K50308, USA Atco SD 36-126). Pete Townshend contributes alongside Benny Gallagher (of Gallagher & Lyle), Kenney Jones and Ian McLagan, plus Billy Nicholls, who can be heard within the background vocals.

Finally, Ronnie Wood replaced Mick Taylor in The Rolling Stones. Ronnie Lane enjoyed a solo career while Kenney Jones and Ian McLagan joined Steve Marriott in The Small Faces reformation.

Rod's Atlantic Crossing into the dire disco hits and miscast Great American Songbook albums represents one of Rock's great wasted voices, frittered away into ridiculous irrelevance. Better by far just to revel in these wonderful group albums...

Side One

'Silicone Grown' (Stewart, Wood) 3:08

Jive boogie piano and choogling guitars, 'I remember you said that we gotta keep abreast of the time, but obviously, you don't know where to draw the line', Rod protests at his suddenly 44" augmented woman. As vocalist with a rocking band, this is Rod at his best.

'Cindy Incidentally' (McLagan, Stewart, Wood) 2:39

Allied to a strong BBC *Radio One Club* on-air take, this track made a memorably powerful single.

'Flags And Banners' (Stewart, Lane) 2:03

Taking a more country-blues slant with Ronnie Lane on microphone and nice guitar harmonies, with Ronnie Wood's rare excursion into electric bouzouki.

'My Fault' (McLagan, Stewart, Wood) 3:07

Relentless full-ahead jogging rhythms, a loose-limbed mainstream Faces lope, with Rod and Ronnie Wood sharing vocals, Rod warns, 'don't try to change me'; he was just born this way and will be responsible for his own faults.

'Borstal Boys' (McLagan, Stewart, Wood) 2:55

With snarling guitar, klaxon intro and Ronald Wood on slide guitar, it delivers some sharp lyrics about life behind the wire. Extended to a full 9:52 minutes on *Live Coast To Coast*, it functions as a good example of the trundle and rumble that Rod calls 'four sets of fingers and one throat' well-lubricated by the juice of the grape and grain.

Side Two

'Fly In The Ointment' (McLagan, Jones, Wood, Lane) 3:52

A nice groove lacking melody or much soloing does not equate good value for an album with a playing time of just 30:22. But it's not hard work to listen to this good-natured group instrumental. 'Speedy' Aquaye plays congas, shakers and percussion.

'If I'm On The Late Side' (Stewart, Lane) 2:39

Rod wrests the vocal spot back for a pretty song with strummed acoustic and slippery slide guitars, emoting 'if I'm late darling, don't hesitate, no, no, go on your lonesome, and I'll catch you there anyway' in a style that could easily have been remaindered from one of his solo albums.

'Glad And Sorry' (Lane) 3:07

There's background conversation beneath the piano-led intro and then Ronnies Wood and Lane share vocals on a more reflective number with pleasant acoustic guitar. 'Can you show me a dream, can you show me one that's better than mine?' Nope. I can't.

'Just Another Honky' (Lane) 3:35

Rod is walking around in circles over loose, sloppy Faces guitars and keyboard, 'you can go if you wanna, I don't own ya', with a lengthy add-on instrumental reprise. The title does not occur in the lyrics, although maybe there are racial undertones to the lover's parting. Who knows?

'Ooh La La' (Wood, Lane) 3:34

The only Faces studio recording to feature Ron Wood's vocals, with acoustic strum and mandolin.

'We cut the track... three times before he (Rod) eventually passed on it, leaving it for Woody to sing', says Ian ruefully. 'It's an acoustic guitar track with both Ronnie and me playing', explained Ron Wood in *Melody Maker* on 3 March 1973, 'there's no bass on it, although it has got a nice backbeat, an old-fashioned harmonium and a piano with drawing pins in it, like up the pub.'

It forms a kind of retro-dialogue with his poor old Grandad about the capricious ways of women, 'I wish that I knew what I know now when I was younger.' This track is where the album's Can-Can imagery comes from. Rod sings his own version on the 1998 *When We Were The New Boys* album as a tribute to Ronnie Lane, who had died a year earlier.

Bonus Tracks On 2015 CD Reissue:

'Cindy Incidentally' 2:26

BBC Radio One Club session, recorded 12 February, broadcast 1 March 1973

'Borstal Boys' 2:46, rehearsal
'Silicone Grown' 3:05, rehearsal
'Glad And Sorry' 2:41, rehearsal

'Jealous Guy' (John Lennon) 4:45
Live on 25 August 1973 at the Reading Festival, with former Free bass player Tetsu Yamauchi stepping in for Ronnie Lane, who had quit the lineup in June.

Related Releases
Cindy Incidentally – Single
'Cindy Incidentally' 2:34 b/w **'Swewiff (Mend The Fuse)'** (Wood, Lane, McLagan, Jones), 5:08
WB16247 UK, WB7681 US
A 1973 single with a non-album B-side that became The Faces' highest charting record reaching the UK number two while only managing a meagre number 48 in America.

Ooh La La – Single
'Ooh La La' 3:35 b/w **'Borstal Boys'** 2:53
Released June 1973, Warner Bros WB 7711
US only single.

Selections From Ooh La La – Single
'Selections From Ooh La La' b/w **'Dishevelment Blues'** (Stewart, Wood, Lane, McLagan, Jones) 4:56
A promotional free flexidisc (SFI-139) issued with the *New Musical Express* dated 5 April 1973. 'Dishevelment Blues' is a blues parody instrumental recorded during the 'Fly In The Ointment' sessions.

Pool Hall Richard – Single
'Pool Hall Richard' (Stewart, Wood) 4:20 b/w **'I Wish It Would Rain'** (Strong, Whitfield, Penzabene) (recorded live at the 1973 Reading Festival, with trumpet) 4:50 (Warner Bros K16341 UK, WBS8066/8102 US)
Reached number eight in December 1973.

You Can Make Me Dance, Sing Or Anything (Even Take The Dog For A Walk, Mend A Fuse, Fold Away The Ironing Board, Or Any Other Domestic Shortcomings) – Single
'You Can Make Me Dance, Sing Or Anything (Even Take The Dog For A Walk, Mend A Fuse, Fold Away The Ironing Board, Or Any Other Domestic Shortcomings)' (Stewart, Wood, Jones, McLagan, Yamauchi) 4:22 b/w **'As Long As You Tell Him'** (4:29) (Warner Bros K16494)
Written by Rod and Ron Wood, credited as Rod Stewart & The Faces, it reached number 12 in December 1974.

Ronnie Lane's Solo Career and With Pete Townsend

Things went rapidly downhill for The Faces after Ronnie Lane quit. 'Ronnie's were huge boots to fill', admits Ian.

Ronnie had an unsuccessful spell at running a 100-acre sheep farm in Fishpool, Wales – only to discover that he wasn't cut out to be a farmer! His easy-going, pleasantly jog-along single 'How Come' b/w 'Done This One Before' (GM GMS011) became a surprise hit, reaching number 11 in January 1974. Written with guitarist Kevin Westlake, Ronnie is completely at ease with both song and musical setting, his voice ambling around Benny Gallagher's accordion and Graham Lyle's mandolin. He sings with a slightly inebriated sway to confess, 'I ain't a superstitious feller, but it worries me' about his spooky girlfriend. The song was later covered by The Pogues on their 1996 album *Pogue Mahone*.

Ronnie put together a new 'floating' band, which became the ironically named Slim Chance – *Anymore For Anymore* (GM Records GML 1013) being the first of their three studio albums, recorded at Fishpool and in Ronnie's Mobile Studio, then mixed at IBC Studios. Released in July 1974, the album includes his song 'Tell Everyone' which The Faces had done on *Long Player*, as well as the charming 'The Poacher', which – issued as a single b/w 'Bye And Bye (Gonna See The King)' (GM GMS 024), became a second hit, reaching number 36 in June 1974. *Q* magazine, in July 1992, was not impressed, 'the music is somehow summed up by the picture of what seems to be a couple of rag 'n' bone men on the cover', although they commend 'Silk Stockings' as a jokey piece of South American nonsense, for the rest 'it's all honky-tonk piano, ramshackle vocals, clunking mandolins and lax steel guitar.'

Ronnie Lane's Slim Chance (Island ILPS9321, USA A&M SP-3638) followed in February 1975, again taking a song from The Faces catalogue – 'Stone', plus covers of Chuck Berry ('You Never Can Tell') and Fats Domino ('Blue Monday), with six new Ronnie songs, and two co-written by wife Kate Lambert. The lineup was different; the Gallagher & Lyle duo had returned to their own successful writing and performing career, while Slim Chance reduced down to Ronnie with Steve Simpson (electric and acoustic guitar, mandolin, violin, harmonica), Ruan O'Lochlainn (piano, organ, soprano alto and tenor saxophones), Charlie Hart (piano, organ, accordion, violin), Brian Belshaw (bass) with Glen LeFleur and session player Jim Frank on drums.

The third album, *One For The Road* (January 1976, Island ILPS 9366), was made up of nine new Lane originals, with a sound that Steve Clarke, in *NME*, says is 'as if the whole thing was put together with a lot of love, affection and the odd tipples in between', with Steve Simpson (guitars, mandolin, fiddle, harp), Charlie Hart (fiddle, harp, whistle, keyboard), Brian Belshaw and Colin Davey on drums. 'I'd rather make my church the open road', he sings in 'Thirty-Second Street', and the band played eccentric but poorly managed and financially disastrous Passing Show tours, taking on a circus-style carnival presentation with Viv Stanshall standing in as ringmaster. The music 'is free-wheeling, windblown and totally unaffected' wrote the *Street Life* reviewer between 7-20 February 1976, 'it's a bit of everything – happy, bittersweet and sad. A passing show perhaps but one leaving substantial memories behind it.'

By this time, Ronnie's health was starting to deteriorate. At first, he put his clumsiness down to the legacy of his drink and drug abuse until he was diagnosed with the same debilitating form of Multiple Sclerosis that had assailed his mother.

Rough Mix – Pete Townshend & Ronnie Lane

Personnel:
Ronnie Lane: vocals, guitars, banjo, ukuleles, mandolins, bass guitar
Pete Townshend: vocals, guitars, banjo, ukuleles, mandolins, bass guitar
John Entwistle: horns (on 'Heart To Hang Onto') and backup vocal (on 'Till The Rivers All Run Dry')
Mel Collins: saxophone (on 'Catmelody')
Peter Hope Evans: harmonica (on 'Nowhere To Run' and 'Misunderstood')
Benny Gallagher & Graham Lyle: accordion and twelve-string guitar (on 'Annie)
John 'Rabbit' Bundrick: Fender Rhodes organ (on 'Nowhere To Run', 'Rough Mix', 'Keep Me Turning' and 'Heart To Hang Onto')
Ian Stewart: piano (on 'Catmelody')
Eric Clapton: electric guitar (on 'Rough Mix'), acoustic guitar (on 'Annie'), dobro on 'April Fool' and 'Till The Rivers Run Dry')
Charlie Watts: drums (on 'My Baby Gives It Away' and 'Catmelody')
Billy Nicholls: back-up vocals (on 'Till The Rivers Run Dry')
Plus:
Dave Markee:double bass, Boz Burrell: bass guitar, Henry Spinetti: drums, Julian Diggle: percussion
Released: 16 September 1977, UK: Polydor 2442, USA: MCA 2295
Producer: Glyn Johns
Highest chart position: UK: 44, USA: 45

'Ronnie was my best friend at the time', says Pete Townshend (in his autobiography *Who I Am*, 2012, Harper Collins). Although 'the recording of *Rough Mix* with Ronnie is now a blur, but I remember some special moments. I played live guitar with a large string orchestra for the first time, my father-in-law Ted Astley arranging and conducting on 'Street In The City'... playing with Charlie Watts on 'My Baby Gives It Away' was also very cool, making me aware that his jazz-influenced style was essential to the Stones' success, the hi-hat always trailing the beat to create that vital swing. Meeting John Bundrick (Rabbit) was also an important event in my life as a musician. He wandered into the *Rough Mix* studio one day, looking for session work. Here was a Hammond player who had worked with Bob Marley and could play as well as Billy Preston. Offstage, he could be reckless and impulsive, drinking too much, asking for drugs and telling crazy stories, but musicians of his calibre didn't come around very often.' Like *Ogdens' Nut Gone Flake*, *Rough Mix* is a passing reference to loose 'shag' rolling tobacco. By this time, Ronnie Lane was enjoying an unconventional itinerant lifestyle, fully at odds with his original sharp little Mod image, as a gypsy traveller and part of his nomadic 'Passing Show.' And it was during these Olympic Studios recording sessions with Pete Townshend – between Winter 1976 and Spring 1977, that Ronnie's multiple sclerosis was first diagnosed, but not generally known. The resulting emotional issues caused some brief disruption between the two musicians, yet they recorded and toured together with this unique collaboration project and did a joint *Old Grey Whistle Test* interview.

The Continuing Adventures Of Humble Pie

Robert Day-Webb has written an excellent *On Track: Every Album, Every Song* (SonicBond, ISBN-13 978-1789522761) on Steve Marriott's adventures with Humble Pie, which therefore does not need repeating here. I would very strongly advise readers to seek out his book in order to give detail to the releases sketched out here.

As Safe As Yesterday Is – Humble Pie

Personnel:
Steve Marriott: vocals, guitar, slide and acoustic guitar, harmonica, organ
Peter Frampton: vocals, guitar, slide guitar, keyboards
Greg Ridley: bass, vocals, percussion, 'happy noise'
Jerry Shirley: drums, harpsichord, piano, 'grins and explosions'
Plus:
Lyn Dobson: flute, sitar
Recorded in the London 'Olympic Studios', arranged by Humble Pie, with producer Andy Johns
Released: 1 August 1969, Immediate IMSP025. American version Immediate IMOCS101
Highest chart position: UK: 32, Netherlands: 6
Side One: 'Desperation' (John Kay) 6:28, 'Stick Shift' (Frampton) 2:22, 'Buttermilk Boy' (Marriott) 4:22, 'Growing Closer' (McLagan) 3:13, 'As Safe As Yesterday Is' (Frampton, Marriott) 6:05
Side Two: 'Bang!' (Marriott) 3:24, 'Alabama '69' (Marriott) 4:37, 'I'll Go Alone' (Frampton) 6:17, 'A Nifty Little Number Like You' (Marriott) 6:11, 'What You Will' (Marriott) 4:20

Melody Maker announced 'Pop Giants' Supergroup: Steve Marriott-Peter Frampton tie-up' in a front-page headline on 26 April 1969, with Chris Welch enthusing 'Peter Frampton and Steve Marriott – together! After weeks of pop world speculation and mystery, the *MM* can now exclusively reveal two of Britain's biggest Pop idols have formed a new supergroup.'

Of course, it wasn't just Steve and Peter. Bass player Greg Ridley had been part of a group lineup that evolved through The V.I.P's into Art before they were signed by Chris Blackwell to Island Records as Spooky Tooth. He played on their first two albums, *It's All About* (June 1968), produced by Jimmy Miller, and *Spooky Two* (March 1969), which included Gary Wright's high-profile song 'Better By You, Better Than Me.' Then Greg quit to join Humble Pie alongside Jerry Shirley, who had been part of Apostolic Intervention. Spooky Tooth carried on without Greg.

When Steve quit The Small Faces for Humble Pie, he wanted Ian to be keyboard player for the new project. The track 'Growing Closer' was written by and rehearsed with Humble Pie by Ian before he opted to go with The Faces instead. To Ian, including the track on the album was 'an attempt at peace-making from Steve and a friendly gesture from Pete.' As such, this ought to be the closest sound-alike to The Small Faces but is paradoxically perhaps the furthest away of them all. Adopting a contagious rapid skiffle style with harmonica, Lyn Dobson's dancing flute, and treated harmony vocals, it's a considerable distance from what was to become Humble Pie's trademark heavy sound.

'Bang!' is one of the two tracks previously recorded by The Small Faces with Johnny Halliday – the other being 'What You Will' – which, although written by Steve, was credited to Marriott-Lane in accordance with their publishing agreement. This is a fast rocker that satirically attacks the 'powers that be' who 'line their pockets with your bread' in a kind of fake news report that aligned with the politics of the newly emerging counter-culture press.

The Humble Pie debut album, wrapped in a sleeve that mimics a postal mail package tied up in string, was promoted with a full-page *NME* cover ad on 3 August, while the US version omitted 'Growing Closer' in favour of the single 'Natural Born Woman.' 'To the question 'is it more like The Small Faces or The Herd?' the answer is neither', judged the *NME* reviewer, 'the only traces of the past are fleeting ones, like when Steve Marriott suddenly loons out on a Faces-like solo and that's a rare occurrence as vocals are mainly delivered by all four singing together heavy campfire style.' The *Disc* reviewer, on 9 August 1969, agreed, 'much of the old Small Faces magic lingers on in numbers like 'Desperation' and 'Nifty' and it's a joy to hear Steve thrashing out those top notes again.'

An untitled eastern-flavoured 2:22-minute instrumental track on Side Two forms an exotic sitar introduction – some of the prettiest moments on the album – that leads into 'I'll Go Alone' which features Lyn Dobson on flute and sitar before it erupts into strong guitar 'Wham Bam Thank You Ma'am' power chords. Peter sings the complex story-lyric with harmony chorus vocal back-up. There are muskets aimed at his head as the preacher asks if he has anythin' to say, and then his hands are bound in a plane goin' down fast, in a kind of Dylan tumble of dream images.

There's a definite Small Faces echo to 'What You Will', from maybe 'Feeling Lonely', with Steve's slightly echoed voice, joined by Peter for aching harmonies. The lyric is both confessional and regretful, 'I'll hide behind a purple pill' while he's 'getting drunk to find some peace and consolation.'

Later CD issues contain bonus tracks 'Natural Born Bugie' and 'Wrist Job.' A 2009 Japanese CD reissue includes additional bonus tracks 'Hello Grass (No Regrets)', 'Road To Ride' and 'I'll Drown In My Own Tears.'

Both debut albums, *As Safe As Yesterday Is* and *Town And Country,* were later combined into the 1972 American double LP *Lost And Found* (A&M Records SP-3513).

Steve remained active in a number of other studio capacities. He played session organ on 'Country Shoes', an Alexis Korner song featured on the July 1973 album *Snape: Accidentally Born In New Orleans* (Transatlantic Records

TRA269). Credited to Alexis Korner & Peter Thorup, it is a glorious Blues celebration featuring Zoot Money, Mel Collins, Mike Patto, Tim Hinkley and 'Boz' Burrell.

Related Releases

Natural Born Bugie – Humble Pie Single

'Natural Born Bugie' (Marriott) 4:15 b/w **'Wrist Job'** (Marriott) 4:17

Personnel:

Steve Marriott: vocals, rhythm guitar, Wurlitzer electric piano

Peter Frampton: vocals, lead guitar

Greg Ridley: bass, vocals

Jerry Shirley: drums

Released: August 1969, Immediate IM 082

Arranged & Produced by Humble Pie

Highest chart position: UK: 4, Austria: 13, Belgium: 9, Netherlands: 6, Germany: 20

'Good Old Rock From Humble Pie' wrote reviewer Bob Dawbarn in *Melody Maker* on 9 August 1969. 'It's a slice of yer real, old-fashioned Rock-and-Roll complete with Boogie Woogie piano (or Bugie Wugie, I suppose, if the label spelling is right) ... I like it, but then I'm just an old-fashioned rocker at heart.'

Record Mirror, on 20 September 1969, went further with a Humble Pie colour cover and an interview explaining 'why we never wanted to hit the top ten.' Yet this, the debut product by what the press were already billing a Supergroup, did just that. It entered the *NME* chart at number 29 on 16 August 1969 – on a chart headed by The Rolling Stones 'Honky Tonk Women.' It climbed through 21, 14, ten and eight before peaking at number five on 20 September beneath Creedence Clearwater Revival's 'Bad Moon Rising.' It went one place higher on the rival *Record Mirror/ Record Retailer* chart before ducking out on 18 October. Humble Pie would not return to the UK singles chart.

'Natural Born Bugie' or 'Natural Born Woman' had that same kind of piano-led rolling retro-rock sound as The Beatles 'Get Back', which seemed to signify a back-to-roots approach, a reaction to the excesses of the Summer of Love. It's sung by Peter from the opening, 'there she is again steppin' out of her limousine, well, looking like the cover of a twenty-dollar magazine', with Steve joining for the chorus and the bridge about 'you can do anything but lay off of my Blue Suede Shoes.' The trad-rock theme extends into 'think I'll move on down to Memphis, pay my money to see a rock 'n' roll show', taken at an attractively loping pace that's both different and distinct from either The Small Faces or The Herd.

There are huge swelling Herd-like organ chords, with maybe Procol Harum cadences and climaxes, for 'Wrist Job' which – despite its throwaway masturbatory slang title – has Steve singing at his most passionately soulful, desolate and left alone by the 'girl that lived here.' It could be argued that making the adjustment to 'living on your own' is a prospect that may well involve a degree of self-comfort. Whatever, the song-pairing presents two diametrically separate faces of Humble Pie, offering any number of future evolutions to come.

Peter Frampton yearned to cast off his teenybopper fan following and be taken seriously as a rock musician. His alliance with Steve Marriott as part of Humble Pie formed his route map to that acceptance. So far, the plan has been working just fine.

Town And Country

Personnel:
Steve Marriott: vocals, guitar, Leslie guitar, sitar, Wurlitzer piano, 'hammer and nail brandy bottle'
Peter Frampton: vocals, guitars (lead, bass and Spanish guitars), Wurlitzer piano, 'plastic cup'
Greg Ridley: bass, vocals, tambourine
Jerry Shirley: drums, saw, tablas, Wurlitzer piano
Recorded at Olympic Studios in London with Andy Johns producing
Released November 1969, Immediate IMSP 027, issued in 1982 in the USA as Recaptured (Accord SN-7192)
No chart position
Tracklisting: Side One: 'Take Me Back' (Frampton) 4:52, 'The Sad Bag Of Shaky Jake' (Marriott) 2:59, 'The Light Of Love' (Ridley) 3:00, 'Cold Lady' (Shirley) 3:22, 'Down Home Again' (Marriott) 2:56, 'Ollie Ollie' (Humble Pie, Andy Johns) 0:50
Side Two: 'Every Mother's Son' (Marriott) 5:43, 'Heartbeat' (Bob Montgomery, Norman Petty) 2:33, 'Only You Can See' (Frampton) 3:38, 'Silver Tongue' (Marriott) 3:20,'Home And Away' (Marriott, Frampton, Ridley) 5:55
Plus Bonus Tracks On CD Edition: 'Seventy-Ninth Street Blues' (Humble Pie) 3:00, 'Greg's Song' (Ridley) 4:29

Within a couple of months of their debut album, Humble Pie were back with a gentler, more bucolic sound; all four members contribute songs, plus a flashback to Steve's earliest influence with a Buddy Holly cover. Steve's 'The Sad Bag Of Shaky Jake', with mournful harmonica, is an off-the-wall semi-comic western tale in which he shot a man when he was just eighteen. Now the Texas Rangers are coming after him to exact the price for that one bad luck mistake. Further evidence of Steve's affection for, and his ability to coin, a good old catchy singalong chorus.

For 'Every Mother's Son', apart from the strange sampled military tack-on at the start, all the references are American, the Mississippi Queen through New Orleans and down the bayou, with molasses-thick country guitar licks and a broken Dylan-style narrative about 'I still had my guitar, so I joined a dirty band, workin' in a smoky downtown bar.' A bitterly powerful track, It would present a useful exercise to compare and contrast this with some of Rod Stewart's earthier folkster shots. Meanwhile, 'Home And Away' sounds as if Crosby Stills & Nash had wandered into the recording session, with its airy, 'Marrakesh Express' acoustic and melodic vocal harmonies, with a lovely coda. This track provides further teasing hints of an alternative path that Humble Pie might have trodden.

Humble Pie

Personnel:
Steve Marriott: guitar, keyboards, vocals
Peter Frampton: guitar, keyboards, vocals
Greg Ridley: bass, guitar, vocals
Jerry Shirley: drums, guitar, vocals
Plus
John 'Willie' Wilson: drums
B.J. Cole: steel guitar
Produced by Glyn Johns with Humble Pie at Olympic Studios
Released: July 1970, A&M Records AMLS986 (UK), A&M Records SP-4270 (USA)
No chart position
Tracklisting: Side One: 'Live With Me' (Humble Pie) 7:55, 'Only A Roach' (Shirley) 2:49, 'One Eyed Trouser-Snake Rumba' (Humble Pie) 2:51, 'Earth And Water Song' (Frampton) 6:18
Side Two: 'I'm Ready' (Willie Dixon) 4:59, 'Theme From Skint (See You Later Liquidator)' (Marriott) 5:43, 'Red Light Mamma, Red Hot!' (Humble Pie, Steve Marriott lyrics) 6:16, 'Sucking On The Sweet Vine' (Ridley) 5:46

Ian had been astounded to discover that, at the height of the group's success with Immediate, The Small Faces were still in debt. There had been a financial settlement to extricate them from Don Arden, and despite being pop stars with a number one album, they were living on a £50 wage.

At the end of 1969, Immediate went bankrupt and officially ceased to exist in 1970, leaving a chaotic financial legacy. Artists received no income, and royalties remained unpaid as a source of continuing legal action that was only resolved in the early years of the new century, by which time many of the deserving claimants were no longer around to benefit. The situation was satirised by Steve Marriott on the track 'Theme From Skint (See You Later Liquidator)', a whining dobro-driven country Blues, 'I ain't got much bread, but it's alright, I got the sun in the morning, got the moon at night.' Dedicated to Mr Banker, Steve generously allows, 'well, Mr Ridley's bought a Bentley, Mr Oldham sold his Rolls, Mrs Winston's fixing guineas, Mr Carter's digging holes, we'd like to thank you people for listening to our song.' It closes with the sound of an exploding bomb. Meanwhile, Humble Pie's new American manager, Dee Anthony, negotiated a deal for the band with A&M. Stateside distribution through Immediate had always been spotty, with a number of brief hook-ups with MGM, United Artists and a licensing deal with CBS. A&M promised the opportunity for more cohesive American promotion. A former road manager for Tony Bennett, Dee Anthony had helped gain

American audiences for British bands Traffic, Jethro Tull, Spooky Tooth and Joe Cocker... he took Gary Wright from Spooky Tooth and was rewarded with a solo American number one with 'Dream Weaver.'

The accepted industry wisdom of the time was that it took relentless touring to break the American market, by paying your dues hard-working on the endless road, building a hard-core following on a town-by-town basis. So, adopting a heavier, tighter live stadium attack, Humble Pie promoted the album with gigs strewn from coast to coast across America, which, given Steve Marriott's already-chronicled proclivity to party hard, with groupies and a variety of stimulants on tap, could only result in the toxic combination that Steve would later term 'Good Booze And Bad Women.'

Melody Maker welcomed the album with 'it would probably be something of an overstatement to say that Humble Pie are the British equivalent of The Band, but this album exactly captures those elements of funk and innate swing that are the hallmark of the American group, in a way that few other British outfits can do.' 'Only A Roach' is a country-tinged ode to cannabis that had preceded the album as the Germany-only B-side of the summer 1970 single 'Big Black Dog.' Jerry Shirley sings and John 'Willie' Wilson plays drums. *Melody Maker* opines 'their success is due essentially to the fact that they have all integrated their separate talents in such a manner that the overall sound has a satisfying tightness and completeness about it. For a start, all four of them sing, even the drummer.'

The distinctive album cover art took an illustration by decadent-era artist Aubrey Beardsley, a *Yellow Book* contemporary of Oscar Wilde, who died aged just 25 of tuberculosis in March 1898, leaving beautifully strange, erotically charged symbolist art. Always a cult figure, he received renewed recognition from the various florid manifestations of the counter-culture press, where his sly but intricate subversion of moral standards made him relevant all over again.

Rock On

Personnel:
Steve Marriott: guitar, keyboards, organ, lead and backing vocals
Peter Frampton: guitar, lead and backing vocals, keyboards
Greg Ridley: bass, guitar, lead and backing vocals
Jerry Shirley: drums
Plus
Alexis Korner: backing vocals
Bobby Keys: saxophone
B.J. Cole: pedal steel guitar
P.P. Arnold, Doris Troy and Claudia Lennear as The Soul Sisters chorus
thanks also to Captain Barry Row & The White Helmets
Plus Jimmy Thomas, Ricky, Cy and Ben Pump.
Released: March 1971, A&M Records AMLS 2013 (UK), A&M Records SP-4301 (USA)

Produced by Glyn Johns with Humble Pie at Olympic Studios, London during January.
Highest chart position: US: 118 (Billboard), Can: 87
Tracklisting: Side One: 'Shine On' (Frampton) 3:00, 'Sour Grain' (Frampton, Marriott) 2:40, 'Seventy-Ninth And Sunset' (Marriott) 2:59, 'Stone Cold Fever' (Humble Pie) 4:08, 'Rolling Stone' (Muddy Waters) 5:57
Side Two: 'A Song For Jenny' (Marriott) 2:34, 'The Light' (Frampton) 3:16, 'Big George' (Ridley) 4:07, 'Strange Days' (Humble Pie, lyrics by Steve Marriott) 6:33, 'Red Neck Jump' (Marriott) 3:05

This album title is slightly misleading. For while they Rock with the best of them there's also a pronounced roundness to their sound, a mellowing that only adds to the sense that this is a *band* in the true sense of the word.

'Shine On' was issued as a Humble Pie single b/w Greg Ridley's 'Mister Ring' (A&M AMS834) – when *Record Mirror* called it 'a mid-tempo beater with lovely rolling guitar riffs. After a somewhat hesitant start, the vocal build-up really makes it worthwhile. It's heavy, but not oppressively so.' Yet the song would reach an even wider audience when it was performed as part of Peter Frampton's mega-selling double live album *Frampton Comes Alive!* (January 1976).

'Sour Grain' is an ode to 'a proud, fierce woman and a jar of whiskey'... that is, moonshine, mountain dew. The embellishments never overdo the strong melody line; the guitar and bass interweave while Jerry's drums pull it all together. There's a dead stop after the first chorus – not many musicians know how to use silence – then the double heartbeat bass drum brings it all to a neat close.

Whereas Jerry Shirley adds boogie piano to Steve's crawling king snake of a song 'Seventy-Ninth And Sunset', promising 'dramas inside your pyjamas tonight' with red-eyed Ruby's nut-crushing boobs. Steve even adds his own 'The Universal' line about 'there's such a lot of good ways to be bad.' Then there's sweet acoustics written for Steve's first wife Jenny Rylance, erupting into vocal backings by The Soul Sisters, reuniting Steve with P.P. Arnold, plus Doris Troy – whose 1963 single 'What'cha Gonna Do About It' had supplied the title for The Small Faces first hit. Like P.P., Claudia Lennear had been an Ikette before working with Joe Cocker, Leon Russell, plus Delaney & Bonnie.

There's laughter and banter behind the playful bop-bop-shoo-waddy-waddy stride piano intro to 'Red Neck Jump', 'the pianist is a freaker too'; Steve throws in a sly tongue-in-cheek 'Freak on! Oh yeah', then makes a passing reference to Lana Turner – star of the first *The Postman Always Rings Twice* (1946), before a hard fifties-style guitar solo and a 'hang it, hang out, hang it all about' fun play-out, to close a varied and frequently inspired album.

Meanwhile, Steve continued his freelancing by playing piano on the BJ Cole song 'Strange Images' on the second album *Swallow Tales* by British Country-Rock band Cochise (1971, Liberty).

Performance: Rockin' The Fillmore

Personnel:
Steve Marriott: guitar, vocals, harmonica
Peter Frampton: guitar, vocals
Greg Ridley: bass guitar, vocals
Jerry Shirley: drums
Released: November 1971, Double album, A&M Records AMLS 63506 (UK), A&M Records SP-3506 (USA)
Produced by Humble Pie, recorded live 28-29 May 1971 at Fillmore East, New York, remixed at Electric Lady Studios
Highest chart position: US: 21 (Billboard), Can: 32, UK: 32
Tracklisting: Side One: 'Four Day Creep' (Ida Cox) 3:48, 'I'm Ready' (Willie Dixon) 8:30 – as featured on the Humble Pie studio album, 'Stone Cold Fever' (Humble Pie) 6:20 – as featured on the Rock On studio album.
Side Two: 'I Walk On Gilded Splinters' (Mac Rebennack as 'Dr John Creaux') 24:30
Side Three: 'Rollin' Stone' (Muddy Waters) 16:10
Side Four: 'Hallelujah (I Love Her So)' (Ray Charles) 5:10, 'I Don't Need No Doctor' (Jo Armstead, Nickolas Ashford, Valerie Simpson) 9:20

Although relationships were already fraying during the recording of *Rock On*, this blockbusting four-sided album was to be the last incarnation of the original Humble Pie lineup. Just as manager Dee Anthony's strategy of breaking into the American market through concentrated live work seemed to be paying off, and this double-set climbed into the *Billboard* charts, Peter Frampton jumped ship. To Chris Welch in *Melody Maker,* this is 'attractively packaged with a series of photographs of the group in action from gigs ranging from Hyde Park to Philadelphia; it's a rocking souvenir of the band that English fans did not hear too often.' Humble Pie would continue as largely a Marriott-fronted band.

Ida Cox, credited as composer for the opening track, was a pioneering blues writer and singer who recorded a song called 'Fore Day Creep', as part of the John Hammond-produced *From Spirituals To Swing* live album recorded at Carnegie Hall with saxophonist Lester 'Prez' Young and trumpeter Buck Clayton. This Humble Pie song bears little resemblance to her song.

When The Small Faces were living together in the Buckinghamshire countryside, in a shared Marlow house, Mick Jagger visited, bringing a gift of albums. Part of his gift was Dr John's *Gris Gris* 1968 debut album, which included 'I Walk On Gilded Splinters', subsequently recorded by Marsha Hunt, The Neville Brothers, The Allman Brothers Band and many others.

Peter sings the first section of 'Hallelujah (I Love Her So)', then Steve takes over, and they continue to alternate, trading Gibson Les Paul licks on this much-recorded item. 'Are you ready for swing time?' asks Steve as they slow into a softer, jazzier sequence. He improvises into a quote from 'Walk Right In', which was a 1963 hit single for The Rooftop Singers, before the big heavy raw energy crescendo. Steve was capable of blowing any other band off the stage, and together, Humble Pie could be awesome. 'I Don't Need No Doctor' is essentially little more than the framework of a repeated power riff with hypnotic title repetitions and fluid guitar side-trips, yet it builds to a furious series of massive climaxes. It had previously been recorded by Ray Charles after J Armstead's own version and was subsequently covered by The Chocolate Watchband and New Riders Of The Purple Sage. Edited to a more concise 3:45 minutes and flipped with 'A Song For Jenny', this was issued as a Humble Pie single, which reached number 73 on the *Billboard* chart.

Smokin'

Personnel:
Steve Marriott: guitar, lead and backing vocals, harmonica, keyboards
Clem Clempson: guitar, lead and backing vocals, keyboards
Greg Ridley: bass, backing vocals
Jerry Shirley: drums, piano
Plus:
Alexis Korner: vocal
Stephen Stills: backing vocal
Released: February 1972, A&M Records AMLS 64342 (UK), A&M Records SP-4342 (USA)
Produced by Humble Pie, recorded at Olympic Studios
Highest chart position: US: 6 (Billboard), Can: 13, UK: 20, Aus: 9
Tracklisting: Side One: 'Hot 'n' Nasty' (Humble Pie, Steve Marriott lyrics) 3:22, 'The Fixer' (Humble Pie, Steve Marriott lyrics) 5:00, 'You're So Good To Me' (Ridley, Marriott) 3:53, 'C'mon Everybody' (Eddie Cochran, Jerry Capehart) 5:11, 'Old Time Feelin'' (Trad, arranged with new words by Steve Marriott) 5:05
Side Two: 'Thirty Days In The Hole' (Marriott) 3:58, 'Road Runner/ Road Runner 'G' Jam' (Holland, Dozier, Holland/Humble Pie) 3:42, 'I Wonder' (Cecil Grant, Raymond Leveen) 8:53, 'Sweet Peace And Time' (Humble Pie, Steve Marriott lyrics) 5:49

Peter Frampton was gone, carving out his own career. A move that thrust Steve Marriott more to the centre, as in came David 'Clem' Clempson from jazz-rock fusion band Colosseum, resulting in the Pie 'cooking better than ever' (according to Chris Welch). Building on the success of *Performance: Rockin' The Fillmore*, this became the band's studio album breakthrough, benefiting from airplay emphasis on the new AOR radio stations (adult-orientated rock).

The album opens with 'Hot 'n' Nasty', a slow-burning R&B workout that was issued as the album's first single, with 'You're So Good For Me' as the B-side. It climbed steadily to number 52 on the American *Billboard* chart and went even higher in Canada to peak at number 35. Stephen Stills, who was also recording at Olympic Studios at the time, dropped in on the session to add guest vocals. The focus shifts to Clem Clempson taking his first Humble

Pie vocals for 'Old Time Feelin'', joined by gravel-voiced blues veteran Alexis Korner, who also plays what at first sounds to be a mandolin, but is, in fact, an instrument known as the Martin Tiple. Some reviewers point out that the track looks back to 'Alabama '69' from the debut Humble Pie album.

But the stand-out track, 'Thirty Days In The Hole', opens with studio banter, laughter and raw acapella rehearsal harmonies before drum-kicking into a guitar attack so intensely vicious there's no stereo system on the market loud enough to do it justice. The album's feature single b/w 'C'mon Everybody' + 'Road Runner' ('Sweet Peace And Time' in the US); it tells the story of Steve's drug bust for possession of various illegal substances, including cocaine, hashish and 'New Castle Brown' – not the Brown Ale but a brand of heroin. There are voice-overs run across the midpoint guitar and harmonica barrage, 'how ya doin' boy?, you're here for thirty days' and 'get your long-hair cut' aping the verdict of the judicial system. 'If you live on the road, there's new highway code', Steve observes with wry bitterness. As a hardcore slice of myth-making rock 'n' roll documentary realism, this has few equals. Steve would carry the song over onto his Packet of Three setlist. Of course, Chuck Berry had recorded a song called 'Thirty Days' as long ago as 1955.

Eat It

Personnel:
Steve Marriott: guitar, lead vocals, harmonica, keyboards
Clem Clempson: guitar, backing vocals
Greg Ridley: bass, backing vocals
Jerry Shirley: drums
Plus:
The Blackberries, Billie Barnum, Clydie King and Venetta Fields
B.J. Cole: pedal steel guitar
Sidney George: saxophone
Released: April 1973, Double album, A&M Records AMLS 6004 (UK), A&M Records SP-3701 (USA)
Produced by Humble Pie, recorded at Steve Marriott's Clear Sounds studio in Moreton, Essex
Highest chart position: US: 13 (Billboard), UK: 34, Aus: 9
Side One: 'Get Down To It' (Marriott) 3:25, 'Good Booze And Bad Women' (Marriott) 3:11, 'Is It For Love?' (Marriott) 4:39, 'Drugstore Cowboy' (Marriott) 5:35
Side Two: 'Black Coffee' (Ike & Tina Turner) 3:09, 'I Believe To My Soul' (Ray Charles) 4:03, 'Shut Up And Don't Interrupt Me' (Edwin Starr, Johnny Bristol) 2:58, 'That's How Strong My Love Is' (Roosevelt Jamison) 3:44
Side three: 'Say No More' (Marriott) 1:58, 'Oh, Bella (That's All Hers)' (Marriott) 3:25, 'Summer Song' (Marriott) 2:42, 'Beckton Dumps' (Marriott) 3:13
Side four (live at Green's Playhouse, Glasgow): 'Up Our Sleeve' (Humble Pie, Steve Marriott lyrics) 4:57, 'Honky Tonk Women' (Jagger, Richards) 4:03, 'Road Runner' (Holland, Dozier, Holland) 13:28

Humble Pie turned in a histrionic performance of the album's stand-out single, 'Black Coffee' (b/w 'Say No More'), as part of their *Old Grey Whistle Test* set in March 1973, with the Blackberries trio pouring impassioned back-up harmonies behind one of Steve's most extreme vocal work-outs, and it was stunning. 'That's where it's at', he stabs at the camera, 'and I know!' Bob Harris nods his approval. It opens with faint but growing chords. Steve's vocals are insanely good. Where Tina Turner sings 'my skin is brown, but my mind is black' on the duo's 1972 *Feel Good* album, Steve autobiographically personalises it with 'my skin is white, but my soul is black', which is surely what he'd set out to prove since his earliest Small Faces days.

The Blackberries, who add to that soul-power, include Vanetta Fields, who – like P.P. Arnold – was a graduate of Ike Turner's Ikettes, with whom she'd recorded respected top 40 hit 'Peaches 'n' Cream.' The Blackberries also included Dallas-born former Raelette Clydie King. Ray Charles had always been a touchstone for brit-soul. Together, they were already respected session artists in their own right, having recorded for Motown's Mowest subsidiary and contributed to The Supremes post-Diana Ross album *The Supremes Produced And Arranged By Jimmy Webb* (1972).

The album itself, a double-set, neatly divides into four distinct sides, with the first consisting of Steve's straight-up rock 'n' roll, the second side made up of R&B covers – including 'That's How Strong My Love Is', most usually associated with Otis Redding, but also done by The Rolling Stones on their 1965 *Out Of Our Heads* album and by The Hollies on their 1966 *Would You Believe?*. Side three reflected Steve's acoustic songs, while the fourth side was a live recording from Glasgow, where roars of applause greet the announcement, 'the finest rock 'n' roll band in the land' – well, maybe, while Steve at his most raucous declares 'even though we get kicked around, won't get caught with my trousers down.' A straight, uncomplicated exercise in rock histrionics.

For 'Good Booze And Bad Women', feedback and harmonica wail as Steve serenades the passions that make touring bearable, 'I wanna stroke ya, choke ya, whisk you up and roll all night.' When The Doobie Brothers sang *What Were Once Vices Are Now Habits*, Steve had already been there and done that. On 'Drugstore Cowboy' he'd played the 'holes' from Bethnal Green down to LA, dealing the rich mythology of the travelling musician, as the back-up voices caution 'remember.' As Ian Hunter writes, it's a mighty long way down rock 'n' roll… Even 'Say No More', which takes the form of a long-distance phone call to wife Jenny Rylance, shows Steve's mellow side, accompanied just by what sounds like mandolin picking. 'I don't need a swimming pool, I don't need to hang records on the wall', he declares, with just a passing mention of 'what I laid down up my snout didn't help me none' to the destructive cocaine that ultimately eroded their relationship. She left him the year of the album's release.

There's an argument that when Peter left Humble Pie he took that certain delicacy with him, that Steve over-compensated by turning the amps up to eleven, with the consequent loss of subtlety. But when that strategy works, it can be formidable. 'At their best, Humble Pie are among the top six Rock bands of an era, ranking alongside The Stones for sheer guts and energy,' said *Melody Maker* on 24 March 1973, 'when they play a song, they absorb it and become it, dragging it into a total mood.'

Thunderbox

Personnel:
Steve Marriott: guitar, lead vocals, harmonica, keyboards
Dave 'Clem' Clempson: guitar, slide guitar, backing vocals
Greg Ridley: bass, backing vocals, lead vocal on 'Drift Away'
Jerry Shirley: drums, backing vocals, piano
Plus:
The Blackberries, Billie Barnum, Carlena Williams and Venetta Fields
Mel 'Al Horns' Collins: horns
Hipgnosis album sleeve design with cut-out keyhole-shaped opening to reveal an inner picture
Released: February 1974, A&M Records SP-3611 (USA), A&M CAM63611 (UK)
Produced by Steve Marriott at Olics Sound 'somewhere east of Guatemala'
Highest chart position: US: 52 (Billboard)
Tracklisting: Side One: 'Thunderbox' (Clempson, Marriott) 5:16, 'Groovin' With Jesus' (Benny Swartz, Gene Barge) 2:18, 'I Can't Stand The Rain' (Anne Peebles, DJ Bernard 'Bernie' Miller, Don Bryant) 4:17, 'Anna (Go To Him)' (Arthur Alexander) 3:42, 'No Way' (Ridley, Marriott) 2:48, 'Rally With Ali' (Marriott, Clempson, Ridley, Shirley) 2:49
Side Two: 'Don't Worry, Be Happy' (Humble Pie) 2:54, 'Ninety-Nine Pounds' (Don Bryant) 2:47, 'Every Single Day' (Clem Clempson) 3:46, 'No Money Down' (Chuck Berry) 4:25, 'Drift Away' (Mentor Williams) 3:57, 'Oh La-De-Da' (Phillip Mitchell) 4:32

Twelve songs. Seven covers. But the UK release was delayed. All was not going well.

With earthy humour intact and just a slight memory of the 'khazi' from 'Lazy Sunday', thunderbox is another archaic slang term for toilet. Arthur Alexander's song 'Anna' was first brought to a wider audience by its inclusion on The Beatles' first album. The Rolling Stones confirmed Alexander's hipness by recording his 'You Better Move On' soon after. Jerry Shirley's piano underlines Steve's raw, anguished vocals on 'I Can't Stand The Rain', which started out as an Anne Peebles Memphis record, produced for the Hi label by Willie Mitchell. John Lennon once called it 'the perfect single.' Steve's voice hits almost woman-tone highs, buoyed by Mel Collins' brass sounds.

Greg Ridley's rough-edged voice gives 'Drift Away' a feel reminiscent of The Band, with Steve yelling encouraging interjections in the background. Most notably recorded by Dobie Gray, a country-soul singer previously best known for his Mod cult classic 'The In Crowd', the song denotes a significant shift in the perception of rock 'n' roll, from its early extrovert teenage celebration of youthful energies, into a more wistful reflective maturity in which the familiarity of rock becomes a source of comfort in increasingly hard times. Rod Stewart included his own version of the song on his *Atlantic Crossing* album. The Rolling Stones attempted a cover for their *It's Only Rock 'N' Roll* album in 1974 but decided they couldn't better Dobie Gray's original, so it was shelved and only issued as a bonus track on the *Tattoo You* CD reissue in 2021. There's an argument that Humble Pie catch the song's mood better than anyone else.

The *Melody Maker* review opines, 'it's a patchy album in terms of material, although the Pie keep to their basic aim of providing good-time rock and funk', while for *New Musical Express*, 'there's nothing actively wrong with the album. The band are sharp and choogle along more strongly than most. It's just another Humble Pie album, made up of all one might expect, but no more.'

Street Rats

Personnel:
Steve Marriott: guitar, lead vocals, harmonica, keyboards, production
Dave 'Clem' Clempson: guitar, slide guitar
Greg Ridley: bass guitar, vocals
Jerry Shirley: drums, except for 'Street Rat', which has Ian Wallace
Plus:
Mel Collins: saxophones
Tim Hinkley: keyboards
Released: February 1975, A&M Records AMLS68282 (UK), A&M Records SP-4514 (USA)
Produced by Steve Marriott and Andrew Loog Oldham at Olympic Studios and Clear Sounds studio
Highest chart position: US: 100 (Billboard)
Tracklising: Side One: 'Street Rat' (Marriott) 2:52, 'Rock 'N' Roll Music' (Chuck Berry) 2:55, 'We Can Work It Out' (Lennon, McCartney) 3:18, 'Scored Out' (Marriott, Clempson) 2:43, 'Road Hog' (Marriott) 3:08, 'Rain' (Lennon, McCartney) 4:00
Side Two: 'Funky To The Bone' (Fred Gowdy, Larry Wilkins), 'Let Me Be Your Lovemaker' (Betty Wright, Clarence Reid, Willie Clarke) 5:57, 'Countryman Stomp' (Clem Clempson, Greg Ridley, Tim Hinkley) 2:20, 'Drive My Car' (Lennon, McCartney) 3:43, 'Queens And Nuns' (Humble Pie) 3:04

This album marked the end of the Humble Pie rainbow – for now. Following the Dee Anthony plan, they'd toured solidly for four years, and there had been corresponding successes, a reward for those twenty-one hard tours. But nothing to compare with the massive American breakthrough achieved by Rod Stewart with Steve's former Small Faces colleagues or the Classic-Rock airplay domination that Peter Frampton reached with the 1976 double-set *Frampton Comes Alive!*, which took 'Shine On' from Humble Pie's *Rock On* album to yet vaster audiences.

Back then, in the pre-streaming age, bands toured to promote albums, and the massive profits resulted from the consequent album sales. And those vinyl sales could be formidable. Before CDs or MP3s, if you wanted to hear that particular album track, the only way you could hear it was to buy the vinyl album and play it on your increasingly sophisticated front-room domestic stereo sound system crammed with woofers and tweeters. From Pink Floyd's *Dark Side Of The Moon* (1973) to *The Wall* (1979), from The Eagles *Hotel California* (1976) to Fleetwood Mac's *Rumours* (1977), this was the era when the album ruled the world.

David Bowie finally 'broke' big in the States only through a hugely expensive series of visually extravagant coast-to-coast tours. As a result of 21st-century streaming, that logic has now been reversed: artists use albums as a way of promoting tours, and it is through ticket sales at venues that vast fortunes can be made.

With touring expenses deducted – hotels, transportation and 'riders' – Humble Pie arrived back in the UK broke, busted and disgusted, already caught up in other solo projects and not intending to work together again. But they were contractually obligated to A&M to deliver another album. Eventually, the label appropriated tapes of works-in-progress, including demos of Steve's solo material and work intended for a Greg Ridley collaboration project. A&M brought former Immediate supremo Andrew Loog Oldham in to re-mix the tracks into some kind of continuity, much as Phil Spector had been requisitioned to salvage an album from the tapes that were to become The Beatles' *Let It Be* album (May 1970). The results are better than might have been expected, considering the circumstances, but it represents a sad end chapter to the high expectations with which the band had started out. So, be humble, and just enjoy this slice of pie.

'Hit it! Hold on! C'mon, now listen' yells Steve on the title track, erupting into a lowlife autobiography of pimps and whores, built around massive riffs that vaguely recall 'Day Tripper', with back-chat dialogue, 'Oh, I know it's bad news, but bad news is good news, eh, you know what I mean?' For an album with an over-reliance on covers, the strength of this track provides considerable counterbalance, 'but I can hear my main man comin' and I'm runnin' outta time / Man, I'm getting' down so far that I'm below ground…' It's a track that draws on all the sleazy street-romance of a Robert Crumb cartoon. Sure, there's a kind of intellectual dishonesty at work as the well-brought-up Cockney boy with lapsed thespian aspirations assumes marketable ghetto poses, but that's never stopped Mick Jagger's mid-Atlantic slur, while Eric Burdon had seldom been outside Newcastle and had no more visited a New Orleans brothel than Bob Dylan had, while Long John Baldry repeatedly insisted he was your Hoochie-Coochie Man when he self-evidently was nothing of the kind. Can De White Man Sing De Blues? That's still a question for academics to tease out.

Bands on the endless tour circuit tend to end up writing songs about touring, motels and overnight groupie angels. Steve injects a major dose of humour into the familiar scenario with 'Queens And Nuns', even when his original cheeky Jack-the-Lad persona occasionally lapses into something a little more unsubtle. Although you could simply read that as honest? He wants to take a leak, but there's a policeman eyeing him; his knees are desperately weak. There's a girl who wears a python coat and it hisses when she comes. It's all delivered in a slow, insinuating talking-blues groove with submerged jazzy horns that sometimes blare. Steve's Cockney comes through on 'hey, is that natives dancing? Naw… it's just a team of tarts!' Then there's a conversational in-joke parting shot directed at Andrew (Oldham?); Steve admits to being the 'oldest has-been' but considers the public should be warned 'that John, George, Paul and Ringo or Linda or Yoko weren't on this bloody record in the first place…' You gotta smile, even as you tap your foot.

Maybe three Beatles songs on one album is stretching it. The *NME* reviewer concedes that 'parts of the record do have rather a valedictory feel about them… it's as if the Pie were going back to 'standards' to show they've achieved classical status – and ushering themselves off-stage in the process?'

'Funky To The Bone', with rich soul horns and minimal lyrics, is a James Brown soundalike originally done by Freddi Henchi & The Soul Setters in 1973 (Reprise REP1175). The track was substituted by the strutting Clempson-Marriott track 'There 'Tis' (3:06) on the American edition, with its call-and-response 'have you got enough woman inside to love me?' vocal jousting and socking horn punctuation. 'Funky To The Bone' was later gathered onto the 'Bonus Tracks' CD of *The A&M Rarities: 1970-1975* Box-set (2022, Universal Music 4588188).

On To Victory

Personnel:
Steve Marriott: guitar, lead vocals, harmonica, keyboards
Jerry Shirley: drums
Bobby Tench: guitar, vocals
Anthony 'Sooty' Jones: bass, vocals
plus:
Cheryl Ashley, Marge Raymond and Lisa Zimmerman: backing vocals
Released: April 1980, Jet Records JETLP231 (UK), Atco Records 38-122 (USA)
Produced by 'The Pie' with Johnny Elijah Wright at Villa Recorders, Modesto, CA
Highest chart position: US: 60 (Billboard)
Tracklisting: Side One: 'Fool For A Pretty Face' (Marriott, Shirley) 4:12, 'You Soppy Pratt' (Marriot, Jones, Shirley) 4:08, 'Infatuation' (Marriott) 3:45, 'Take It From Here' (Marriott) 3:39, 'Savin' It' (Tench, Marriott) 4:41
Side Two: 'Baby Don't You Do It' (Holland, Dozier, Holland) 4:41, 'Get It In The End' (Marriott, Jones, Shirley) 2:41, 'My Lover's Prayer' (Otis Redding) 4:02, 'Further Down The Road' (Marriott, Tench, Jones, Shirley) 4:29, 'Over You' (Allen Orange, Clarence Toussaint) 2:22

Ironically titled, heading into a sad downward spiral. After the failed Small Faces reunion, Ian was off playing with Glen Matlock's Rich Kids, then recording – playing Wurlitzer electric piano on 'Miss You' – and touring with The Rolling Stones, while Steve convened a new Humble Pie lineup for two more albums.

Issued as a single 'Fool For A Pretty Face' b/w 'You Soppy Pratt' (11 April 1980, Jet 180), it reached number 58 in the US. The story is that the song was written by Steve and Jerry Shirley in New York over the course of a weekend after being told by Aerosmith manager David Krebs that he would get them another record deal if they could come up with a hit single. Krebs liked it, and Humble Pie were signed to Atco. 'Steve liked to record the vocals 'live' and instead of recording the group standing around the mic, he miked us individually', recalls Marge Raymond (who sang with Flame on two 1977 and 1978 albums).

'Over You' is a song from Aaron Neville's Minit Records catalogue, a strong Ray Charles feel with a New Orleans bounce buoyed on bass and pattering percussion. The original 1960 single opened with piano chords from Chopin's 'Funeral March', as Aaron threatens to kill his woman if she dares leave him. Humble Pie remove the doomy intro but retain the questionable lyric. Steve's voice sounds suitably broken in contrast to Neville's bright clarity.

In an interesting case of compare and contrast, 'Baby Don't You Do It' goes back to the very earliest Small Faces sets because Jimmy Winston sings a version of this Marvin Gaye hit on *From The Beginning*. But, as Ian McLagan pointed out, 'where (Steve had) been so soulful and ahead of his time for a white boy in the sixties, by the mid-seventies he'd become so flash and vocally gymnastic, it wasn't as good on the ears.'

The album cover art shows a World War II blitz dogfight with a Spitfire shooting a Luftwaffe bomber going down in flames. It's debatable whether Humble Pie is the victor or the loser on this LP. Critical reception was poor. 'Just what the world needed, a Humble Pie revival!' sneered *Sounds* on 24 May 1980, 'the famed raw vocals of Mr Marriott are pushed to such extremes that they're totally incomprehensible for half the album's duration, that's duration as in endure.'

Go For The Throat

Personnel:
Steve Marriott: guitar, vocals, harmonica, keyboards
Jerry Shirley: drums, percussion
Bobby Tench: guitar, keyboards, vocals
Anthony 'Sooty' Jones: bass, vocals
plus:
Robin Beck, Maxine Dixon, Dana Kral: backing vocals
Released: June 1981, Atco Records 38-131 (USA), issued in the UK in 2019 as The Store For Music SFMCD534

Produced by Gary Lyons at Mediasound and Soundworks, New York City
No chart position
Tracklisting: Side One: 'All Shook Up' (Otis Blackwell, Elvis Presley) 2:40, 'Teenage Anxiety' (Marriott) 4:44, 'Tin Soldier' (Marriott, Lane) 3:09, 'Keep It On The Island' (Marriott, Shirley) 3:54, 'Driver' (Marriott) 3:19
Side Two: 'Restless Blood' (Richard Supa) 4:04, 'Go For The Throat' (Marriott, Tench) 3:59, 'Lottie And The Charcoal Queen' (Marriott, Shirley) 4:37, 'Chip Away The Stone' (Richard Supa) 4:55

Steve and original Humble Pie drummer Jerry Shirley, with Bobby Tench, whose roots go back to the Jeff Beck Group, and New York musician Anthony Jones holding down the bass.

'Chip Away The Stone' – one of two Richard Supa compositions, is a rougher, less polished cover of the swaggering 1978 Aerosmith single. Heavy metal was not a popular designation, even among those you'd class as practitioners. Jon Lord of Deep Purple told me he preferred the term 'Heavy Rock.' Humble Pie veer towards heavy metal at betraying moments, but Steve was always too savvy, too aware of rock and soul roots to surrender to blind volume-bludgeoning riffola. Yet the Aerosmith production is cleaner, and arguably, Steve Tyler's voice has certain melodic advantages over Steve Marriott's wrecked croak.

Rod Stewart had also recorded 'All Shook Up' as part of The Jeff Beck Group's second album *Beck-Ola* (June 1969, Columbia SX6351).

With a piano introduction, 'Teenage Anxiety' is Steve's John Lennon tribute written shortly after 'they shot my hero in the street'; it's one of Steve's better late songs. The shooting prompts intimations of his own mortality, asking if I had my time again, I guess I'd do it just the same and 'hide behind the bullshit I live by.' While 'Tin Soldier' is a rather redundant reworking of The Small Faces hit, which basically follows the original blueprint without adding anything significantly new, nevertheless issued as a single, it reached number 58 on the US charts. Only the line 'so now I've lost my way, I need help to show me things to say' takes on an added layer of meaning.

It had only been twenty long and eventful years since a chirpy young Steve Marriott played in Lionel Bart's *Oliver* stage production. Now, on 'Keep It On The Island', he engagingly reprises his Artful Dodger 'Jack the Lad' cockney roots, as he opens with 'Aye Aye' before launching into 'I've been up and I've been down, I've been happy and sad, didn't take me very long to take the good times with the bad.' The track closes with muted laughter.

The sad vampiric cover art is neither big nor clever. While dogged by bad luck, tour dates supporting Judas Priest were cancelled due to Steve's 'ill-health', complicated by his crumbling marriage. Humble Pie were dropped by the record label and broke up soon after.

Afterglow: Return Of The Small Faces

Itchycoo Park – Single

'Itchycoo Park' (Marriott, Lane) 2:45 b/w **'My Way Of Giving'** (Marriott, Lane) 1:58
Re-released: December 1975, Immediate IM 102
Produced by Steve Marriott and Ronnie Lane
Highest chart position: UK: 9 (on chart for 11 weeks)

There was a groundswell of rediscovery and an appreciation of what had come before.

NEMS bought up the old Immediate masters and re-released the single. At Tony Calder's urging, the group reconvened to film a new promotional video, with the result that 'Itchycoo Park' returned to the UK chart at number 28, 20 December 1975 and climbed the lap over into the new year to find itself at number nine on 17 January 1976 in a chart dominated by Queen ('Bohemian Rhapsody'), Abba ('Mamma Mia') and former Immediate colleague Andy Fairweather Low with his plaintive 'Wide Eyed And Legless.'

In the USA, Sire Records issued a generous gatefold double-vinyl compilation, *History Of British Rock* (1974, SAS3702), which featured 'Itchycoo Park' among other tracks by The Hollies, Status Quo, The Pretty Things and Manfred Mann. 'Lazy Sunday' was featured on Vol.2 (1974, Sire SASH3705-2) alongside The Beatles 'Ain't She Sweet', Billy J Kramer With The Dakotas, The Searchers and The Kinks.

'Itchycoo Park', with a John Peel voice-over, would return in mid-1990 as a TV ad for Andrex!

Lazy Sunday – Single

'Lazy Sunday' (Marriott, Lane) 3:08 b/w **'(Tell Me) Have You Ever Seen Me?'** (Marriott, Lane) 2:14
Released: March 1976, Immediate IM 106
Produced by Steve Marriott and Ronnie Lane
Highest chart position: UK: 39 (on chart for five weeks)

Again, there was a new video. Once the shoot was completed, Marriott quipped, 'See you in five years' time, lads. Next time, we'll do it on ice.'

Although it was only in the top 40 for the single week of 3 April, it shared the chart with a re-issue of The Beatles 'Hey Jude' and Elton John's reworking of The Who's 'Pinball Wizard.'

The Best Of The Nice, The Small Faces, Humble Pie, Eric Clapton And John Mayall – Various Artists

German gatefold double-vinyl compilation: Immediate 1C 148-92 661/662

Available only on import, of the four sides, the first is devoted to The Small Faces with Marriott-Lane tracks, 'Itchycoo Park', 'Tin Soldier', 'Lazy Sunday', 'The Universal', 'Afterglow Of Your Love' and 'Wham Bam Thank You, Ma'am.' Side Two consists of The Nice, while side four features 'The Best

Of The British Blues' with various lineups of John Mayall's Bluesbreakers featuring Jimmy Page and Eric Clapton. But side three is made up of a selection of Humble Pie tracks, 'Natural Born Bugie' (Marriott), 'The Sad Bag Of Shaky Jake' (Marriott), 'As Safe As Yesterday Is' (Marriott, Frampton), 'Alabama '69' (Marriott), 'Wrist Job' (Marriott) and 'Cold Lady' (Shirley). Steve told *NME* 'Humble Pie were a more serious rock 'n' roll band, as were The Faces. In The Small Faces, we had a sense of humour all of our own.'

Playmates

Personnel:
Steve Marriott: lead guitar, vocals, harmonica
Rick Wills: bass, backing vocals
Kenney Jones: drums, vocals
Ian McLagan: keyboards, vocals
Plus:
Dave Hynes, Greg Ridley, P.P Arnold and Vicky Brown: backing vocals
Joe Brown: mandolin, acoustic guitar and backing vocals
Mel Collins: saxophone
Produced by 'Kemastri' (Kenney, Mac, Steve, Rick)
Released: August 1977, Atlantic Records K 50375/ SD 19113
No chart placings

Remarkably, this was only the fourth full-length studio album recorded by The Small Faces.

And why 'Playmates'? Diminutive comedian 'Big-Hearted' Arthur Askey was frequently heard on 1950s radio with his nonsense song 'The Bee', and a compilation of his silly songs was issued in 1957 under a collective title using his popular catchphrase 'Hello Playmates' (Oriole MG 20017). His eccentric performance of the song, in which he'd buzz back and forth across the stage like a man possessed, flitting, fizzing and flapping like a demented insect to the amusement of audiences everywhere, was maybe something – not unlike Stanley Unwin – that was uniquely appreciated only by those of certain age, young enough at the time to find it endearing. The four Small Faces were of that generation. They used the radio 'Workers Playtime' theme played through the PA as a stage fanfare.

Towards the end of his eighteen-month tenure as WEA Records 'Director of Special Projects', former Beatles PR officer Derek Taylor was party to the final demise of the Faces. Their former vocalist was already enjoying huge success as a solo artist and had announced to the *Daily Mirror* that his relationship with the band was over. Ron Wood was due to join the Rolling Stones, although it hadn't yet been officially announced. The remaining group members, Kenney Jones and Ian 'Mac' McLagan, were invited to Warner Brothers' East End office 'for a little chat' with Derek and American record executive Mo Ostin.

'Derek had only recently become the head of Warner Bros in England and had worked closely with the Beatles for years. Nevertheless, the proposition on offer wasn't promising. Why not reform a group with Steve Marriott? We looked at each other in disbelief, and I told him it was the last thing I wanted to do, and left the office in a black mood' (quoted from Ian's book *All The Rage*, Sidgwick & Jackson, 1998).

'He (Derek Taylor) was a lovely man', recalls Ian now. Although they saw each other infrequently, 'he was a gentleman.' But perhaps Derek was right?

Steve Marriott was by some considerable distance a better interpretive singer than Rod Stewart. And, despite Ian's denial, The Small Faces did indeed reform, with Steve Marriott, in June 1976, around the time the reissued 'Itchycoo Park' returned them to the top ten. With 'Itchycoo Park' enjoying renewed success, there was an imperative to shoot a promotional video to aid its inexorable return to climb up the charts. So, there was an external incentive for the four members to get together, and the reunion worked well enough for them to enjoy jamming together. Although the internal group-chemistry had always been both good and creative, there had been incessant record label and management issues to distort their work together. There was still unrealised potential, with energies to match. Freed of such contractual restraints and other commitment obstacles for virtually the first time, indications seemed positive. Inevitably, it was not going to be as simple as that. First there was an unfortunate falling out with Ronnie Lane. He was there for filming the videos, then he 'went off for a packet of fags and didn't come back.' The hook-worthy Lane-Marriott axis had been vital to the first phase of The Small Faces career. As a writing and performing partnership, they were matchless. But suddenly, things were different.

Steve, Ian and Kenney at first assumed that Ronnie was simply not handling his alcohol intake too well. Perhaps he'd eventually come around? In fact, it was evidence of the first symptoms of the cruel multiple sclerosis that was to drag him down. Could they continue without Ronnie? Would it still be The Small Faces without him? Well – The Rolling Stones had continued without Brian Jones. The Who would continue without Keith Moon. Reluctant to abandon the project that had begun with such positive vibes, the other three recruited Rick Wills into the lineup. He had played bass with Roxy Music, but perhaps more significantly, he'd worked with Peter Frampton too, on his first three post-Humble Pie albums, the last being *Somethin's Happening* (1974), for which he co-wrote 'Doobie Wah' which was later featured on the mega-selling live double-album *Frampton Comes Alive!* (A&M Records, 1976).

The sleeve logo design for *Playmates* was by an (uncredited) 'Barney Bubbles', who Ian first knew as Colin Fulcher when they were both at 'Twickers' art college together. The cartoon image shows a cheeky, grinning schoolboy brandishing a board with the album name on it, with a suitably shocked schoolgirl in pigtails with red ribbons, carrying books, an old-style wooden ruler and a politically unsound golliwog toy. Both children wear neat sandals with white ankle socks. Under Colin's assumed guise, this 'bright and talented' designer went on to become art director for Stiff Records. Meanwhile, live support gigs for the album were not entirely untroubled. During their first night at the Finsbury Park Rainbow their dressing room was pilfered of credit cards, passports, address books, four new songs, and £1000 in cash, while reviewers were not kind. On 7 May 1977, in the *NME*, Tony Stewart wrote about 'Stevie and the boys bullying 'Itchycoo Park', stomping on it and it's spillin' all over the bleedin' stage like stuffing from an old armchair.'

Appointed manager, promoter Mel Bush explained how, after rumour and speculation, the album had been completed six months earlier but was being released to coincide with the tour, that with Ronnie Lane, 'it didn't work out – he wasn't compatible', but that the get-together was not a one-off, but a permanent reunion. A sentiment confirmed when Steve was so delighted by the response at a Munich Easter Rock 'n' Blues Festival that he yelled, 'it's good to be together again. This band's gonna be together for fuckin' years.' As if.

Side One

'High And Happy' (Marriott) 2:42

A semi-autobiographical statement of intent from Steve in which he declares he's 'been on the road for about ten long years, I've seen spring in Des Moines, I've seen laughter and tears', which is an obvious reference to the endless cross-America touring he'd done with Humble Pie, accompanied by 'good booze and bad women.' And with the horns and the wailing back-up girl vocals it could be said the track cleaves more to Humble Pie than it does to The Small Faces legacy. The narcotic preferences he declares, about 'drinkin' snortin' anything to please me' and let's 'do another line', flags up warning signals about the state of his head. Kenney's drums play in, leading to a pleasing swell of Ian's keyboard, and there's a strong, sweaty funk boogie acceleration, emphasised by handclaps and saxophone; it seems an almost effortless ooze of musicians coming together quite naturally. He's high, and he's happy. Isn't that enough? Is it churlish to ask for more? Charles Shaar Murray, for one, reviewing the album for *NME* on 3 September 1977, thought, 'yeah well, if they'd drunk, smoked and snorted a little less, they might have realised what a fatuous piece of guff 'High And Happy' is.' For an appearance on BBC-TV's *The Old Grey Whistle Test*, introduced by 'Whispering' Bob Harris – 'let's go back to the sixties', – the reformed Small Faces open with a slow soulful 'All Or Nothing', 'that was one of our more successful records that we never got paid for, now I'd like to sell you a few postcards', says Steve dressed as a moustachioed dodgy geezer in a grey-blue jacket, black shirt and white tie, before linking into 'High And Happy' 'from the next album, which we hope we'll get paid for!' Steve turns to watch Ian as he plays a sharp keyboard solo, then stands back to play a neat guitar solo of his own before they close with a leg-kicking flourish.

'Never Too Late' (Marriott, McLagan) 3:50

With a keyboard interplay that closely resembles The Rolling Stones' 'Fool To Cry', this is a slow blues showing Steve's voice at once restrained but with controlled power. 'Have to find a new song', he exhorts, to 'help your days along' as it moves into an attractive acoustic guitar break, closing with gospel support voices, only to return for an extended fade. This is a track that delivers above expectations, proving that no... it was not too late.

'Tonight' (McLagan, John Pidgeon) 2:47
Again, the mood is subdued, with Ian's blue-eyed soul vocal melding smoothly into a slickly textured soft groove as gentle as 'your breath on my face' that, while it might not suggest a perfect fit for The Small Faces of old, demonstrates a healthy and not illogical evolution. This is The Small Faces, just not as we once knew them! Co-written with music journalist John Pidgeon, who not only wrote for *New Musical Express*, but for *Let It Rock* and *Melody Maker* too, the song was later covered by Ringo Starr on his album *Bad Boy* (1978).

'Saylarvee' (Marriott) 2:17
Boogie-woogie rolling piano. 'Oh, how we danced on the night that we met…' A strange amalgam of ragtime Country and exaggerated tongue-in-cheek Jerry Lee Lewis phrasing. A rockabilly guitar break. Then a 'Oh, how we mmmmmm, how we did it…' C'est la vie is a French expression that means 'such is life.'

'Find It' (Marriott, McLagan, Jones) 6:01
Prowling guitar, Kenney's regular drum-thump, the girls wail out the title phrase as Steve hits his trademark raucous vocal heights; you don't see his 'ass for dust.' The strutting guitar break defines the term raunch. Just when you think it's over – it isn't, there's a cutting harmonica solo taking it into the fade.

Side Two
'Lookin' For A Love' (JW Alexander, Zelda Samuels) 3:13
This must have been high on Steve's favourites list; he'd already done it as a guitar-based thrash single from his *Marriott* album. The song itself had started out as the breakthrough hit on Sam Cooke's SAR indie label for Bobby Womack's family group The Valantinos (who also originated 'It's All Over Now' as done by The Rolling Stones), and later it was a solo hit for Bobby Womack himself. Womack was something of a cult figure for the Soul fraternity, the last of the muscular, old-style, gritty blue-collar R&B shouters from an era before the genre sophisticated into insipid, vacuous gloss. The Small Faces take the song tighter, with Steve singing 'I'm lookin' for love' into a slowed-down mid-section, with organ trimmings, a harmonica break, and girl-voice interjections. The J Geils Band had also done a fast, propulsive version of the song.

'Playmates' (Marriott) 3:37
Steve extends a seductive invitation to come around his house and share a cold be; he's got some coke on ice, too, all set to a funky down-home rhythm track with scintillating guitar. They'd been playmates; why not talk over those old memories one more time? A sweet, laidback, unhurried groove

with Steve perfectly at ease with the moment. To writer Roland Schmitt, its 'reflective walking blues is again Memphis bound – but Mac's Hammond makes sure there is a Small Faces element in there, too. Steve's lyrics seem autobiographical, 'we're playmates of the millionaires' seems like the bitter truth behind all the contractual confusion that preceded the release of these recordings' (in his book *The Small Faces And Other Stories*).

'This Song's Just For You' (Marriott, McLagan) 4:06
A sensuously slow 6/8-time Stax groove, his woman's just left, he's all alone and he's missing her already; he kills time with another beer, one more cigarette. There's a definite feel of The Rolling Stones in their Southern country-soul mode, with a deliciously simmering organ break, cracked vocal harmonies and stinging guitars, with a soupçon of Otis Redding's 'I've Been Loving You Too Long.'

'Drive-In Romance' (McLagan, Pidgeon) 5:11
Something closely resembling the 'Find It' riff comes around again, with Ian's keyboard to provide a binding lubrication. He has so many words inside, but you can't make love on a telephone wire – in those days before cellphones, with a slow drifting melodic middle-eight. This is the pain of separation for a touring band. When musicians are endlessly touring, they end up writing songs about the Hotel Hell of endlessly touring.

'Smilin' In Tune' (Marriott, McLagan) 4:44
Strolling pub piano, a vague continuity from 'Queens And Nuns' on Humble Pie's *Street Rats*, in that it's an ironic crying-in-my-beer on-the-road lament, a slinky rhythm punched out by Kenney's 'Honky Tonk Women' drums and limned by little flashes of harmonica, with lyrical reach-backs to earlier days, 'I've been looking for a bookin' on this 'Lazy Sunday' afternoon' and 'it's been light, it got dark, gates were locked in 'Itchycoo Park'.' But there's an optimistic note in 'now we're all back where we all belong, and the four of us can't be wrong.' Albeit without Ronnie Lane!

Related Releases
Lookin' For A Love – Single
'Lookin' For A Love' (Alexander, Samuels) 3:10 b/w **'Kayoed (By Luv)'** (McLagan, Pidgeon) 3:28
Released: August 1977, Atlantic K10983
The A-side was jointly produced by Shel Talmy with 'Kemastri.' The B-side opens with slinky keyboard before Steve confesses he's been 'dirty with some girls in my time', but now he's ready to throw in the towel; as the backing harmonies chant the title, there's an effective tempo-change mid-section, a fine Jimmy McCulloch guitar solo and burbling sax enriching the mix. More Humble Pie that it is Small Faces, but powerful for all that.

Stand By Me – Single
'Stand By Me (Stand By You)' (Marriott) 3:22 b/w **'Hungry And Looking'** (McLagan, Jones, Wills, Marriott) 2:31
Withdrawn single, November 1977, Atlantic K11043
A cool keyboard-led instrumental with keening harmonica, the rare and uncollected B-side echoes the band's earlier forays into free Booker T & The MGs jazz-funk. No posturing or ego-tripping; everything works in perfect synergy, and it ends way too soon.

Sha-La-La-La-Lee' and **'What'cha Gonna Do About It' – The Small Faces Single**
'Sha-La-La-La-Lee' and **'What'cha Gonna Do About It'** b/w **'All Or Nothing'**
Released: 1977, Decca F 13727
Advertised as 'A triple A-side single, of the best known 'Faces' songs – being played on their current tour (see music press for dates).'

78 In The Shade

Personnel:
Steve Marriott: lead guitar, vocals
Rick Wills: bass, backing vocals
Kenney Jones: drums, vocals
Ian McLagan: keyboards, vocals
Plus:
Jimmy McCulloch: guitar
Vicki Brown, Helen Chappelle, Lavinia Rogers, Madeline Bell, Liza Strike, Sam Brown, Jimmy McCulloch, Stephen Smith, Greg Cobb, Nick Webb: backing vocals
Released: September 1978, Atlantic Records K 50468.
No chart placings

Jimmy McCulloch joined the lineup briefly after his tenure with Paul McCartney's Wings. Brothers Jimmy and Jack had moved from Scotland to London in 1966 to record as part of One In A Million; their 'Fredereek Hernando' b/w 'Double Sight' (December 1967, MGM 1370) was described by David Wells as an 'astonishing, skull-busting example of the crash-and-burn end of the British psychedelic spectrum, marrying acid-ravaged lyrics and a psychotropic lead vocal to a blitzkrieg sonic assault led by Jimmy McCulloch, astonishingly just fourteen years old at the time.' Then Jimmy became part of Thunderclap Newman, a group protégé of The Who created and produced by Pete Townshend as a vehicle for Speedy Keen's talents, which was rewarded with a one-off number one hit, 'Something In The Air.' After its demise, Jimmy was a session player and a member of Stone The Crows before joining Paul & Linda in time for their October 1974 single 'Junior's Farm', and to play on their *Wings At The Speed Of Sound* (1976) album, even writing and singing 'Wino Junko' at the close of Side One. Yet his working relationship with the formerly Fab Paul was proving problematic, so he jumped ship in time to catch The Small Faces' final spasm.

Playmates had not been the success it might have been. It was released and promoted across a period of time that coincided with the rise of the 'No More Heroes' punk movement... 'no Elvis, Beatles or the Rolling Stones in 1977' said The Clash by way of a manifesto. No room for The Small Faces either. The Jam might extol the virtues of The Who and The Small Faces, but the general critical consensus was a rejection of all the excesses of Rock's past (while selectively pilfering from it!).

They missed Ronnie Lane's counterbalancing wit and intelligence. His continuing absence was an ache that would not heal. The creative core of the sixties Small Faces lineups had been the Marriott-Lane writing partnership. Since the 1969 split both Ronnie and Steve had gone on to work in other writing partnerships which had yielded solid catalogues of songs, but arguably, neither had produced material as distinctively inventive as 'All

Or Nothing' or 'Tin Soldier.' Now, Ronnie had declined to participate in the reunion, so there would be no new Marriott-Lane songs to fuel the two albums that resulted. Perhaps if Ronnie had been there, the old spark could have been rekindled, and things might have worked out differently. But that must be left to speculation.

The first Small Faces tracks had all been tight, sharp and crammed to the grooves with high energy – no room for self-indulgence, all the virtues that punk claimed to champion. Yet this new Small Faces incarnation had traded that tightness for a more relaxed approach that fed on the American Humble Pie touring schedule, where lengthy instrumental improvisation and virtuoso soloing was very much the desiderata to which to aspire.

This was The Small Faces in a different gear. During the Decca phase, they were part of the Mod subculture. Through the Immediate era, they reflected burgeoning psychedelic awareness. Now, they were adrift. What they represented was nothing more than a kind of skewed nostalgia.

Side One

'Over Too Soon' (Marriott, McLagan) 3:07

Brief studio chat. Then there's a stripped quality about this opener track, with a clipped guitar figure and girl vocalists to back up forcefully behind Steve's slightly phased talk-preaching vocals. And yes ... it is over too soon, in every sense. The track itself, the band reunion that it is part of … and Steve Marriott's life. On the surface, the lyric is about finding love, 'I used to be a loner, don't you know that?', but times slip away, and 'I know that time is limited, 'cause we would've done all the things we did.' Maybe it's just the fore-knowing that adds poignance when the girls chant, 'don't let me feel that it's over too soon.' Yet it carries an unmistakable sting. There's a down-home American edge, a Muscle Shoals feel, with a vicious guitar run across the line 'feel I'm going closer to me, Heh', with Steve's voice almost taking on the characteristics of a female Stax/Volt vocalist. Something he would have been extremely happy about. The records the early Small Faces had adored had been those American Soul R&B singles.

'Too Many Crossroads' (Marriott, McLagan) 2:18

The tired down-and-out feel of Dobie Gray's classic 'Drift Away', and while he's stuck at the crossroads of life and fortune, there's humour in that his sister has joined the circus and his mother has run off with a sailor. The Crossroads carries a special significance in Blues mythology, going back to the Faustian pact attributed to Robert Johnson, and The Small Faces were well aware of playing with those multiple levels of meaning.

'Let Me Down Gently' (McLagan, John Pidgeon) 3:38

Ragged harmonies that recall a gospel Evangelical-Revival tent prayer meeting, with Steve adopting his most American soulman persona, it develops into a kind of Delaney & Bonnie routine with a genuine Southern country-rock feel that has everything to do with Steve's Humble Pie tours – as the girls' back-up voices take on the Blackberries role very effectively, and has little to do with The Small Faces legacy. But this is the band's new default setting.

'Thinkin' About Love' (Wills) 3:46
A slow melodic crying-tears-in-my-beer country blues, with a lovely organ duel break with Jimmy McCulloch's articulate lead guitar. The lovers broke up; now they're back together again. The Small Faces broke up, too. Now they're (briefly) back together. But if potential record-buyers were hoping to find more of the sharp little Mod dynamics of 'All Or Nothing' or the Brit-Psych invention of 'Tin Soldier', they were going to be disappointed. This is not that Small Faces at all.

'Stand By Me (Stand By You)' (Marriott) 3:26
Chiming guitars lead into a mid-paced soul-stirrer with Steve pledging his mutual-support love. Through battered days, they find paradise in each other's arms, with solid guitar and organ interplay behind his hoarse vocals. The instrumental break aches with longing. 'I won't let you down', he promises, with just a suspicion that human frailty will yet thwart his best intentions. It nevertheless takes the album's first side out on a fragile high.

Side Two
'Brown Man Do' (Marriott) 3:02
Stabbing electric piano and all-around organ as Steve does his 'Black Coffee' tribute to the social role played by brown men… and brown women too! Although genuinely well-intentioned, intending to right wrongs and draw attention to the neglected contribution made by what was still considered the 'immigrant community', it could be seen as patronising to the woke awareness. They brush the streets while you're still in your bed and work all night driving your bus, but they also 'sell the best things that get to your head.' It makes you wonder what a Wilson Pickett cover would have sounded like.

'Real Sour' (McLagan, Pidgeon) 3:55
A percussive workout employing Kenney's full drum arsenal, little phrases of jazz-touched piano, and Ian's own slightly phased voice riding chiming down-home country guitars. 'Funny how the joke's on me, but I'm not laughing', he snipes back at his inconstant lover. It's a pleasant enough track that bears little resemblance to anything that the original lineup had ever attempted.

'Soldier' (Joe Brown) 4:04
A lyrically sensitive acoustic anti-militarism song – 'don't ask me what I'm fighting for' – starts out harking back to the group adapting Tim Hardin songs, then builds into an over-embellished gospel-intense climax. It comes

teasingly close to greatness. A solo Steve Marriott version of this Joe Brown song, recorded in 1976 accompanied by the Los Angeles Philharmonic Orchestra, is marginally better. Included on the *Rainy Changes* 2CD set – 'a collection of rare recordings 1973-1991' from the Darlings of Wapping label (2005, DWWLCD03), it's also featured on their *Midnight Of My Life* posthumous compilation (2015, DWWLCD011).

'You Ain't Seen Nothing Yet' (Marriott, McLagan, Wills) 2:59
A vaguely skanking rhythm and a heavy Rolling Stones-style riff, with lead guitar from Jimmy McCulloch. Steve's voice is at its most raggedly raw; Ian plays liquid organ squiggles until soul-voice harmonies feed in support. Taking its title from the Al Jolson 'Jazz Singer' movie quote ('you ain't heard nothin' yet'), this song is nothing remotely similar to the Bachman-Turner Overdrive hit record of a similar title.

'Filthy Rich' (Marriott) 2:39
If I was a rich man, an ironic Cockney vaudeville strut poking fun at his own state of penury. It opens with the kind of *Opportunity Knocks* TV-organ play-in – then a burp, and Steve wishing he was famous like his best mates, conjuring various wealth-fantasies, a dirty great house, half a dozen cars, a private yacht, Italian suits and handmade boots, a girlfriend with Jane Mansfield's (posthumous) tits, with jibes at Mick & Bianca. There's a nice country steel guitar sound, a merry whistle and a mock Elvis talking bit into the communal singalong fade. 'Give the boy the money', Steve quips in an accent that might just recall Don Arden from The Small Faces' earliest days and the sound of a spinning coin. This is fun, with an edge of bitterness.

Related Releases

Filthy Rich – Single
'Filthy Rich' (Marriott) 2:38 b/w **'Over Too Soon'** (McLagan, Marriott) 3:02
Withdrawn single, August 1978, Atlantic K11173

Tin Soldier – Single
'Tin Soldier' (Marriott, Lane) 3:18 b/w **'Tin Soldier (Live)'** 3:24 and **'Rene'** (Marriott, Lane) 4:28
Released July 1980, Virgin VS367

Sha-La-La-La-Lee – Single
'Sha-La-La-La-Lee' b/w **'Whatcha Gonna Do About It'**
One of three singles reissued on the Old Gold label, on OG9344 (October 1983), plus 'Lazy Sunday' b/w 'Tin Soldier' (January 1985, OG9465) and 'Itchycoo Park' b/w 'Here Come The Nice' (January 1985, OG9466). Then, in 1989, a CD-mini and single format 'Itchycoo Park', 'Lazy Sunday' and 'Tin Soldier' (OG6119).

Marriott Solo

Marriott

Personnel:
Steve Marriott: lead guitar, vocals
Dennis Kovarik & Greg Ridley: bass
Mike Baird & Ian Wallace: drums and percussion
Ben Benay & David Spinozza: guitars
David Foster: keyboards
Red Rhodes: pedal steel guitar
Mickey Finn: rhythm guitar
Ernie Watts: saxophone
Released: 1976, A&M Records AMLH 64572, CD release July 2005 Lemon Recordings CD LEM68
No chart placing

Following the sad collapse of Humble Pie, Steve's first solo album was made up of a 'British' side featuring Greg Ridley, including 'Lookin' For A Love', produced by Shel Talmy, and an 'American' side.

Talmy writes:

After he became successful with The Small Faces, I met Steve several times over the years at the band clubs we frequented, mainly the Rev (Revolution) and the Speak (Speakeasy). In 1976, when I was about to produce a solo album by one of my favourite singers, Vicki Brown, premier member of female backing vocalists The Breakaways. Her husband, Joe Brown, a friend of Steve's, asked him to come play guitar and maybe some harp (harmonica).

The sessions for the LP went great, and apparently, Steve was impressed with my production, as he then asked me to do two songs for him that he had always wanted to record – 'Lookin' For A Love', first recorded by Bobby Womack, and 'Don't You Lie To Me', written by Tampa Red and made popular by Chuck Berry. Those two songs were recorded at IBC in 1977. The band for this session was the original Small Faces, with keyboardist Ian Maclagan and drummer Kenny Jones. The exception was Rick Wills on bass, as original bass player Ronnie Lane decided not to participate as he felt ill.

'Lookin' For A Love' was released as an A-side in August 1977 and created a lot of excitement, so Steve then asked me to produce a 'solo' LP. I need to insert here that Steve was now his own worst enemy, featuring his increased usage of drugs that might at one time have resembled a mild wind but now had blown up to gale force. I thought long and hard about accepting but afterwards, realised I shoulda thought longer and harder!

The album was to be made at Steve's house in Chigwell, Essex, with recording taking place in a remote truck parked outside his home. So began one of the most frustrating sagas I and the rest of the band, Mac, Kenney and Rick Wills, had ever experienced!

Allegedly, we were to begin each night's recording at 8 pm, and all of us were making the long daily drive to always arrive on time, as we were all 'pros.' But we never got started before midnight because Steve had some bad habits that took precedence over the four of us and the remote truck crew, so we were cooling our collective heels for hours. After midnight, when we were supposed to begin recording, all we wanted was to head home; the sessions, unfortunately, were a travesty. Steve could barely sing and much of it was off-key. I think we put up with it for three nights when we all agreed it was time to return to 'normal' lives!

The more bluesy American side, recorded at the LA Record Plant between October and December 1975, features slick players with assorted guests. On 15 May 1976, journalist Phil McNeil of the *NME* said 'throughout the album, Steve's lead work is really good – not the stuff of which guitar heroes are made, but, like that other East End Rocker, Marc Bolan, touchingly intuitive and surprisingly effective.'

Steve did a promotional tour of America with a pick-up band named The All-Stars but was never happy to be out front as a solo artist, as explained by Rick Wills to the *NME* on 30 April 1977: '... he was like a mercenary, paying everybody's wages. He came home pissed off. He went through it and said he'd never do it again.'

Side One ('British' Side)

'East-Side Struttin'' (Finn, Marriott) 4:47

As though, once released from the high pressures of Humble Pie, Steve had recharged his creative energies, this is struttin' with considerable brashness, 'the streets ain't paved with silver, in fact, they ain't paved at all.'

'Lookin' For A Love' (Alexander, Samuels) 3:47

NME reviewer Phil McNeil calls this 'the only one really superb track... where the British team attempts to play like the American guys and comes up with a racing R&B track featuring great Lesleyed guitar from the old feedback merchant.'

'Help Me Through The Day' (Leon Russell) 5:55

Anguished vocals are underscored by just jazzy keyboard, joined by tasteful guitar quivers and a steady drum throb. The song had previously been done with strings by Freddie King in 1973.

'Midnight Rollin'' (Geoff Stephens, Marriott) 3:30

An unlikely collaboration with the prolific commercial songwriter behind not only Dave Berry's 'The Crying Game' and Manfred Mann's 'Semi-Detached

Suburban Mr James', but The New Vaudeville Band project too! Yet Steve seems effortlessly at home on this rollicking anthem about being on the road with a rock 'n' roll band.

'Wham Bam Thank You Ma'am' (Lane, Marriott) 3:54
This Small Faces song was also the opening track on a 1999 double-CD compilation *Clear Through The Night* (NMC Music Pilot 22) where it's credited to Steve Marriott's All Stars.

Side Two ('American' Side)
'Star In My Life' (Wallace, Marriott) 3:30
Also issued as a single b/w 'Midnight Rollin'' (AMS 7230) where the production credits specify Kenny Kerner and Richie Wise, there are electro squonks, gospel voices and country touches. Greg Ridley and Carlena Williams are also present and correct.

'Are You Lonely For Me Baby' (Bert Berns) 3:52
A composition from the writer responsible for 'Hang On Sloopy' and 'Under The Boardwalk', originally recorded in 1966 by Freddie Scott. Steve takes the song with jerky stabbing instrumentation, spry horns and gospel voice backup.

'You Don't Know Me' (Cindy Walker, Eddy Arnold) 4:56
Benefitting from the lusher production textures of the American studio, this is the classic country-soul song best known for its Ray Charles interpretation, which was also done by Elvis Presley, among countless others. Steve invests it with a more gutsy soulful treatment with weaving saxophone.

'Late Night Lady' (Ridley, Marriott, Hinkley) 3:00
Funk wah-wah rhythms that reunite elements of Humble Pie with Ernie Watts' sax. Steve can't find his late-night lady despite looking here, there and everywhere while he's sucking on the sweet vine – in a lyric reference going back to Greg's song on the 1970 *Humble Pie* album. As a solo project, this is still very much a collective effort.

'Early Evening Light' (Marriott) 3:48
Swirling strings cushion a sensitive, heartfelt lyric, 'I already said goodbye to all the seasons that I knew, if I gotta love somebody, baby, why in heaven's name can't it be you', that builds with the addition of gospel voices into an impassioned repeating climax.

Packet Of Three – Steve Marriott
Personnel:
Steve Marriott: vocals, guitar, producer
Jim Leverton: bass

Fellon Williams: drums
Released: 1984 on Aura AUL729
Recorded live at Dingwalls, 6 July 1984
No chart placing
Tracklisting: Side One: 'What'cha Gonna Do About It' (Potter, Samwell) 3:21, 'Bad Moon Rising' (Fogerty) 6:00, 'All Shook Up' (Otis Blackwell, Elvis Presley) 3:03, 'The Fixer' (Clempson, Ridley, Marriott) 7:00
Side Two: 'All Or Nothing' (Marriott, Lane) 5:12, 'Five Long Years' (Eddie Boyd) 7:17, 'I Don't Need No Doctor' (Ashford, Simpson, Armstead) 11:04
Extended Reissue: 'What'cha Gonna Do About It' (4:16), 'Fool For A Pretty Face' (5:19)
'Shame On You' (4:06), 'Bad Moon Rising' (6:31), 'The Cockney Rhyme' (0:47), 'All Shook Up' (3:17), 'The Fixer' (7:24), 'All Or Nothing' (5:48), 'Five Long Years' (7:42)
'Thirty Days In The Hole' (10:57), 'I Don't Need No Doctor' (12:46), 'Big Train Stop At Memphis' (5:24), 'Walkin' The Dog' (4:03)

Wary of managers and suspicious of record companies, Steve commenced a number of small-scale projects, retreating to more informal performances in small venues, bringing an up-close-and-personal intimacy that the huge American stadia of Humble Pie days did not permit. It returned him to the kind of gigs he'd once played with Steve Marriott's Moments

Pete Frampton recalled how they got together to play a one-off date at the Half Moon Pub in Putney. 'This is the first time we played live since I left the Pie. Unfortunately, we were to lose Steve the following year. It's the only time we played 'Natural Born Bugie' live. Humble Pie never played it while I was in the band. It was a special night.' His 1994 album *Peter Frampton* (Relativity REL 475876-2) included 'Out Of The Blue', a track co-written with – and sung by, Steve Marriott, a tragic past-echo recorded during a 1991 hook-up.

The *Packet Of Three* album was reissued in expanded form in 1991 as *Dingwalls 6.7.84* (Mau Mau MAUCD609). This album is a live souvenir from what Johnny Black, in *Q* magazine in January 1992, calls the late career phase of 'a hard-working entertainer and all-round diamond geezer.'

Another Walkman-recorded *Packet Of Three* album captured at Finsbury Park's Sir George Robey, complete with chirpy between-song banter, was issued as *Live 23-10-85* by Zeus CD2.

The Legendary Majik Mijits – The Majik Mijits

Personnel:
Steve Marriott: guitar, vocals
Ronnie Lane: bass guitar, vocals
Mick Green: guitar
Mick Weaver: keyboards
Jim Leverton: bass guitar
Dave Hynes: drums
Sam Brown: backing vocals
Producers Steve Marriot and Ronnie Lane
Recorded 1981, Released: 2000, NMC Music PILOT58
No chart placing

In 1981, Steve made a deliberate effort to contact a now wheelchair-bound Ronnie Lane, and they convened a pick-up band including the mighty Zoot Money and sax-player Mel Collins, with Jim Leverton (bass), the legendary Mick Green (guitar), Mick Weaver (keyboards) and Dave Hynes (drums, 1937-2000). There was Sam Brown on backing vocals, but no new Marriott-Lane originals on the subsequent album – *The Legendary Majik Mijits* – which lay unreleased until 2000 when it was rescued by the NMC Music label, with bonus track 'All Or Nothing' recorded live from the Bridgehouse Pub in Canning Town.

A subsequent edition by Alchemy Entertainment expanded it to a 2CD set with nineteen outtakes or previously unissued tracks:

'Lonely No More' (Marriott) 2:18

An easy jog-along song with a nagging guitar motif, Steve's sat here by the fire with my dog on the floor, 'got a woman, got a kid, got a whole lot more', as though he's finally reconciled to the vicissitudes of life, no stress, no straining for effect, with a comfortable handclap-driven organ groove, and a hint of sax in the fade.

The song is a gentler reconfiguribng of 'Lottie And The Charcoal Queen' on the last Humble Pie album.

'Chicken (If The Cap Fits)' (Lane) 3:51

Quivering keyboards, jumpy rhythms with a honking sax solo, as Ronnie taunts 'you're chick-chick-chicken', with a barrage of barbed vitriol aimed in a tongue-in-cheek manner. Although the object of his derision is not specified, clues include the stink of smack and rock 'n' roll and a total absence of balls, on the principle that the target will self-identify – hence 'if the cap fits.'

The motive on this album is not to set the world on fire, not to compete or score points, just to have some good-natured fun making music with an old friend.

And curiously, that's all it needs.

'Toe Rag' (Marriott) 1:09
Acoustic hoe-down nursery rhyme sung to Steve's two-year-old child, 'I'm your dad… that's your mum, you're my son and this is my guitar – keep yer bleedin' hands off!', affectionately happy-bad and good-and-sad. 'Oi, no – let it go, put it down, be told!' Rock stars can be embarrassing when they start serenading their offspring, but this is a fun glimpse into Marriott's Sawbridgeworth domesticity. In years to come, son Toby (born 20 February 1976) would become a respected musician in his own right with The Strays.

'Bomber's Moon' (Lane) 3:07
Using a title that borrows a term from the blitz, Ronnie tries on his 'Slim Chance' mode one more time for a nostalgic glance back. He's thinking about 'how young we were', with time held in the palm of his hand like quicksilver, now he's 'trying to catch the way it was between us.' Superficially, the story is about crossing the Rio Grande, but conclusions about the reunion of the magic midgets are inevitable.

'Birthday Girl' (Marriott) 2:52
Steve with a big bump and grind tribute to a lady who they say is 50; she says 45, but he knows she's 57. It slows to a piano trickle, then erupts into a blaring sax solo as Steve hits the vocal highs for which he's deservedly renowned on the 'Happy Birthday' chorus. It closes with a burlesque flourish.

'Last Tango In NATO' (Lane) 3:16
Bouncing funk bass, snarling guitar and a genuine doomsday end-of-the-world tango as Ronnie wakes to find the sky is black, 'I knew it, I deja-vu-ed it.' Lest we forget, this was still a time of Cold War superpower confrontation, paid for by 'your tax and VAT.' Although Ronnie doubtless had CND No-Nukes sympathies, this track plays it more as ironic satire than protest.

'How Does It Feel?' (Marriott) 2:43
Slinky crawling blues that opens 'I hope that you burn in hell', and seems to be aimed at the music industry apparatchiks who had systematically screwed him up across the years, 'you didn't care if I was dead or alive' as long as they got their 90%. The vehemence is blunted by a dee-down-dee-dee-down chorus and a screw-do-wop reprise that affectionately harks back to more innocent fifties rock 'n' roll days.

'That's The Way It Goes' (Lane) 2:45
He's got two black eyes and a broken nose. He's got a dirty mouth and a filthy mind. But this Cockney knees-up is a cheerful survivor's celebration. The organ solo is interrupted by a yell of 'Green Bottle' that then extends into what resembles a twangy Jew's harp sequence until Steve yells 'all together' into the sing-along fade.

'You Spent It' (Marriott, Leverton) 3:34
A strident, moody rocker that rides a strong guitar riff that owes a debt to Joe Walsh's 'Life's Been Good To Me (So Far)' while it also sounds like something left over from Steve's Humble Pie days. 'I don't care what I had when I was Jack the Lad', he asserts as he inserts a cutting harmonica solo and bewails the woman who spent it all while he held the bank balance. A storming back-to-form R&B workout that proves Steve could still be Jack the Lad when he so chose.

'Son Of Stanley Lane' (Lane) 2:13
Stanley Lane was Ronnie's Forest Gate lorry driver father, who worked long hours and then nursed Ronnie's mother Elsie as she fought her own cruel battle with multiple sclerosis. Ronnie takes an echoey rockabilly sound with Trad horn interjections to declare, 'one of these days, I'm gonna be famous, they'll put a blue plaque outside my basement.' And yes, maybe there should be a blue plaque outside 385 Romfort Road, where Ronnie spent his childhood years.

'Be The One' (Marriott, Leverton) 2:29
An unambitious plea to a lover to be there for him, taken at an easy demo-quality pace, the vocals are off-hand, rising only into the middle-eight and lifted further by a raunchy sax solo. It's a pity that this album wasn't better. It's a pity that their last collaboration could not have lived up to our wildest expectations. But it is what it is. Two old friends trading songs in an informal, relaxed, home-taping way.

'Ruby' (Lane) 3:35
The album's regular mix of strummed guitar carried on a bed of oozing organ, although Ronnie's voice is not really at its best as he declares his love for 'Ruby.' There's a sense of painful vulnerability in the song's flawed delivery, which creates an unintended intimacy. This indicates another factor determining the album's fate: that Ronnie's deteriorating health made any live promotion impossible. So, the tapes were simply shelved until their rediscovery and eventual release.

'All Or Nothing' (Marriott, Lane) 2:14
A live reprise, recorded during a Canning Town gig and tacked into the album as a bonus track. It becomes almost an audience singalong, closing with Steve saying, 'thank you kindly, god bless ya and keep you' and over-enthusiastic applause. As the compere punningly announces 'the great Mariarty!'

Rod Stewart Solo During The Faces Era

An Old Raincoat Won't Ever Let You Down – Rod Stewart

Personnel:
Rod Stewart: vocals, guitar
Ronnie (Good Looking) Wood: bass, guitars, harmonica
Martin Pugh: guitars
Martin Quittenton: acoustic guitar
Ian McLagan: piano, organ
Michael 'Micky' Waller (ex Jeff Beck Group): drums
Released: November 1969 as The Rod Stewart Album Mercury SR61237(US), and February 1970 as Vertigo 847-200VTY (UK)
Produced by Rod with Lou Reizner at London's Olympic and Lansdowne studios.
Highest chart placing: US: 139 (Billboard)
Tradcklisting: Side One: 'Street Fighting Man' (Jagger, Richard) 5:04, 'Man Of Constant Sorrow' (Trad: arranged by Rod) 2:30, 'Blind Prayer' (Stewart) 4:36, 'Handbags And Gladrags' (Mike d'Abo) 4:22
Side Two: 'An Old Raincoat Won't Ever Let You Down' (Stewart) 3:02, 'I Wouldn't Ever Change A Thing' (Stewart) 4:45, 'Cindy's Lament' (Stewart) 4:28, 'Dirty Old Town' (Ewan MacColl) 3:40

As early as June 1969, a try-out lineup for what would become The Faces played at the Cambridge University Ball under the flag-of-convenience name Quiet Melon, with Rod Stewart and Ron Wood allied to Ian McLagan, Ronnie Lane and Kenney Jones, plus guesting musicians Art Wood – Ron's older brother – and Kim Gardner from The Creation. An EP, *Art Wood's Quiet Melon*, was eventually released in 1995 (Lost Moment Records LMCD051), with two Art Wood numbers, 'Diamond Joe' and 'Engine 4444' plus a 3:47-minute group 'Instrumental.'

But in the meantime, Rod had also signed a separate deal as a solo artist for £1,300, with the Mercury label. This album, which took a week and a half to record, was issued in the USA first, where it was considered Rod had established a following of sorts from the Jeff Beck Group tours.

Although it's impossible to top the rumbling menace of The Rolling Stones' own version, his cover of 'Street Fighting Man' achieves something of its own dirty bedraggled sound; less a palace revolution, more a minor skirmish, it was issued as a December 1969 single. Rod plays acoustic guitar on 'Man Of Constant Sorrow', a song Bob Dylan recorded on his debut 1962 album, an LP that had a life-changing effect on young Rod. 'No other album has worked on me this way since', he recalls in his *Rod* autobiography. Ron Wood's fills are hardly subtle but don't detract when stacked against Rod's conviction. Writer and former Manfred Mann vocalist Mike d'Abo plays rippling piano arrangement on 'Handbags And Gladrags', which was issued as a May 1970 American single. In March 1968, Rod Stewart recorded another Mike d'Abo song 'Little Miss Understood' as a failed single, Immediate IM060, b/w 'So Much To Say' co-written by Mike with Rod.

'Dirty Old Town' is a song from the politically radical folk clubs, uniting 'angry young man' urban romance with working-class lyricism. Written in 1949 by Ewan MacColl (father of Kirsty MacColl), it is set amid the gasworks and grimy old Lancashire industrial canal system. The Dubliners had done the song before, and The Pogues would make it a minor hit single in 1985. Rod had been familiar with the song for years, and he retains the song's folk purity, while Ron Wood adds harmonica.

Martin Pugh plays guitar on the album; he'd played alongside Martin Quittenton in Worthing-based prog-blues band Steamhammer on their eponymous June 1969 debut album, which is sometimes retitled *Reflection* (CBS S-63611). Rod had seen Steamhammer play at The Marquee, and he'd been impressed.

The original *NME* review points out that 'Rod 'The Mod' Stewart commands a lot of respect among pop people for his unusual blues voice, and this album does him full justice.'

Gasoline Alley – Rod Stewart

Personnel:
Rod Stewart: lead vocals, acoustic guitar
Ronnie Lane: bass, backing vocals
Ronnie Wood: lead, bass and acoustic guitars
Kenney Jones & Mick Waller: drums
Ian McLagan: Hammond organ, piano
Martin Quittenton: acoustic guitar
Released: 12 June 1970, Vertigo 6360-500 (UK), Mercury SR-61264 (USA)
Produced by Rod Stewart with Lou Reizner at Morgan Studio, London
Highest chart position: US: 27 (Billboard).
Tracklisting: Side One: 'Gasoline Alley' (Stewart, Wood) 4:00, 'It's All Over Now' (Bobby & Shirley Womack) 6:23, 'Only A Hobo' (Bob Dylan) 4:20, 'My Way Of Giving' (Lane, Marriott) 4:10
Side Two: 'Country Comforts' (Elton John, Bernie Taupin) 4:45, 'Cut Across Shorty' (Wayne P Walker, Marijohn Wilkin) 6:30, 'Lady Day' (Rod Stewart) 4:15, 'Jo's Lament' (Rod Stewart) 3:35, 'You're My Girl (I Don't Want To Discuss It)' (Beth Beatty, Dick Cooper, Ernie Shelby) 4:30
CD Bonus Track: 'It's All Over Now' single edit (Womack, Womack) 3:35

The sixties was a decade that told a story in ways that other decades do not. The tip-over from the sixties into the first few years of the seventies was a firebreak moment in the history of Rock. The landscape was changing irrevocably in unsuspected ways. The Beatles were no longer there. Brian Jones, Jimi Hendrix, Otis Redding, Mama Cass Elliot and Jim Morrison were all gone; Syd Barrett, Peter Green and Brian Wilson were teetering on the edge. Rock 'n' roll must be the Saturn of the arts – it exacts the very highest price from the children who serve it most ably and loyally. The Small Faces were gone too, while artists who had been hanging around through the dying embers of the previous decade, overshadowed by events, were sensing the opening drumbeat of a new epoch and finding their moment to shine.

David Bowie found new guises beyond the one-hit-wonder status he'd briefly enjoyed with 'Space Oddity' in September 1969. Marc Bolan had flirted with the charts as part of John's Children, then went underground with the cult Tyrannosaurus Rex but only broke big with 'Ride A White Swan' at the end of 1970. Paul Raven arrived in a new incarnation as Gary Glitter. Elton John had been releasing a steady stream of critically approved singles but only hit big with 'Your Song' in early 1971.

And then there was Rod Stewart, who had been on the sidelines, temptingly close, the dishevelled rake slumped against the cracked concrete wall on this album's centrefold. 'A rebel with a Post Office savings account, the beatnik who went back to his mum's' as he autobiographically admits. He only really happened with the onset of the seventies. And this is where his career begins to pick up momentum. 'The offer from Mercury Records to go into a studio and make an album of my own was a last shot at the big time', he says in retrospect, 'screw this up and who knows? It would probably be cruise ships forever after...'

The Small Faces had specialised in a series of tightly constructed hit singles, from two minutes in length and seldom exceeding three minutes. Singles were still important, although that market had been in part ceded to teeny bands, while more grown-up record buyers opted increasingly for albums. This was the new arena for bands to compete.

The title track is an intriguing blend of acoustic and slide guitar, with reviewer Richard Williams opining, 'Rod's voice is an extraordinary tool, seemingly shot to pieces and at times barely seeming to exist, yet retaining a power and depth of communication with which few can compare.' There's a Blues earthiness here that proves just how effective his voice could be when 'yearnin' for my own backyard', with what *NME* terms 'the splendidly evocative guitar' creating 'a jangle of inventive and unusual chords, setting the pattern for what is to follow.' There's another example of Rod's 'headful of Dylan', where the *NME* reviewer allows Rod 'his downtrodden vocal timbre to work wonders' on this early Dylan lament from his *Witmark Demos 1962-1964* catalogue, 'only a hobo, but one more is gone, leavin' nobody to sing his sad song, leavin' nobody to carry him home', with both song and interpretation falling on the correct side of bathos. 'My Way Of Giving' usefully supplements Ronnie's songwriter royalties while throwing up unfortunate comparisons between Steve Marriott's original vocals and Rod's own more rounded version, from which the latter inevitably loses out. Ian closes the track with some ornamental organ doodles.

'Country Comforts' was written by the struggling songwriter formerly known as Reg Dwight, and it's the song's first recorded outing, although there would be another in September by Orange Bicycle before Elton's own version appeared on his third studio album *Tumbleweed Connection* (October 1970).

Both factions of what had been The Small Faces were drawing on the same essential roots influences – Chuck Berry, obviously, plus old shared soul, blues and R&B favourites, as well as rock and rockabilly pioneers. Rod always had a penchant for the smooth tones of Sam Cooke. But they all drew on Eddie Cochran too; Humble Pie would do Eddie's 'C'mon Everybody' on their *Smokin'* album, while Rod got in first with his humorous modern retelling of Aesop's fable 'about the turtle and the hare' with a country boy named Shorty beating city boy Dan to win Miss Lucy's hand, showing country cunning triumphing over city slickness. The song would be done live on The Faces *Coast To Coast: Overture And Beginners* album, while Rod and Ron Wood would reunite to perform it again as part of his *MTV Unplugged* session and its 1993 spin-off album.

The album was recorded in two weeks on a tight schedule, on a 24-track Ampex machine. Lou Reizner was essentially a back-seat producer who allowed Rod his head. So, credit must be apportioned accordingly. *Melody Maker*, on 12 September 1970, welcomed the album, 'with *Gasoline Alley* Rod Stewart has given us a statement to rank with his first solo album... as an expression of personal truths and experiences', and *NME* proclaimed it as Rod's 'coming of age.' While less grandly, on the liner notes, Ron Wood said, 'everyone had a good time, nobody came without being invited, and no one arrived who didn't come.' Yes, exactly.

Every Picture Tells A Story – Rod Stewart

Personnel:
Rod Stewart: lead vocals, acoustic guitar
Ronnie Lane: bass, backing vocals
Ronnie Wood: lead, bass and pedal steel guitars
Kenney Jones & Mick Waller: drums
Ian McLagan: Hammond organ
Martin Quittenton: acoustic guitar
Ray Jackson: mandolin (credited as mandolin player in Lindisfarne)
Danny Thompson: upright bass
additional 'vocal abrasives' by Maggie Bell, Long John Baldry, Madeline Bell & Friends
Released: 28 May 1971, Mercury 6338-063 (UK), Mercury SRM 1-609 (USA)
Produced by Rod Stewart at Morgan Studio, London
Highest chart position: UK: 1, US: 1 (Billboard)
Tracklisting: Side One: 'Every Picture Tells A Story' (Stewart, Wood) 5:58, 'Seems Like A Long Time' (Theodore 'Ted' Anderson) 4:00, 'That's All Right/ Amazing Grace' (Arthur Crudup/ traditional) 6:02, 'Tomorrow Is A Long Time' (Dylan) 3:44
Side Two: 'Maggie May' (Stewart, Quittenton) 5:46, 'Mandolin Wind' (Stewart) 5:32, '(I Know) I'm Losing You' (Cornelius Grant, Eddie Holland, Norman Whitfield) 5:22, 'Reason To Believe' (Tim Hardin) 4:07

Tim Hardin's song 'Reason To Believe' was the original A-side (Mercury 6058-097) – The Small Faces had already recorded two of Tim's songs, but airplay and consumer reaction soon fell in favour of the intended flipside, 'Maggie May', and it soared. For the chart published 9 October 1971, it effortlessly nudged last week's chart-topper aside (The Tams' old reissue 'Hey Girl Don't Bother Me') to claim the top slot for five weeks, eventually toppled by Slade's stomping 'Coz I Luv You.' And Rod had arrived, big time. At one point, he occupied the number one spot on both singles and albums charts on both sides of the Atlantic.

To put things into perspective, there had been a traditional scouse 'Maggie May' song about a different 'docker's delight', a forty-second fragment of which The Beatles tacked onto the end of the *Let It Be* album. And much later the 'wake up Maggie' chant was used by protesters demonstrating against Prime Minister Thatcher's policies, something that Conservative voting Rod might not have fully approved of. Meanwhile, this is the song that made Rod a star.

Elsewhere, Maggie Bell and Long John Baldry join vocal responses in the album's compulsive uniquely-constructed title song that dispenses with rhyme or chorus, a lesson in technique learned from Bob Dylan, yet it builds into a beat travelling-man narrative of time spent in Paris, Rome, and across the Peking ferry, 'my body stunk but I kept my funk.' His songwriting seldom got better. There's an obligatory Dylan cover. Reviewer Richard Williams wrote that 'Rod has such a true feeling for acoustic music, and the instrumental sound he extracts from his musicians is something totally new. These songs have the feeling of honest autobiography which he extends into the compositions of others, like Dylan's 'Tomorrow Is A Long Time'.'

Related Releases

(I Know) I'm Losing You – Single

'(I Know) I'm Losing You' b/w **'Mandolin Wind'**

(Mercury 73244)

1971 single credited to Rod Stewart With The Faces, which reached US number 24. The B-side is credited to Rod Stewart only.

Never A Dull Moment – Rod Stewart

Personnel:

Rod 'Stewarty' Stewart: vocals, acoustic guitar

Ronnie 'It wasn't me' Lane: bass on 'True Blue' and 'Angel'

Ronnie Wood: electric and acoustic guitars, slide and pedal steel guitars

Kenney 'You Queer' Jones: drums on 'True Blue'

Micky 'I'm not feeling very well today' Waller: additional drums

Ian 'I'm Fantastic' McLagan: Hammond organ, piano

Martin Quittenton: acoustic guitar

Ray Jackson: mandolin

Spike 'I prefer Jazz' Heatley: upright bass
Neemoi 'Speedy' Aquaye: congas
Gordon Huntley: steel guitar
Dick 'Tricky Dicky' Powell: violin
Pete Sears: piano, bass
Released: 21 July 1972, Mercury 6499-153 (UK), Mercury SRM 1-646 (USA)
Produced by Rod Stewart at Morgan and Olympic Studio, London
Highest chart position: UK: 1, US: 2 (Billboard)
Tracklisting: Side One: 'True Blue' (Stewart, Wood) 3:28, 'Lost Paraguayos' (Stewart, Wood) 3:58, 'Mama, You Been On My Mind' (Dylan) 4:26, 'Italian Girls' (Stewart, Wood) 5:01
Side Two: 'Angel' (Hendrix) 4:04, 'Interludings' (Art Wood) 0:40, 'You Wear It Well' (Stewart, Quittenton) 4:21, 'I'd Rather Go Blind' (Billy Foster, Ellington Jordan) 3:53 'Twisting The Night Away' (Sam Cooke) 3:15

Every Picture Tells A Story had created high expectations, and largely, *Never A Dull Moment* delivered. The *Melody Maker* review judges 'if you want comparisons, let's just say that this set is a little more relaxed, the sound a little less dense than previously. Really, though. It's pretty much the mixture as before, which is reassuring.' The album sleeve shows Rod morosely slumped in an armchair in a 'bring a bottle over here' state. His line on 'Lost Paraguayos' 'Darling, please don't cry, you know I wouldn't tell you no lie' is followed by a self-deprecating laugh.

Although the instrumental arrangement of 'You Wear It Well' suggests that this track was styled to be the album's 'Maggie May' follow-up, this letter-form story song is strong enough to stand without such comparisons. Edited down to 4:09 and issued as a single b/w 'Lost Paraguayos', it hit number one in the UK and number 13 in the USA. While 'Interludings' is a brief showcase for Ronnie's acoustic guitar written by Art Wood, who, as well as being Ronnie's older brother, was the leader of cult Mod group The Artwoods.

Every time I use Angel tube station on the Northern Line, I think of this lovely Jimi Hendrix song 'Angel' 'about the sweet love between the moon and the deep blue sea', which Rod respectfully reinterprets, double-tracking voice with touches of xylophone. Speedy plays congas. For a *Top Of The Pops* performance of 'Angel', Ronnie Lane was absent, so he was replaced by a life-size cardboard cut-out. 'Angel' became the album's second single b/w 'What Made Milwaukee Famous', a maudlin alcoholic's non-album track written by Glenn Sutton and first done as a country rocker for Jerry Lee Lewis.

Smiler – Rod Stewart
Personnel:
Rod Stewart: vocals
Ron Wood: bass guitar, acoustic and electric guitars
Martin Quittenton: acoustic guitar
Spike Heatley & Willie Weeks: bass guitar

Elton John: piano
Pete Sears: piano, harpsichord, celeste
Ian McLagan: Hammond organ
Kenney Jones, Micky Waller and Andy Newmark: drums
Ray Jackson: mandolin
Ric Grech & Dick Powell: violin
plus The Memphis Horns, The Chris Barber Jazz Band and The Tropic Isles Steel Band
Released: 4 October 1974, Mercury 9104-001 (UK), Mercury SRM 1-1017 (USA)
Produced by Rod Stewart at Morgan Studios and The Wick (Ronnie Wood's Richmond home studio)
Highest chart position: UK: 1, US: 13
Tracklisting: Side One: 'Sweet Little Rock 'N' Roller' (Berry) 3:44, 'Lochinvar' (P Sears) 0:30
'Farewell' (Quittenton, Stewart) 4:31, 'Sailor' (Stewart, Wood) 3:38, 'Bring It On Home To Me/ You Send Me' (Sam Cooke) 4:02, 'Let Me Be Your Car' (John, Taupin) 5:02
Side Two: '(You Make Me Feel Like) A Natural Man' (Goffin, King, Wexler) 3:54, 'Dixie Toot' (Stewart, Wood) 3:30, 'Hard Road' (Vanda, Young) 4:30, 'I've Grown Accustomed To Her Face' (Lerner, Loewe) 1:32, 'Girl From The North Country' (Dylan) 3:54, 'Mine For Me' (McCartney) 4:02

The Buxton Festival happened over the 5-6 July weekend at Booth Farm in Derbyshire and included Humble Pie as 'Special Guest Stars' on the same Saturday bill as The Faces (with Tetsu). The Humble Pie set included 'What'cha Gonna Do About It', 'Thirty Days In The Hole', 'C'mon Everybody' and 'Let Me Be Your Lovemaker.' When The Faces refused to return for an encore, the stage was bombarded with bottles.

The front cover of this album's gatefold sleeve begins Rod's flirtation with tartan. At the same time, his involvement with The Faces reduces here. Ronnie Lane is gone. Kenney Jones and Ian McLagan play here and there. While Ron Wood hung on, despite having released his first solo album – *I've Got My Own Album To Do* in September 1974 (Warner Bros K56065 UK, Warner Bros BS2817 USA), which included contributions from Ian McLagan, Mick Taylor, Rod Stewart, Keith Richards, a song co-written with George Harrison ('Far East Man'), and another by Gig Gilbeaus of The Flying Burrito Brothers called 'Big Bayou.' Woody's voice is all scratched up, but that's part of its charm. A conflicted Nick Kent, in *NME* on 14 September 1974, writes, 'this album is awful – but I like it'). He followed it a year later with *Now Look* (BS2872), which also features Kenney and Ian McLagan.

Ron Wood had helped write 'It's Only Rock 'N' Roll (But I Like It)', a song built up around his throwaway quote for The Rolling Stones. Ron put the song together on guitar, with Jagger (vocals), David Bowie (background vocals), Kenney Jones (drums) and Willie Weeks (bass). It was recorded at Ron's Richmond house, 'The Wick.' Some guitar parts were later added by Keith, who left some of Wood's twelve-string on it. Bowie and Weeks remained on the final product. Although Ron received no writing credit for 'Its Only Rock 'N' Roll' he did get invited to join the Stones. Following Mick Taylor's departure from the band in December 1974, he recorded and toured with The Stones while still technically a member of The Faces until The Faces announced their split in December 1975, freeing him to be confirmed as a full member of The Rolling Stones.

Meanwhile, for this album, Rod's 'voice does wear a smile, but it's most like the smile of Smokey Robinson's jester… it seems to be a mask' says *Melody Maker* reviewer 'GB.' It's an album spattered with contributions from Elton John and Paul McCartney, which indicates the status level Rod's name had achieved. Yet it's an indication of what was to come. Rod's next album – *Atlantic Crossing* (August 1975) constituted a decisive break with the past, recorded in American studios using American musicians. Middle-of-the-road anthems, absurd disco flirtations, blonde bombshells… and an eventual knighthood loomed.

Ian sums up, 'Steve (Marriott) needed to feel you were agreeing with him or he couldn't function, being a very insecure person on many levels. But I never felt Rod needed us in that way. He was cocksure.' For what it's worth, in my opinion, Rod The Mod did his best work during his period with The Faces. And, quoting a line from a TV sitcom of the time, I'm unanimous in this.

Compilations

The Small Faces: The Singles A's & B's

Released 1990, See For Miles SEECD293. No chart placings

It comprehensively gathers all twenty-eight sides, although *Record Collector* magazine says that 'considering that The Small Faces only released three studio LPs in the sixties, it's safe to regard the flood of repackages that have surfaced over the years with some suspicion.'

A 1989 compilation – *Pop Into The Sixties* (See For Miles SEE243), reaches back even further to resurrect Steve Marriott's 'Give Her My Regards', which *Record Collector* terms 'his best teenage Adam Faith impression.'

The Best Of Small Faces

Released: 1995, Summit Records SUMCD 4001. No chart placings

Mike Oldfield wrote a touching obituary to Ronnie Lane in *The Guardian* on 6 June 1997 in which he praised the Marriott-Lane writing partnership as 'they never tried to change the world but noted its idiosyncrasies with wry humour and compelling emotion in songs that have lingered in a fond afterglow.' Inevitably, there had already been a number of 'Best Of' compilations, but arguably, this 16-track collection gathering fourteen Marriott-Lane songs alongside 'Every Little Bit Hurts' and 'Sha-La-La-La-Lee' is the definitive one.

The Immediate Years – The Small Faces

Released 1995 (Germany), Charly Records CDIMM BOX1. No chart placings

An 86-track 4CD box-set that opens with 'You Really Got Me' and 'Money Money' by The Moments, then contains every Small Faces recording ever issued by Immediate Records in England, Germany or the US, with mono and stereo mixes, a 52-page band history booklet, family tree and track-by-track notes from the compiler. A previously unreleased lively Booker T-style instrumental, 'The War Of The World' (3:39), is included – likely a studio jam that ends messily – plus instrumental takes of 'Tin Soldier' and 'The Hungry Intruder', alternate mixes of 'Red Balloon' and what is retitled 'Donkey Rides, A Penny, A Glass' with brass overdub, and 'Wham Bam, Thank You Ma'm' using guide vocals only. After a couple of false starts, the slower instrumental 'The Pig's Trotters' (3:09) is a showcase for Ian's fluid organ improvisation that later evolved into Humble Pie's 'Wrist Job.' What John Harris, in *Q Magazine* in January 1996, calls 'as exhaustive a dossier of the band's truly purple period as could be imagined.'

Long Agos And Worlds Apart: A Tribute To The Small Faces – Various Artists

Released: 27 August 1996, Nice Records NYCE 001CD

Tracklisting: Side One: 'Understanding' – Primal Scream featuring P.P. Arnold (5:03), 'I Can't Make It' – Dodgy (2:58), 'It's Too Late' – B.L.O.W. (3:32), 'My

Mind's Eye' – Northern Uproar (2:05), 'I've Got Mine' – Mantaray (3:48), 'Afterglow' – Changing Man (3:54), 'The Universal' – Sixty-Foot Dolls (3:37), 'Become Like You' – Granny Takes A Trip (1:54)
Side Two: 'Song Of A Baker' – Ocean Colour Scene (3:14),'Rollin' Over' – Whiteout (2:13), 'Almost Grown' – Kenney J All Stars (3:00), 'Talk To You' – Hyperglo (3:59), 'Here Comes The Nice' – The Buzzcocks (2:55), 'That Man' – Ride (3:17), 'Autumn Stone' – Gene (4:40)
In July 1986, at the end of a Rod Stewart Wembley Stadium concert, there was a one-off Faces reunion, with Ron Wood, Ian, Kenney, and Ronnie Lane 'terribly frail now and with a cane, but smartly suited and happy.' This was a well-intentioned fund-raising tribute project for Ronnie, who was struggling to pay Texan medical bills for his multiple sclerosis treatment. The Kenney J All Stars were Kenney Jones with Marco Nelson, Mick Talbot and Paul Weller, while Changing Man was also Mick Talbot with Steve McNerney of The Pleasers.

The Decca Anthology 1965-1967

Released: 1996, Deram Records 844-583-1. No chart placings

The Faces: All Shapes And Sizes Family Collection

Released: 1996, Connoisseur Collection VSOP CD231. No chart placings
Tracklisting: 'Afterglow' – The Small Faces, 'For All That I Am' – The Creation, 'In A Broken Dream' – Python Lee Jackson (Rod Stewart), 'Black Coffee' – Humble Pie, 'Reason To Believe' – Rod Stewart, 'Sorry, She's Mine' – Jimmy Winston & His Reflections, 'Cindy Incidentally' – The Faces, 'Heartbreaker' – Free, 'How Come' – Ronnie Lane & Slim Chance, 'I Can Feel The Fire' – Ron Wood, 'Ready Or Not' – Kenney Jones, 'Find It' – The Small Faces, 'La Da La' – Ian McLagan, 'Waiting For A Girl Like You' – Foreigner, 'What'cha Gonna Do About It (Live)' – Steve Marriott, 'Won't Get Fooled Again (Live)' – The Who
A strange anthology charting the band's family tree, although centred around the later success of the Rod Stewart-fronted Faces. Ronnie Wood was briefly a member of The Creation. Kenney Jones played with The Who following Keith Moon's death and was also part of the early 1990s band The Law with Paul Rodgers of Free. Rick Wills, who played on both Small Faces 1970s reunion albums, had gone on to record a series of albums as part of the radio-friendly British-American band Foreigner. It all ties in and gathers some oddities and curios along the way.

Running With The Pack – Humble Pie

Released: 1999, New Millennium Communications PILOT48, reissued 2008 as Alchemy Entertainment PILOT198. No chart placings
Tracklisting: 'Think', 'This Ol' World', 'Midnight Of My Life', 'Lovemaker', 'Rain', 'Snakes And Ladders', 'Good Thing', 'A Minute Of Your Time', 'Charlene', 'Think (two)', 'Four Day Creep' (live), 'Stone Cold Fever' (live), 'C'Mon Everybody' (live), 'I Don't Need No Doctor' (live)

Tracks recorded at the same 1975 sessions that resulted in the *Street Rats* album, but previously unissued, consisting of songs written by Steve – a big voice in a small body – and/or Greg Ridley, as well as James Brown's 'Think', The Beatles' 'Rain', and four tracks tacked on from the Pie's last-ever US show in Philadelphia, December 1973.

The Darlings Of Wapping Wharf Launderette: The Immediate Anthology – The Small Faces

Released 1999, Immediate/ Sequel Records NEECD311.

Billed as the 'first official Immediate anthology approved by The Small Faces, a double-CD remastered from the original tapes, with colour foldout booklet.' Reviewer Paolo Hewitt said for *Melody Maker*, 'their music bore traces of humour, inspiration and energy, founded like The Who's, on the silver spirit of youth.'

Fifty tracks drawn from three albums and six singles, plus outtakes; this is not to be confused with the earlier vinyl twelve-track compilation called *For Your Delight, The Darlings Of Wapping Wharf Launderette* (1980, Virgin V2178).

The Small Faces: The BBC Sessions

Personnel:
Steve Marriott: lead guitar, vocals, harmonica
Ronnie Lane: bass guitar
Kenney Jones: drums, vocals
Ian McLagan: keyboards, vocals
Plus:
Jimmy Winston: keyboards and tracks 1-3
P.P. Arnold: backing vocals on tracks 13 and 15.
Released: 15 November 1999, Strange Fruit Records SFRSCD087
No chart placings.

'Whatcha Gonna Do About It' (Potter, Samwell) 2:15
The first three tracks and the first interview are taken from 'Saturday Club', produced by Peter Harwood (recorded on 23 August, but broadcast on 4 September 1965), with the original Jimmy Winston lineup.

'Jump Back' (Rufus Thomas) 1:39 – with a rare Jimmy Winston lead vocal.
'Baby Don't You Do It' (Holland, Dozier, Holland) 2:25
'Shake' (Sam Cooke) 3:12 – with Ronnie Lane singing lead.
The second three tracks and interview are taken from 'Saturday Club' (recorded on 14 March but broadcast on 19 March 1966).

'Sha-La-La-La-Lee' (Lynch, Shuman) 2:48
'You Need Loving' (Dixon) 2:34

'Hey Girl' (Marriott, Lane) 2:07
The next three tracks and interview are taken from 'Saturday Club' (recorded on 5 May, but broadcast on 7 May 1966).

'E To D' (Marriott, Lane) 4:11
'One Night Stand' (Marriott, Lane) 1:53
'You'd Better Believe It' (Lynch, Ragovoy) 2:22
The next three tracks and interview are taken from *Saturday Club* (recorded on 30 June, but broadcast on 2 July 1966).

'Understanding' (Marriott, Lane) 2:32
'All Or Nothing' (Marriott, Lane) 3:00
'If I Were A Carpenter' (Hardin) 2:29
The next three tracks, and the Kenney Jones interview, are taken from *Top Gear,* produced by Bernie Andrews (recorded on 14 April, but broadcast on 20 April 1968), with PP Arnold providing backing vocals.

'Lazy Sunday' (Marriott, Lane) 3:17
'Every Little Bit Hurts' (Ed Cobb) 3:57 – with Steve Marriott playing impassioned piano.
Four interviews with Steve Marriott.
Interview with Kenney Jones.

Signed Sealed – Steve Marriott
Released: April 2003, Alchemy Records, Start Up/Big Daddy Records STRTR165, Universal Int 450166
No chart placing
A patchy compilation described by journalist Ian MacDonald in *Uncut* magazine in August 2003 as a 'slung-together bargain-priced selection' that 'gives an idea of the music he made in his later years, but offers nothing by way of documentation.'

'Midnight Rollin'', 'Wham Bam Thank You Man'

'Oh Well'
Credited to Steve Marriott & The Official Receivers, a powerful cover of Peter Green's Fleetwood Mac song, with variant lyrics and female backing vocals.

'Lonely No More', 'Cocaine' (with Tim Hinkley and Greg Ridley), **'It's All Over', 'Shake', 'Street Rat', 'Ruthy'**
Credited to Steve Marriott's All Stars, opens with a stuttered 'R-R-R-Ruthy', about a girl who takes her gear off for anyone who picks a guitar, 'the first time I heard Ruthy's voice, I was travelling through Ontario, and she was on the radio.' Recorded during January 1976 at Steve's own 'Clear Sounds' studio.

'Stay With Me Baby', 'You Sport It', 'Don't Need No Doctor', 'Tin Soldier'

The Small Faces: Ultimate Collection

Released: 2003, Sanctuary Records TDSAN 004
Originally issued in multi-format as a 1990 double-vinyl by Castle Communications (CTVLP 004), as a CD (CTVCD004) and cassette (CTVMC004)
No chart placings
Tracklisting: Side One: 'All Or Nothing', 'Don't Burst My Bubble', 'Rene', 'My Mind's Eye', 'Afterglow', 'Ogdens' Nut Gone Flake'
Side Two: 'Itchycoo Park', 'Tell Me Have You Ever Seen Me', 'Wham Bam Thank You Ma'am', 'Tin Soldier', 'The Universal', 'Every Little Bit Hurts'
Side Three: 'Lazy Sunday', 'Call It Something Nice', 'Song Of A Baker', 'Hey Girl', 'Colliboshe r', 'Autumn Stone'
Side Four: 'Sha-La-La-La-Lee', 'Red Balloon', 'Rollin' Over', 'What'cha Gonna Do About It', 'Here Come The Nice', 'If I Were A Carpenter' (Live)

Writing the cassette insert notes, Will Birch – journalist, record producer and former member of The Kursaal Flyers – says that 'The Small Faces are remembered by most Sixties scene makers as the definitive Mod group… they were one of the most creative groups in a highly creative area and their music still sounds fresh and vital nearly a quarter of a century after the last true Mod roared out of Soho and into the sunset.'

The Small Faces: Live 1966

Released: 3 September 2021, Nice Records NRCD001
Two sets recorded on 9 January 1966 at the Twenty Club, Mouscron, Belgium.
No chart placings

Endings: Long Agos And Worlds Apart

Ronnie, 'the darling of Wapping Wharf laundrette, Ronald Leafy a-Lane', travelled to Florida in the early eighties and began experimenting with remedies, including hyperbaric oxygen treatment, in desperate attempts to treat his condition. Musical allies such as Pete Townsend, Eric Clapton, Jeff Beck, Steve Winwood, Kenney Jones, Bill Wyman, Charlie Watts and Andy Fairweather-Low rallied and helped support his charity ARMS (Action Research into Multiple Sclerosis), which raised over $1,200,000 in benefit concerts for the cause. A branch of the charity was established in the USA, but 90% of the proceeds were frittered away in 'administrative costs', with long-standing litigious repercussions.

Ronnie relocated to Austin, Texas in 1987, believing that the climate would prove beneficial, and it was there he met his third wife, Susan Gallegos, of Hispanic/Native American heritage. As his condition worsened, he began to withdraw socially. He played his final gig in 1992, at 'The Terrace' in Austin, joining Ronnie Wood and Ian McLagan on stage to sing 'Ooh La La.' In 1994, the couple moved to the relatively remote settlement of Trinidad in the Colorado Rockies (population of 5,000). By now, Rod Stewart and Ronnie Wood were beginning to take care of his medical bills, and royalties from the music he'd created over two decades earlier began to trickle in. Ronnie's mobility and speech rapidly deteriorated and he died, at age 51, of the same disease that killed his mother on 4 June 1997. He was buried in a private ceremony just hours afterwards.

Ian McLagan's graduation into session work is awesome, requiring a full chapter in its own right, taking in Bob Dylan and Chuck Berry as well as The Rolling Stones. But it meant that he released his debut album – *Troublemaker* (Mercury 7142-731), as late as 1979, picking up from his contributions to Ronnie Wood's solo work and his tour with Keith Richards, The New Barbarians lineup. Very much an old-pals routine, Ringo Starr and Keith Richards guest as well as Ronnie Wood. It was followed by *Bump In The Night* (January 1981, Mercury SRM-1-4007), which formed the basis of Ian's subsequent Bump Band, with Ronnie Wood and sax player Bobby Keys adding depth. Relocating to Austin, Texas, his next album, *Best Of British* (March 2000, Maniac Records MRCD-0001), was dedicated to Ronnie Lane, with the track 'Hello Old Friend' documenting their friendship.

It was followed by *Rise And Shine* (March 2004, When Records WENCD 222), with guest contributions by singer-writer Patty Griffin. The touching *Spiritual Boy* (April 2006, Maniac Records MRCD0006), issued on his own label, is subtitled 'An Appreciation Of Ronnie Lane' and consists of new versions of songs written or co-written by Ronnie, including 'Itchycoo Park' and Ian's own tribute 'Hello Old Friend.'

Ian was married to Kim Kerrigan, the former wife of Keith Moon, but she was killed in an auto wreck in 2006. For Ian, there was one further album – *Never Say Never* (February 2008, Maniac Records MRCD0007), recorded in his

Texas studio 'The Doghouse' and featuring 'Scrappy' Jud Newcomb (guitar, vocals), Mark Andes (bass), Don Harvey (drums) and Patty Griffin (vocals) with Glyn Johns mixing and mastering. Ian died of a stroke on 3 December 2014, aged 69. His 2CD album *United States* (Yep Roc Records YEP2388) was issued the same year.

Meanwhile, Kenney Jones had joined The Who in November 1978 to fill Keith Moon's drum chair – despite a rival offer from Phil Collins. Pete Townshend insisted, 'I wanted Kenney Jones. He was my friend. I had worked with him quite a bit, and I liked the idea of having a drummer who kept strict time, so I didn't have to do it. I felt Kenney's work with The Small Faces had been inventive but restrained; 'cool' is the word... winning the point over Roger (Daltrey). I had insisted Kenney be made an equal partner in The Who. He would get a 25 per cent share.' Kenney played on The Who albums *Face Dances* (1981) – including their hit single 'You Better You Bet' – and *It's Hard* (September 1982), as well as on the soundtrack album for Roger Daltrey's movie *McVicar* (1980), on which Billy Nicholls contributes. He is one of the drummers who play on Pete Townshend's solo album *Empty Glass* (April 1980), including the single 'Rough Boys', and he plays on the soundtrack album for the Ken Russell movie version of *Tommy* (March 1975), including Tina Turner's 'Acid Queen' with Ronnie Wood, and 'Eyesight To The Blind' with Eric Clapton and Arthur Brown.

Kenney played on the band's tours from 1979 to 1982, as well as their four-song set at the Live Aid concert at Wembley Arena on 13 July 1985. In 2001, he re-united with Rick Wills to form The Jones Gang with vocalist Robert Hart (who has a history of taking in stints with Bad Company). They played a set at the 'Ronnie Lane Memorial Concert' at the Royal Albert Hall on 8 April 2004, which included their version of 'Tin Soldier' with Sam Brown standing in for P. P. Arnold. Their album *Any Day Now* (2005, BUT! Records CDBUT24, US AAO Music AAO40501) has Ron Wood cover art and features well-received power-ballad single 'Angel' (AAO4405PM2) co-written by Hart and Russ Ballard.

'Steve Marriott – hair flying, jaw set at an aggressive angle, knees akimbo and arms flailing over his jutting guitar, is one of the most characteristic and easily identifiable spectacles in rock' wrote Chris Welch in *Melody Maker* in March 1974. 'Tough, wiry, hard-working, alternately moody and wide-open, Marriott has hauled himself along by the guitar-strap, come hell or disaster, through punch-ups and cock-ups to ultimate success and happiness – we hope.'

Yet by 31 December 1988, Steve Marriott & The DTs were supporting Doctor Feelgood at the London Town & Country New Year's Party. To Ian McLagan, Steve 'wanted so much to be accepted as a serious musician that he fought stardom all the way to relative obscurity', yet the legacy he created through the Mod Decca Small Faces period and the Brit-Psych Immediate Small Faces period are the ones that are valued by subsequent generations of musicians, not the 'seriously heavy' Humble Pie material.

Had he not succumbed to the lures of High and Happy!

Shel Talmy recalls how 'Steve Marriott's excesses finally caught up with him a few years later in the early hours of 20 April 1991, when, full of whatever, he chose to leave where he was housed for the night and took a taxi home. The coroner's take on the events that were to unfold was that heavy smoker Steve, 'loaded, lit a cigarette, went to bed and promptly fell asleep. The cigarette ignited the bedding and the ensuing fire spread very quickly throughout the very old house.

The official verdict was that it was an accidental death where the victim, woken by the fire and partially overcome with smoke, made an attempt to escape but turned the wrong way toward the wall instead of the door. Steve was found on the floor between the bed and the wall. This very talented guy with some personal demons, Steve Marriott, was only forty-four years old.'

'He was 900 years old in Steve Marriott years', Ian told *NME* on 15 July 1995 that 'he *lived* his life: he lived three days to everyone else's one. He was a very… what's the word?... *electric* bloke.'

As Steve wrote on 'The Autumn Stone', 'yesterday is dead, but not my memory…'

Sources

Small Faces: The Young Mods' Forgotten Story – Paolo Hewitt
(1995, Acid Jazz Books, second edition November 2010, ISBN-10: 095-2393-530)
'A rattling, fast read, peppered with candid opinions from everyone significant, including a posthumously published interview with Marriott, this official biography covers everything from the acid casualties, the rucks, high jinx and arty statements like *Ogdens' Nut Gone Flake*' said reviewer Max Bell in *Vox* in August 1995.

Steve Marriott: All Too Beautiful – The Life & Times Of Steve Marriott – Paolo Hewitt and John Hellier
(December 2005, Helter Skelter Books, 352pp, ISBN-13 978-1900924733)
Respected *NME* journalist Hewitt and Hellier, who edited The Small Faces fan club magazine, collaborate in an 'honest appraisal of a flawed genius' at a time when Steve 'remains a pivotal figure, with Oasis, Paul Weller and Pete Doherty borrowing freely from his wardrobe as well as his songbook.' Stuart Clark, reviewing the book in *Hot Press* on 14 July 2004, said, 'if things had panned out a little differently, Steve Marriott would be as revered as Keith, as big a hit with the ladies as Rod and as filthy rich as Sir Paul.'

All Or Nothing: The Authorised Story Of Steve Marriott – Simon Spence
(March 2021, Omnibus Press, 480pp, ISBN-13 978-1787601840)
Simon Spence collaborated with Andrew Loog Oldham on *Stoned* and *2Stoned*, his memoirs of the Immediate label; this oral history is drawn from interviews with those closest to Steve, his sister, his first two wives, children, bandmates and friends.

All The Rage – Ian 'Mac' McLagan
(1998, Sidgwick & Jackson, ISBN 0-283-06334-3)
Mac's own story is immensely energetic, funny and at times poignant, richly anecdotal, astute and irreverent.

Let The Good Times Roll: My Life In Small Faces, Faces And The Who – Kenney Jones
(2018, Blink Publishing, ISBN-13: 978-1911600091)
Despite supporting the Conservative Party and the controversial Countryside Alliance pressure group, which supports so-called 'blood sports', Kenney has a luminous history and was inducted into the Rock & Roll Hall Of Fame in 2012. At the time of writing, he is the solitary surviving member of The Small Faces.

The Small Faces: When The Screaming Stopped: Live 1965-1969 – Guy Mowbray
(2023, Red Planet Publishing, 304pp, ISBN-13: 978-1912733354)
Dedicated to the fantastic roller coaster contribution The Small Faces

made to live 1960s music: Steve Marriott, Ronnie Lane, Kenney Jones, Ian McLagan and Jimmy Winston. Also, the brass boys – Lyn Dobson, Derek Wadsworth, Don Fay, Eddie Thornton, Johnny Marshall, Brian Smith, Peter Coe and Harry Beckett.

Small Faces: All Or Nothing – Kenneth Marriott
(November 2021, Lulu.com, 214pp, ISBN-13 978-1794835535)
A poor collection of dubious authenticity.

Happy Boys Happy!: Rock History Of The Small Faces And Humble Pie – Uli Twelker and Roland Schmitt
(1997, Sanctuary Publishing Ltd, 320pp, ISBN 978-186074-1975)
Although it centres on The Small Faces, it extends out to cover the members' subsequent careers in equal detail, with Ronnie's Slim Chance, Ian's Bump Band, Kenney's time with The Who, The Faces plus Steve's Humble Pie, Packet Of Three and the rest.

Who I Am – Pete Townshend
(2012, HarperCollins, ISBN 978-0-00-746603-0)
The powerful and disturbing autobiography of the troubled leader of The Who. He and Ronnie Lane were both followers of the guru Meher Baba and had collaborated on a limited-edition 1970 LP in his honour, *Happy Birthday* (Universal Spiritual League/ Eel Pie Records), which includes the track 'Evolution' with words and music by Ronnie.

Rock On Wood: The Origin Of A Rock & Roll Face: Ron Wood – Terry Rawlings
(1999, Boxtree, ISBN 0-7522-1164-1)
By the author of *All Our Yesterdays*, the earliest account of The Small Faces' story.

Rod: The Autobiography – Rod Stewart
(2013, Arrow Books, ISBN 978-0099574750)
What the Daily Telegraph called 'an entertaining romp through fifty years of bad behaviour.'

Small Faces: Darlings Of Wapping Wharf Launderette
Issues of the expertly-produced glossy fanzine from John Hellier of Canvey Island, with cuttings and interviews.

Record Collector: 100 Greatest Psychedelic Records – David Wells
(2005, Diamond Publishing, ISSN 1746 8051)

Revolt Into Style: The Pop Arts In Britain – George Melly

(Allen Lane 1970, Penguin paperback, 1972, ISBN 0-14-00.3394-7)
The Neophiliacs: The Revolution In English Life In The Fifties And Sixties – Christopher Booker
(1969, Wm Collins, 1992, Pimlico edition ISBN 0-7126-5505-0)

Plus, a multitude of features, reviews and press-cuttings from *New Musical Express*, *Melody Maker*, *Record Mirror*, *Disc*, *Fabulous* and other sources, with issues, dates and writers specified in the text wherever possible. Apologies and thanks where sources have proved impossible to trace, and thanks to those other contributors who prefer to remain anonymous.

On Track Series

Allman Brothers Band – Andrew Wild 978-1-78952-252-5
Tori Amos – Lisa Torem 978-1-78952-142-9
Aphex Twin – Beau Waddell 978-1-78952-267-9
Asia – Peter Braidis 978-1-78952-099-6
Badfinger – Robert Day-Webb 978-1-878952-176-4
Barclay James Harvest – Keith And Monica Domone 978-1-78952-067-5
Beck – Arthur Lizie 978-1-78952-258-7
The Beatles – Andrew Wild 978-1-78952-009-5
The Beatles Solo 1969-1980 – Andrew Wild 978-1-78952-030-9
Blue Oyster Cult – Jacob Holm-Lupo 978-1-78952-007-1
Blur – Matt Bishop 978-178952-164-1
Marc Bolan And T.rex – Peter Gallagher 978-1-78952-124-5
Kate Bush – Bill Thomas 978-1-78952-097-2
Camel – Hamish Kuzminski 978-1-78952-040-8
Captain Beefheart – Opher Goodwin 978-1-78952-235-8
Caravan – Andy Boot 978-1-78952-127-6
Cardiacs – Eric Benac 978-1-78952-131-3
Nick Cave And The Bad Seeds – Dominic Sanderson 978-1-78952-240-2
Eric Clapton Solo – Andrew Wild 978-1-78952-141-2
The Clash – Nick Assirati 978-1-78952-077-4
Elvis Costello And The Attractions – Georg Purvis 978-1-78952-129-0
Crosby, Stills & Nash – Andrew Wild 978-1-78952-039-2
Creedence Clearwater Revival – Tony Thompson 978-178952-237-2
The Damned – Morgan Brown 978-1-78952-136-8
Deep Purple And Rainbow 1968-79 – Steve Pilkington 978-1-78952-002-6
Dire Straits – Andrew Wild 978-1-78952-044-6
The Doors – Tony Thompson 978-1-78952-137-5
Dream Theater – Jordan Blum 978-1-78952-050-7
Eagles – John Van Der Kiste 978-1-78952-260-0
Earth, Wind And Fire – Bud Wilkins 978-1-78952-272-3
Electric Light Orchestra – Barry Delve 978-1-78952-152-8
Emerson Lake And Palmer – Mike Goode 978-1-78952-000-2
Fairport Convention – Kevan Furbank 978-1-78952-051-4
Peter Gabriel – Graeme Scarfe 978-1-78952-138-2
Genesis – Stuart Macfarlane 978-1-78952-005-7
Gentle Giant – Gary Steel 978-1-78952-058-3
Gong – Kevan Furbank 978-1-78952-082-8
Green Day – William E. Spevack 978-1-78952-261-7
Hall And Oates – Ian Abrahams 978-1-78952-167-2
Hawkwind – Duncan Harris 978-1-78952-052-1
Peter Hammill – Richard Rees Jones 978-1-78952-163-4
Roy Harper – Opher Goodwin 978-1-78952-130-6
Jimi Hendrix – Emma Stott 978-1-78952-175-7
The Hollies – Andrew Darlington 978-1-78952-159-7
Horslips – Richard James 978-1-78952-263-1
The Human League And The Sheffield Scene –
Andrew Darlington 978-1-78952-186-3
The Incredible String Band – Tim Moon 978-1-78952-107-8
Iron Maiden – Steve Pilkington 978-1-78952-061-3
Joe Jackson – Richard James 978-1-78952-189-4
Jefferson Airplane – Richard Butterworth 978-1-78952-143-6
Jethro Tull – Jordan Blum 978-1-78952-016-3
Elton John In The 1970s – Peter Kearns 978-1-78952-034-7
Billy Joel – Lisa Torem 978-1-78952-183-2